CONCEPTS OF IDENTITY

CONCEPTS OF IDENTITY

Historical and Contemporary
Images and Portraits of Self and Family

KATHERINE HOFFMAN

Westview
PRESS
A Member of the Perseus Books Group

11/13/09
Lan
$38 —

Peseus Publishing is a member of the Perseus Books Group

First published by HarperCollins Publishers, New York

ISBN 0-06-433332-9   ISBN 0-06-430211- 3 (pbk)

10 9 8 7 6 5 4

For My Family
With Love

Human beings are too important to be treated as mere symptoms of the past. They have a value which is independent of any temporal processes—which is eternal and must be felt for its own sake.

Uninterpreted truth is as useless as buried gold; and art is the great interpreter. It alone can unify a vast multitude of facts into a significant whole, clarifying, accentuating, suppressing, and lighting up the dark places of the imagination.

LYTTON STRACHEY

Art, even the art of fullest scope and widest vision, can never really show us the external world. All that it shows us is our own soul, the one world of which we have any real cognizance. . . . It is art, and art only, that reveals us to ourselves.

OSCAR WILDE

Let us try to impart to our children not only facts but a perspective on how important it is to know and understand others, to reach out, to put yourself in others' shoes, walk as they walk, and feel their pain. That is our challenge. . . .

Let us live so that in dying each of us can say: "All my conscious life and energies have been dedicated to the liberation of the human mind and spirit."

MAYA ANGELOU

Contents

List of Illustrations

The number in italics refers to the page on which the illustration appears.

Acknowledgments

This book has a variety of roots that extend to the workplace and to home. I wish to thank the clerical and library staff at St. Anselm College for their continuous help in locating research materials. In particular, I would like to thank Denise Beaule for her expertise on the computer. I also wish to thank the staff members of various museums and galleries from which I obtained illustrations and other sources. A faculty summer research grant from St. Anselm College allowed me the luxury of a summer devoted to research. A 1994 summer grant from the New Hampshire Council for the Humanities allowed me to write full-time that summer. My editor, Cass Canfield, Jr., has evidenced continuing patience and support for this project, which took far longer than was initially intended. His words, "You need to jump out of the nest and fly," helped me spread my wings. To him, I extend an ongoing thank you. Some of the material for this book grew out of, or was derived from material used for, a previous book, *Explorations: The Visual Arts Since 1945*, for which he also served as editor.

And to my family, for simply being who they are, I extend a heartfelt thank you—to my children, Kristen, Geoffrey, and Ashley, who have seen too much of life's difficulties in their short lives; to my own parents; and to my husband, Graham Ward, whose love and support made it possible for me to finish this book.

Preface

W̶e need stories, visual and verbal, fiction and nonfiction. His/story or her/story, persons' stories are all part of discovering who and where we are; where we've come from; and where we are going, individually and collectively. Histories and stories can stimulate our imagination; stories can jar or provoke us and raise questions. Stories can give us a sense of peace, of repose, or become a metaphor for greater things beyond our everyday lives.

Several family "stories" from the twentieth-century literary world come to mind quickly. In 1901, Thomas Mann completed his famous *Buddenbrooks: The Decline of a Family*, which chronicles in majestic detail the joys and sorrows of the Buddenbrook family during the years 1835–77. At times, the novel is somber and depressing, with repeated images of decadence, such as decaying teeth. But it is also about events and the feelings that go with them that we all know about—births, deaths, christenings, betrothals, and marriages. The novel is framed by the works of Tony Buddenbrook. The opening words of the book, *"Was ist das?"* ("What is it?"), are spoken by Tony, as a young eight-year-old girl, sitting on her grandfather's knee. The novel ends forty-two years later, a few moments after Tony speaks for the last time, answering her own question posed at the beginning of the novel. *"Es ist so."* ("It is so.")

In 1971, Wallace Stegner also chronicled four generations of family life in his novel *Angle of Repose,* in which retired historian Lyman Ward, confined to a wheelchair because he has only one leg, decides to write the story of his grandparents' days on the American western frontier. His research reveals as much about himself and his life as it does about his grandparents' lives. His son, Rodman, a sociologist, is at first skeptical. Ward, the narrator, writes at the beginning of the novel that his son was born "without a sense of history," that,

> like other Berkeley radicals, he is convinced that the post-indus-trial, post-Christian world is worn out, corrupt in its inheritance, helpless to create by evolution the social and political institutions, the forms of personal relations, the conventions, moralities, and systems of ethics (insofar as these are indeed necessary) appropri-ate to the future. . . . Marriage and the family as we have known them are becoming extinct. . . . He [Rodman] sits in with the sit-ter-inners, he will reform us malgré our teeth, he will make his omelet and be damned to the broken eggs. Like the Vietnam Commander he will regretfully destroy our village to save it.[1]

Near the end of the novel Stegner, in the voice of Lyman Ward, refers to the "angle of repose," originally an image of a rock balanced on a mountain rock slide, as an angle at which a man or woman finally lies down in what appears to be a metaphor of bal-ance, of a certain harmony, rest, and acceptance.

More recently, in 1992, Donald Katz, in *Homefires: An Intimate Portrait of One Middle-Class Family in Postwar America,* chronicled the life of the Gordon family from the end of World War II to the early 1990s. This book, however, is not a novel, but a journalist's account of the Gordon family's evolution after four years of regular interviews with them and several thousand pages of transcribed discussions with friends, ex-spouses, teachers, colleagues, rabbis, and so forth. In his preface, Katz referred to a poll that indicated that 97 out of 100 Americans want a "happy family life" and notes that a study commissioned by the Massachusetts Mutual Life Insurance Company called the family "the most central element in the lives of most Americans."[2] He noted, "The family is the pri-mary lens that filters the early and lasting light of every life."[3]

Although not a family chronicle, one more story may be mentioned—Fannie Flagg's *Fried Green Tomatoes at the Whistle Stop Café*, both a novel (1987) and a movie (1991). This poignant narrative, which is both humorous and tragic, tells of family and friends on two levels—of Evelyn and Mrs. Threadgoode in the 1980s and of Idgie Threadgoode and her lover-friend, Ruth Jamison, in the era of the Great Depression of the 1930s in Whistle Stop, Alabama. The stories that Idgie frequently told became so important to Ruth that while on her deathbed, dying young of cancer, she asks Idgie to retell one of them. In the movie, Idgie looks out the window, with her back to the camera. There are no camera close-ups on either Idgie or Ruth; rather, the focus is on the story. This is the story:

> One time there was this lake. And it was right outside of town, and we used to go fishing and swimming and canoeing in it. So, one November this big flock of ducks came in and landed in that lake. And then the temperature dropped so fast that the lake just froze right there and the ducks flew off, you see, and they took that lake with them and now that lake is somewhere over in Georgia [transcribed from movie].

By the time the story is over, Ruth has died peacefully, able to do so after hearing the story, which had become a mirror and a lamp for her. The lake; the free-flying ducks; and the friends and family who went canoeing, fishing, and swimming were everywhere and nowhere but in the richness of the mind's eye, which in this moment carried Ruth to her death.

I have mentioned these stories because this is a book about family "stories" told by visual artists or, in more formal terms, an exploration of artists' portraits and images of self and family, focusing primarily on the twentieth century. It is, though, a book not only about visual images and their stories, but about you and about me—how we may perceive ourselves and others, how we construct or deconstruct our identities, as a result of viewing some of the works shown or discussed in the following pages.

As Thomas Mann did, I, too, would like to pose the question, *"Was is das?"* ("What is it?") in relation to our understanding and perceptions surrounding the family and images of it. Unlike Thomas Mann, however, I will not be able to end the book with a definitive *"Es ist so"* ("It is so"), for our world is too complicated or complex for such absolutes, and I intend to raise as many or more questions than I answer for the reader and the viewer.

Like Wallace Stegner, I hope that some "angle of repose" will be reached. Using the words of Donald Katz, I hope there will be further light for the "lens," the family, that "filters the early and lasting light of every life." And, as for my children, or Idgie and Ruth, I hope that the following visual images and "stories" may move and carry you to a new place in your own lives, a place of increased understanding, tolerance, and sense of who you are and who we are as we live in diverse family structures and prepare to enter the twenty-first century.

KATHERINE HOFFMAN
Peterborough, New Hampshire
1995

Introduction:
Of Families and Portraits

We search these faces, the silvery shadows, the garish Kodachrome surfaces, the yellow streaked early Polaroids, the elegant studio portraits. . . . Dialogue begins, is born fresh out of our own deep, dread yearning. Somewhere in that dialogue is hidden the clue to who I am, if I could but understand the language in which it is written. Your history is here, too . . . written in fat faces and lean faces, happy and sad; written in rejection and acceptance, mother love, lust or honest passion. . . .

DAVID GALLOWAY

. . . Come my friends
'Tis not too late to see a newer world
Push off, and sitting well in order smite
The sounding farrows; for my purpose holds
To sail beyond the sunset, and the baths
Of all the western stars, until I die. . . .

HOMER, *Ulysses*

We look at portraits and images of others to learn about our roots, about similarities and differences in our own circles of friends and families and in images of others who are total strangers. Portrayals of past "seasons" of our lives and others may help us better understand our present and prepare for the future. Family images may provide some sense of immortality of blood lines; family images may call up pleasant and/or unpleasant memories or current situations. But there can always be a "journey" to "see a newer world" that may be clearer and richer as a

1

result of having looked at and been moved by images of others and thereby to understand our own individual identities and the families we are a part of or close to.

But what is a family? What is a portrait? There is no one answer to either question. The Latin root of the word *family,* familia, refers to servants in a household. *Webster's Unabridged Dictionary* defines family as "1) the collective body of persons who live in one house, 2) a father, mother, and their children, 3) the children of the same parents, 4) one's husband (or wife) and children, 5) a group of people related by blood or marriage; relatives, 6)those who descend from one common pro-genitor, 7) descent, lineage."

Definitions of family have expanded and changed in recent years, particularly since World War II. Lifestyles that involve single parents with children, gay couples with children, unmarried couples with children, and communities of adults with no children are all part of family configurations in our current society. The wider definition of family, adopted by Family Service America in its 1992–93 *Family Agenda,* is perhaps appropriate: "A family consists of two or more people, whether living together or apart, related by blood, marriage, adoption, or commitment to care for one another." In recent years the American family has been described as beleaguered, as disintegrating, as torn asunder, and even as dead. Today, we are frequently told that traditional family life, which once consisted of a nuclear unit, sometimes with an extended family of multiple generations, is no longer viable. Recent reports by two bipartisan national commissions—the National Commission on Children, in its 1991 *Beyond Rhetoric,* and the National Commission on America's Urban Families, in its 1993 *Families First*—stated that the disintegration of the American family is a significant concern for our society and that family decline is a variable in some of our most urgent social problems. The steady breakup of the two-parent home is seen by many as a major factor in family decline.

There are counterarguments to these assertions, though. Works, such as historian Stephanie Coontz's *The Way We Never Were,* sociologist Judith Stacey's *Brave New Families,* and psychologist Arlene Skolnick's *Embattled Paradise,* suggest that changes in the contemporary American family structure are not of such great concern and that it is necessary to move beyond the high divorce rate (currently, approximately 50 percent of all first marriages fail) and even to celebrate "alternative" lifestyles. For some of these scholars, changes in the family are being blamed unfairly for poverty, crime, the crisis of our youths, and other serious social problems. For others, there was never an ideal picture-book, harmonious family, as suggested by the television media of the 1950s in such programs as *Leave It to Beaver, Ozzie and Harriet*, and *Father Knows Best*. According to Coontz, in the 1950s, prior to food stamps and public housing programs, one in four Americans was poor, and incidents of family violence remained unspoken and hidden and therefore unknown to the wider public. For example, wife battering was not considered a real crime by most people.

Whatever one's opinion, a war is being waged over the family, involving how children are raised, conflicts between sacrifice and self-fulfillment for parents, and our governmental and corporate programs and structures that have an impact on family life.

The term *family values* is charged with social, political, economic, and emotional connotations as discourse in political campaigns, press conferences, editorials, and other places centers on crises in our nation that relate to our children and family life. Indeed, "evidence suggests that we may have the first generation of children and youths in our history who are less well off—psychologically, socially, economically, and morally—than their parents were at the same age."[1]

The word *family* is no longer simply singular, either. There are diverse families—in configuration, ethnicity, and class. The word family has also been extended to descriptions of small town communities, to national identities, and even to international networks made possible by computers and telecommunications. Issues directly and indirectly related to the family are clearly all around us. We frequently read and hear news commentators, politicians, sociologists, historians, economists, and others offer various perspectives and opinions on the history and current status of the family. Less frequently do we see and hear artists' perspectives. Artists through the ages have dealt with images of the family in diverse ways, in both form and content. These voices, too, need to be seen and heard, as part of the complex tapestry that consists of multiple strands, woven together to form pictures of who we are, individually, and in relation to various family structures.

The most obvious form of artistic statement related to family imagery is the portrait, although other artistic content and forms, such as advertising, movies, television, architectural structures and environment, toys, clothing, and objects belonging to family members, may shed significant light on family images and identities, either in isolation from or connected directly to the individuals in question. This book seeks to bring together some of these artistic strands from the visual arts, from both popular culture and the fine arts.

The word *portrait*, as well as the word *family*, is not quickly and readily defined. Although not as emotionally or politically charged, the word, or genre, is filled with complexities that may not be readily acknowledged or seen at first glance. The root word of *portrait*, from the Latin, *protrahere*, means to draw forth. Webster's *New Unabridged Dictionary* (1979) defines portraiture as "1) originally a drawn, painted or carved picture of something, 2) a picture of a person, especially of his face, drawn, painted, photographed, etc. from life, 3) a description, dramatic portrayal, etc. of a person." A portrait may assist in drawing forth the person, both for himself or herself and for the viewer. In today's world, the technologies of computers, photography, and printmaking, for example, have allowed us to push beyond its original destination suggested by Webster. The well-known critic and art historian E. H. Gombrich said, "All art originates in the human mind, in our reactions to the world rather than in the visible world itself. . . . The correct portrait, like the useful image, is an end product on a long road through schema and correction. It is not a faithful record of a visual experience, but the faithful construction of a relational model. . . . The form of a representation cannot be divorced from its purpose and the requirements of the society in which the given visual language gains currency."[2] The painter Édouard Vuillard remarked, "One begins a portrait without knowing the model. When it is finished one knows the model, but the portrait no longer resembles the model."[3] The art historian Marcia Pointon noted that "at its most abstract, portraiture is a question of the relationship between the self *as* art and the self *in* art."[4]

There is a wide diversity of approaches to discussions of portraiture, and the relationship between the artist and the subject is
an important part of the essence of portraiture. The portrait made
is of someone, and a relationship is thus set up between the artist,
his or her subject, and the viewer of the portrait. For a portrait to
be a portrait, there must be a specific referent, a specific or real
person. The scholar John Pope-Hennessy wrote about this relationship in his book, *The Portrait in the Renaissance:* "Portrait
painting is empirical. The artistic problem it presents is one that
we can all envisage no matter how distant the time and context
where it occurs, and a great part of its fascination is due to the fact
that it results from the interaction of two forces, artist and sitter,
and not from the action of one."[5]

Two literary accounts, although fictional and somewhat
extreme, may serve to illustrate further, sometimes unseen or
unrecognized aspects of the relationship between an artist and his
or her subject or sitter. Edgar Allan Poe, in his poignant short
story, "The Oval Portrait," recounted the eerie story of an artist
who paints his wife, "a maiden of rarest beauty, and not more
lovely than full of glee." But "having already a bride in his art," he
does not see his young wife slowly deteriorate physically and spiritually in the weeks she poses for her artist-husband, who becomes
obsessed by the work. Upon completing the work, the painter,
standing entranced and proud before his portrait, shouts, "This is
indeed life itself," only to find as he turns to regard his beloved:
"She was dead!"

Oscar Wilde's *The Picture of Dorian Gray*, both novel and
movie, in its melodrama, speaks of the depths in which artist and
sitter can become intertwined with one another on many levels. In
the opening scenes, the young artist in question, Basil Hallward, is
reluctant to exhibit a portrait he has recently completed of Dorian
Gray, a handsome young society figure in late nineteenth-century
London. Basil says to his friend and supporter, Lord Henry Wot-
ton,

> Every portrait that is painted with feeling is a portrait of the artist, not of
> the sitter. The sitter is merely the accident, the occasion. It is not he who
> is revealed by the painter; it is rather the painter who, on the colored can-

vas, reveals himself. The reason I will not exhibit this picture is that I'm afraid that I have shown it in the secret of my own soul.[6]

The story of artist, sitter, and portrait unfolds in a fantastic manner as Dorian Gray, a Faust-like hedonist, is willing to sell his soul for eternal youthful beauty. "If it were I who were to be always young and the picture to grow old. . . . I would give my soul for it."[7] Such is the pact. In the end both artist and sitter die, Basil at the sword of Dorian, and Dorian at his own hands, no longer able to live with himself and the living, aging portrait.

Clearly, such examples are extreme, yet they may serve as catalysts to question the very nature of a portrait and of the relationships among the artist, the person portrayed, and society. Since tradition has frequently suggested that portraits have some degree of likeness to the "sitter," let me briefly consider this concept. Likeness usually suggests that a thing resembles something else. If the resemblance is not identical, then likeness presupposes there is a degree of difference and therefore contains some degree of "falseness." Likeness, then paradoxically, may imply falseness.[8] Indeed, "in German, Dutch, and English, portraits were often called 'counterfeits' and the word carried its modern meaning also."[9] Through much of the nineteenth century, however, a close likeness to the portrayed was essential for a good portrait.

The concept of likeness may be expanded, though, beyond physical resemblance or likeness, to the world of feelings. As R. G. Collingwood suggested: "The true definition of representative art is not that the artifact resembles an original . . . but that the feeling evoked by the artifact resembles the feeling evoked by the original . . . when a portrait is said to be like the sitter. What is meant is that the spectator, when he looks at the portrait, 'feels as if' he were in the sitter's presence."[10]

The problem of likeness becomes further complicated when one asks, likeness of what? an outer self, or an inner self if one delves into psychological realms? Is there even a true self, or are there many selves? Do time, place, dress, activity, etc. influence what aspect of self is to be depicted? Is there a "protean self," as Robert Jay Lifton described in his 1993 book of that title, where a resilient self (like Proteus, the Greek sea god of many forms) is able to change shape in response to crises and to create new psychological sensibilities to immerse oneself in new endeavors throughout one's lifetime? As Lifton observed: "We are fluid and many-sided. Without quite realizing it, we have been evolving a sense of self appropriate to the restlessness and flux of our time. . . . The protean self emerges from confusion, from the widespread feelings we are losing our psychological moorings. It makes use of bits and pieces here and there and somehow keeps going."[11] Today, some would argue that there is no longer a "core" self, but that in the late twentieth century, we are fragmented, oversaturated, deconstructed human beings.

So who or what may be or is to be portrayed? Is it possible to "unmask" a sitter, to reveal any sense of "true" self not yet discovered? Diane Arbus wrote that "a photograph is a secret about a secret. The more it tells you, the less you know."[12]

Yousuf Karsh would have us understand the reverse, that it is possible to uncover and to portray a true psyche. "All I know is that within every man and woman a secret is hidden, and as a photographer it is my task to reveal it if I can. The revelation, if it comes at all, will come in a small fraction of a second with an unconscious gesture, a gleam of the eye, a brief lifting of the mask that all humans wear to conceal their innermost selves from the world. In that fleeting interval of opportunity, the photographer must act, or lose his prize."[13]

In the past few pages I have talked of some of the complexities involved in discussing and defining families and portraits. Definitions of families and portraiture have evolved and changed over time. Portraits of and images related to family life have also changed over the course of history. At some points in time family portraits have been exalted and placed in positions of honor. At other points, they have been consigned to a lonely garret, to be covered and collect dust for a generation or more. Some portraits, beginning in the eighteenth century, have been called "conversation pieces"—not simply in the vernacular sense, but more formally, in the sense that they have two or more identifiable people, contain a background that represents the surroundings of the family group and some kind of gesture signifying conversation or some type of communication within the group, and show some aspect of private life (versus a public or official function). In our world of the twentieth century, there are all kinds of "conversation pieces," both related and unrelated to family life, but images of the family clearly still provoke different types of conversation.

The following pages contain some of the portraits and images of family life that have been significant or representative voices from a variety of historical periods with emphasis on the twentieth century. The images from earlier periods are included to serve as "roots" from whence we came and as points of comparison for the more recent imagery of this century. In a book of this type, it is not possible to present numerous examples from all periods and cultures. Therefore, those that I selected represent simply a sampling of differences and similarities in family-related imagery in various periods, focusing on our own modern and postmodern eras and dealing primarily with Western and middle- and upper-class culture.

In viewing these images, one cannot discount the role of memory—the personal memories of the viewer that may somehow be triggered by the work, the role of memory for those being portrayed, and the role of memory for the artist. What is seen and what is remembered or re-membered by the artist in the process of creating the work of art or shown by the camera in photography, film, and television? Memory, including both remembering and forgetting, may be viewed, in part, as a socially and culturally constructed process. It does not have to be a passive blank slate waiting to be "written" or acted upon. It can be a significant interactive process involving various layers and levels of individual and social "forces" that intersect or are intertwined.

The images that follow are to be viewed in the context of the larger social fabric and culture, as a mirror or a lamp, that make up any given period. If one considers aspects of the philosopher Martin Heidegger's aesthetic, then such works may provide some sense of home, of shelter in a chaotic world. "In the Heideggerian aesthetic, creation and safekeeping, composition and conservation are absolutely indivisible. Even the most revolutionary work of art, if it is authentic, will conserve and give to Being a dwelling and a sanctuary such as it can find nowhere else."[14]

It is hoped that the images that follow may enhance your sense of identity and being and help you see where we have come from, where we are, and where we are going as we struggle with diverse concepts of individual and family identities at the turn of a tumultuous twentieth century.

PART I

From Whence We Came

1

The Ancient and Medieval World

A s early as 3000 B.C., Egyptian funerary monuments were erected to preserve the remains of the dead, and to celebrate a journey to the afterlife that included evidence of family life. Left in the elaborate tombs were artifacts and wall paintings that show us that even long ago there was a search for the eternal through art and that tensions between the ephemeral and the eternal, between individual and type, were a part of Egyptian portraiture, as they have been in later cultures. The Egyptian artist's approach was conceptual, not entirely perceptual, because he painted not only what he saw, but what he knew was there. In a typical, well-known scene depicting the use of leisure time, a whole family is gathered among tall papyrus reeds along the Nile River, fishing and hunting (the Tomb of Nakht at Thebes, Eighteenth Dynasty). On the left, a nobleman is hurling sticks at a flock of geese; his wife clings to his waist, while his daughter clings to his leg. On the right, another nobleman appears to have just thrown a spear. His wife and daughter also cling to his waist and leg, providing a definite symmetry and order to the scene. This protective image of a husband, wife, and child was a stylized way of depicting the family group. One quickly sees the image of male dominance in the size of the figures. The husband is much larger than his wife or daughter, and the daughter is seated securely and firmly in the triangular space between her father's legs. The wife's legs are also in that same triangular space, and she stands under her husband's raised arm. It is interesting to note that females, although inactive, appear in the hunting-sports scenes. In some cultures families would not have participated as a whole in such an activity.

A somewhat different image, a relief on a limestone stele, shows Akhenaten and his family—his wife Nefertiti and their three children [1]. Found in his tomb at Tell el-Amarna, the relief may be one of the first "conversation pieces" in art, for the royal family seems engaged in some kind of domestic conversation as the couple face each other in profile, holding their children in their arms. One of the two children Nefertiti holds gestures toward her father. The symmetry of the relief brings a sense of harmony and well-being to the family group. These figures appear to be more individualized than the painted family scenes. Both images, however, contain a significant amount of writing (hieroglyphics), for writing the name, or making the name become alive, was funda-

1. *Akhenaten and His Family,* Tell el-Amarna, c. 1372–1355 B.C. Staatliche Museen, Berlin.

mental to Egyptian thought. It was believed that while the name lived, the person lived.

Although scenes such as these depict a family scene, they are perhaps not true portraits, for their concerns are not mainly with the subjects as whole persons or as a family unit, but rather with the family as part of a funerary practice. They appear to be more important as instruments of magic—for protecting the living and for protecting and sustaining the dead. As Panofsky noted, "An Egyptian tomb statue, intended to be occupied by its soul, is not what a Greek or Roman statue is. It is not a representation (mimesis) of a living being—body plus soul, the former animated by the latter—but a reconstruction of the body, waiting for animation."[1]

Greek portraiture in general contained more re-creations of a person in terms of temperament and achievement than an accurate rendering of a person's physical appearance. A story by Pliny, however, of a potter's daughter tracing the outline of her lover's shadow on the wall implies a desire and ability to achieve a good likeness of the person portrayed. From the fourth century B.C. on, Greek portraiture became more precise. Besides the soldiers and political leaders, there also appeared likenesses of intellectuals, poets, and philosophers. Plato's thinking (circa 427–347 B.C.) also had an impact. In Plato's philosophy, the soul took on a new significance and was thought to be the center of the human personality. Plato argued that there was an individual personal immortality that continued after the death of the body. Hellenistic portraits thus began to show stronger emotions than the gentle sorrow of earlier grave reliefs. The whole body became important, not simply the face, as the revealer of personality. The figures were no longer types, but individuals. Since there was an increase in private wealth during the Hellenistic period, and on into Roman times, portrait sculptors grew rich. Some were able to purchase property, thereby raising their social status from that of manual laborers. Beyond famous historical personalities, there was an increase in commissions for local personalities. This tradition of the portraiture of private citizens, as well as renowned figures, was a new one that would become an important legacy passed on from the Greeks to the Romans. Yet with this attention to portraiture, there is little evidence that high priorities were given to women and family life, which were not the subjects of "official" portraits.

The lives of women and children, in general, were quiet. As the playwright Menander commented, "The loom is women's work and not debate." When husbands entertained guests at dinner, women were expected to stay upstairs in their own quarters, anointing their bodies with sweet oils and perfumes. There are, however, depictions of tenderness and family love in vase paintings and sculptures. One image, a stele from the fifth century B.C. (Kerameikos Museum, Athens), shows evidence of extended family relations—a grandmother tenderly holding a grandchild, gazing admiringly at the baby. The tombstone inscription describes the grandmother's happiness at having held the child.

Family life was not always depicted as harmonious, however. For example, in an image on an Attic red-figure jug [2], a husband, drunk with wine at the end of a party, stands, his arm raised with the handle of his torch, hammering at the doorway. His young wife, with a lamp in her hand, stands trembling on the other side of the door. Thus one sees very early allusions to domestic violence in the realm of the visual arts.

In general, visual imagery related to family life and the role of women is to be viewed as much for what is not portrayed as for what is portrayed—that family and more intimate imagery was not as significant as were images of public and idealized forms and images.

In early Rome, the family was the basic unit, both socially and legally. Kinship was considered most important. In early Republican Rome, the head of the house, the male (or "pater familias") had control over all aspects of his household and the legal right to punish any member of his household with death. By the first century A.D., however, family councils began to replace the absolute authority of the pater familias. Roman portraiture tended to be realistic in depicting physical qualities as well as social roles. Particularly, images related to rulers were at times more idealistic or more youthful than reality and served propagandistic ends. In Republican days, the Roman sense of self was strongly connected to one's ancestors, and ancestor portrait busts and death masks played a large role in religious, family, and political funerary customs in Rome. Images of ancestors were frequently paraded at

2. Attic red-figure vase (image of husband and wife at doorway), 5th c., c. 430 B.C. Metropolitan Museum of Art, New York.

funeral rites. A portrait of a Roman nobleman might well include ancestral busts in his arms (for example, the statue of a Roman nobleman with ancestral busts, late first century B.C., Rome, Palazzo dei Conservatori). These early Republican images were veristic and realistic and included the wrinkles and blemishes of aging, for instance. Frequently, older men were portrayed in an attempt to show the old Roman virtues of *gravitas, dignitas,* and *fides* passed on to the conservative aristocracy from their ancestors.

Under Augustus, elected pontifex maximus in 12 B.C., there was a great building program, a program for the regeneration of religion and morality, incentives for having children. In 2 B.C., Augustus was formally given the title of "Father of the Fatherland" (*pater patriae*). Although he was not officially deified until after his death, he was frequently referred to as *divi filius*, the son of the deified Julius Caesar. Thus, the very nomenclature used in the political-public realm reinforced the stature and structure of the family realm. The magnificent Ara Pacis (Altar of Augustan Peace) is filled with numerous allusions to the family unit [3]. The south side shows members of Augustus's family, while the north side shows magistrates and their families. A panel, carved in the Hellenistic tradition, depicts Mother Earth with children in her lap and the personification of ocean and water at her side. Mother Earth embraces her children tenderly and assertively. The panel, with its lyrical and delicate images of flora and fauna in high and low relief, suggests tranquillity and fertility. The altar was a commemoration in marble of an actual event—a procession and sacrifice in 13 B.C. following Augustus's safe return from a tour of the Roman provinces. It is important to note that the altar is propaganda, intended to celebrate a leader's heroism and a land at peace, with the family as the centerpiece, that the Father of the Fatherland had brought. It is interesting to compare such propaganda with the photographs of the National Association of Manufacturers (NAM) and the Farm Security Administration (FSA) in the twentieth century as family images became linked with the American economy.

Beyond the royal family, other images reflected the activities of the everyday lives of other citizens. Some illustrated intimate moments, such as the delivery of a child by two midwives (Archaeological Museum, Ostia) or of a woman, seated in a high-backed armchair, a sign of privilege, nursing her baby, while the father looks on (detail from a mid–second century A.D. sarcophagus, the Louvre, Paris). In addition to sculptural works, a number of paintings and mosaics have been excavated that provide us with further images related to family and daily life. One of the most famous images, known as *The Baker and His Wife* (A.D. 50–75, Museo Nazionale, Naples), was found at Pompeii, the city that was cov-

3. *Procession* from the *Ara Pacis Augustae*, 13-9 B.C., portion of frieze. D. Anderson, Editorial Photocolor Archives, Inc.

ered by the eruption of Mt. Vesuvius. The painting is so titled because it was discovered in a house next to a shop selling bread. The young woman holds a writing table, and her husband holds a scroll. These objects do not necessarily mean that the couple could read and write, since they were popular symbols of culture and common in portraits of the middle class. Some scholars believe that the scroll indicates that the man was some kind of municipal magistrate. The portrait is vivid, and the viewer is drawn to the pleasing symmetry of the faces and the young couple's partially raised hands. The husband and wife appear contemplative and constrained, perhaps aware there is a spectator, perhaps even asking who the spectator is. And the spectator begins to sense the possibility of an inner presence in those who are portrayed. This perception of the inner human experience, of an inner self, was new. And as Sheldon Nodelman pointed out, "This new conception, conferring upon the portrait an unprecedented capacity to articulate and project the interior processes of human experience, made possible the achievement in the ensuing six centuries of what is surely the most extraordinary body of portrait art ever created, and forms the indispensable basis for the whole of the later European portrait tradition, from its rebirth in the thirteenth and fourteenth centuries to its virtual extinction in the twentieth."[2]

Although the image and significance of the family was clearly emphasized in both the public and private realms of Roman life, there were cracks in the institution and in the image at the height of the empire and into its decline. By the end of the first century A.D., many Roman marriages were childless. Indeed, the emperor Nerva was chosen for his celibacy; his successors Trajan and Hadrian, although married, had no legitimate children. Writers, such as Martial in his *Epigrams* and Juvenal in his *Satires,* pointed to incidents of adultery. Divorce became prevalent. Some women began to rebel against the constraints of traditional "family values." In his sixth satire Juvenal presents a series of verbal portraits that refer to women giving up embroidery, reading, and playing the lyre and attempting to rival men in their education and more public activities.[3] (Such "stories" of rebellion and divorce were to become familiar in the twentieth century.) In general, Roman portraiture and images related to the family are perhaps the most significant in their awareness and presentation of an essence of humanity and of an inner presence.

The inner life appears to have become dominant in early Christian art. The expression of the eyes is an important part of portraits of this period, since a gaze seems to be fixed on the transcendent, the eternal. Less attention is paid to the worldly, physical attributes of the portrayed. For the early Christians, the true self was to be found in the soul, not in the body or its clothes. Early Christian faith was an important factor in the journey to find one's soul and sense of self. Among the earliest Christian portraits of private individuals and of a family (rather than of Christ and his disciples) is a third-century glass miniature of the Vunnerius Keramus family on which the figures are painted in gold leaf (Museo Civico Cristiano, Brescia). Unlike the Pompeiian baker and his wife, the mother, son, and daughter peer into the distance, beyond this world toward a transcendent world. The baker and his wife are part of this world and hold tools of a worldly culture. But one sees no worldly props in this miniature. Indeed, the miniature was ultimately placed at the center of a seventh-century gold cross.

When the Emperor Constantine declared Christianity to be the official religion of the empire, church and state gradually merged, and a new more symbolic art began to develop. The mosaics at San Vitale, A.D. 547, in Ravenna, which depict Justinian and his Empress Theodora, show the royal couple as a union of political and spiritual authority. Justinian and Theodora are each surrounded by attendants—officials, local clergy, and ladies in waiting—watching as if they were in a palace chapel. Their bodies are tall and slim, and they have large staring eyes. Their robes are beautifully patterned. There is little sense of movement, but a strong frontal image that gives way to a sense of the transcendent in the church space. Indeed, Justinian may be viewed as analogous to Christ and Theodora, to the Virgin. The hem of Theodora's mantle is "embroidered" with the three Magi carrying gifts to the newborn Christ and his mother Mary. Justinian is surrounded by twelve figures, who may be analogous to the twelve disciples. Six of the figures are soldiers who stand behind a shield with the monogram of Christ. The figures are slightly individualized, but there is a "family" resemblance in that they all have the same large dark eyes, small mouth, or long narrow nose that are to reappear in Byzantine art.

The early Middle Ages saw the death of individual portraiture. The medieval artist or illuminator tended to draw a type. The individual identity crises that have beset modern culture simply did not exist. Medieval society was much more rigidly structured, and possibilities for flexibility were almost nonexistent. Identity of family and self was usually fixed at birth—on the basis of lineage, gender, home, and social class. Marriage and age-related transitions, such as from childhood to adulthood, brought about changes in identity, but the individual was usually passive, and marriages were usually arranged. One of the major reasons for lack of emphasis on individuality was the firm medieval faith in Christianity, which considered life on earth simply an imitation or derivation of an ultimate transcendent reality. More important were the larger struggles of good and evil, honor and dishonor, virtue and vice—forces in which the individual was simply a player in a larger cosmos, with little uniqueness. Imagination was viewed as a kind of mirror, and any acts of creation were thought of as mirroring the original, which was seen as emanating from God. The arts, which developed primarily out of this Christian faith, were to draw on the light and reason of the Holy Scriptures.

The depiction of family life was thus marginal or subservient to the larger Christian faith. Images of European family life literally decorated the margins of Books of Hours (collections of psalms and short prayers). Families are shown at work or at rest, defining their place in society, economically and socially. In the Cleves Book of Hours (fifteenth century, Pierpont Morgan Library), one sees a family baking bread on a page that is devoted mainly to an image of St. Philip the Apostle, while the text is beneath the richly patterned image surrounding the apostle. Although the family is clearly portrayed in the act of baking bread, which indicates their economic position as tradesmen, it is significant that this particular trade is illustrated in juxtaposition to the biblical figure, given the role of bread in biblical stories and its importance in the sacrament of communion. Thus, sacred and secular are clearly and closely intertwined in a manuscript such as this. In another Book of Hours, the Da Costa Book, one again sees a family preparing a meal before a large open fire [4]. A lit candle on the table, with painted rays of light, appears to be not only a physical earthly light, but a light of the Holy Spirit, symbolized in the flame imagery, which was seen as warming, sustaining, and transcending earthly life. Images such as these are filled with harmony and a sense of well-being. The family's unity and sense of self appears to be based not only on work, but on an inward harmony that mirrored a heavenly spirit and place.

By the thirteenth century, the growth of towns in Europe created a new class of women with managerial skills that they developed due to inheritance, and privileges that allowed them to carry on family businesses after the death of their husbands or fathers. Women are shown working in a variety of occupations in a sculptural series known as the "Active Life," on the north porch of Chartres Cathedral. The *Book of Trades*, written by Étienne Boileau in the thirteenth century, lists at least six occupations out of one hundred that were governed by female guilds. Men and women frequently worked side by side in guild workshops. Thus, women were not entirely connected with the realm of the home, and the

4. *January: Dinner Scene* from the Da Costa Book of Hours, 15th c. Pierpont Morgan Library, New York.

family could be seen as an economic, social, and spiritual entity, though one that fit into its place in God's universe. The imagery in the medieval era is related, above all, to the glory of God and Christianity, as the encyclopedic, majestic Gothic cathedrals, in which painting, sculpture, and architecture came together in a magnificent whole, attest to. Men, women, and families were but small players on the medieval stage. Indeed, the word *self* did not become a noun until late in the Middle Ages, and even then, it had a negative connotation. At first, the *Oxford English Dictionary* (circa 1400), was to quote, "Oure own self we sal deny. And folow oure lord God al-myghty." Initially, the word self was a reflexive pronoun and adjective that meant "own," as in ownership and "same."

At the end of the Middle Ages, the spread of religious dissent and the possibility of some social mobility began to have an impact on concepts of human identity. Questions about a Catholic monopoly on the Truth, which led to the Protestant Reformation, created cracks in the model of a single, unquestioned guide for living one's life. The growing schism between Protestantism and

Catholicism could lead only to unrest concerning any fixed sense of self. Social rank became dependent not only on birth, but on wealth and lineage, which could come into conflict with one another. No longer could the older norms of social interaction by class, birth, and the like always hold true. Hence, public life involved some possible stress, as self-definition became more dependent on achievement and interaction in a commercial world. This stress could have contributed to the increasing emphases on privacy and on the home and family as distinct from public life that were to occur in the Renaissance.

2

From the Renaissance to the Nineteenth Century

It was during the Renaissance, as man—not God—became the
center of thought and the role of the individual became increasingly important in the society at large that there was a great
increase in painted and sculpted portraiture. As John Pope-Hennessy stated: "Portraiture, like other forms of art, is an expression of
conviction, and in the Renaissance, it reflects the reawakening
interest in human motives and the human character, the resurgent
recognition of those factors which make human beings individual,
that lay at the center of Renaissance life. It is sometimes said that
the Renaissance vision of man's self-sufficient nature marks the
beginning of the modern world. Undoubtedly it marks the beginning of the modern portrait."⁴ One's ego, personality, and sense of
individual worth were given new importance. There was a renewed
interest in the classical world of Greece and Rome. Everyday life of
this world, rather than life in the next world, was emphasized. Correct perspective and proportion were developed.

An early Renaissance painting related to family life, although
stylistically perhaps better connected with late Gothic art, was the
Flemish wedding portrait of Giovanni Arnolfini and his bride,
Jeanne Cenami, by Jan Van Eyck [5]. Van Eyck, as did a number
of Flemish artists, attempted to depict as exactly as possible what

5. Jan Van Eyck, *Wedding Portrait of Giovanni Arnolfini and His Wife*, 1434. National Gallery, London.

his eye saw. Thus, in the portrait, there is great attention to the details of texture—of the fur of the dog, the man's coat, the surface of the fruit, the chandelier, and the slippers. And beneath these details there was a search for individual character. Who was this Arnolfini, and what does one learn from his wedding portrait? Clearly, from his dress, one sees he was affluent, an Italian financier among the foreign residents who resided in the growing Flemish centers of trade and international banking—Tournai, Ghent, and Bruges—and therefore commissioned a Flemish painter. The young couple are exchanging vows in a secular space, the bridal chamber. Although, at first glance they appear to be alone, through the mirror on the back wall, one quickly learns that two other people are part of the scene. Of the two figures reflected faintly in the mirror, one is possibly Van Eyck's assistant. The other is the artist, as is evidenced by the elegant writing above the mirror that reads, when translated into English, "Jan Van Eyck was here," along with the date 1434. Van Eyck thus becomes a witness to the ceremony and at the same time raises questions about the relationship of the artist to his subjects. Although the setting is domestic, there are subtle symbols that convey the significance of the sacrament of marriage. A single candle burning in the chandelier alludes to the Spirit of Christ, whose Passion is referred to in the scenes on the mirror frame. The couple has removed their shoes as a reminder that they are participating in a holy sacrament. Yet the shoes remain in the room, both pairs clearly visible in the front and rear of the painting. The little dog is seen as a symbol of marital fidelity, and the fruit may well be related to fertility. The finial of the bedpost is a tiny statue of St. Margaret, the patron saint of childbirth. From the finial hangs a whisk broom, symbolic of domestic care. The natural world and the world of the holy seem to be integrated into a balanced whole of unity and graceful beauty.

A larger family-group portrait, executed forty years later in Italy also to honor newlyweds, was the large-group family portrait of the Gonzaga family, for the Camera degli Sposi, at the Ducal Palace in Mantua in 1474, by Andrea Mantegna. In this "Room of the Newlyweds," Mantegna represents members of the House of Gonzaga welcoming home from Rome a son, Francesco, recently made a cardinal of the Roman Catholic Church. Mantegna had been Marchese Ludovico Gonzaga's official painter in 1459 after Gonzaga had amassed both wealth and land by defeating his enemies in Venice and Milan. In the trompe l'oeil fresco, he paints larger-than-life-size figures, magnificently costumed, as if they seem to be stepping out of a small terrace into the palace room. The marchese's right foot and the hem of the marchesa's dress appear to project beyond the floor of the terrace where the family sits. The figures are somewhat casually portrayed, in both domestic and landscape settings, conveying the familiarity of a family reunion. On the entrance wall are three frescoes at eye level, the right one filled with portraits. In the foreground are the male members of the family: Ludovico Gonzaga; his eldest son, Federigo, in profile; and his second son, Cardinal Francesco Gonzaga, in the center in almost full face, clearly the center of attention. At the back are six other figures, four in profile, all placed in positions similar to a Roman Aurelian relief. The second fresco above the chimney piece shows the marchese and his wife, Barbara of Brandenburg, seated with members of the family and court, awaiting an emissary. The painting is a glorification of Gonzaga, his family, his wealth, and his power, and of fifteenth-century court life. It is also the century's only major depiction of a current event. Mantegna has integrated the architecture of the room with his painting. The lunettes are filled with garlands and medallions similar to those of classical antiquity, recalling earlier ages of splendor and power. The room's decoration, with the *di sotto in su* perspective of a ceiling from which painted spectators and strongly foreshortened amorous cupids look down form the illusion of a high arched ceiling and set a mood for the room. Thus, the room, in more modern terms, is an environment, and the portrait has become three dimensional in a sense. Important, too, is the fact there are spectators, an audience, in the room, those looking down from the ceiling and, of course, those who are entering the room. The ceiling figures—non-family members, particularly a black, turbaned figure—all glorify the Gonzaga family. Unlike earlier frescoes of court life, the family is strongly depicted as representative of power and wealth and is portrayed on the stage set of history with allusions to classical antiquity. In the spandrels beneath the ceiling are Roman emperors, and above the Gothic arches are scenes from classical mythology.

Public image was clearly important. Portraits dealt with both public image and events of private significance that then took on a public face, as in wedding portraits. Portraits could also be used for the purposes of "social climbing." Imaginary portraits of ancestors, sometimes themselves imaginary, could do something to enhance the grandeur of a family, and living persons might be painted in poses and clothes that made them seem more than they may in fact have been. As Lorne Campbell noted, "In 1584 the Italian theorist Lomazzo complained that 'merchants and bankers who have never seen a drawn sword and who should properly appear with quill pens behind their ears, their gowns about them and their day-books in front of them, have themselves painted in armour holding generals' batons.'"[5]

The development of trade and capitalism and the emergence of the modern state affected economic, social, and family relationships in Renaissance Italy. There was increased loyalty to the state and an emphasis on individualism and to one's religious sect as people gradually ceased to feel that their identities were tied to and determined by family lineage. Rather than the medieval organization of localities comprised of families, interests turned toward the state as the growth of capitalism brought greater wealth for some. In addition, privatization of the family increased, particularly in relation to women's roles outside the home. Women were not as much a part of the "production of culture" as they were in the medieval era or were frequently relegated to unskilled activities in various guilds. The division between public and private led to the perception and practice of art as primarily a male, public activity. Women were more frequently represented as the subjects/objects of male artists.

The discovery that childhood, particularly later childhood from about age six to puberty, was different from adult life did not become widespread, according to Philippe Ariès in *Centuries of Childhood* (1962) until the sixteenth century. It was then that children were first seen as both amusing and handsome or beautiful and to be doted on. Children were also considered, as Alberti noted, to be unformed, in need of adult guidance to grow up to be "good" adults. In practice, this "guidance" sometimes meant harsh discipline by family members or the school. Along with the recognition of individual potentiality, there arose issues of choice for parents and children.

The sixteenth century also brought with it the concept that there was a hidden internal space that was not always reflected in outward actions or appearances. Contrasts between appearances and realities existed in a number of cultural areas, from figures as diverse as Machiavelli, whose "ends justified the means," and Shakespeare, with his plots of mixed and missed identities.

This manifestation of a hidden self is seen in the beginnings of psychological portraiture with the portraits of Leonardo da Vinci and his attempt to paint "the motions of the mind." In Leonardo's well-known painting, *Virgin and Child with Saint Anne* [6], although the subject is the Holy Family, the sense of a hidden self is felt in the presence of both Mary and her mother, Anne. Here is a family scene that is filled with warmth and intimacy, as Mary reaches for her baby frolicking with the symbolic lamb, while her mother, somewhat emotionally distanced, looks fondly at her daughter and granddaughter. The classical pyramid structure of the figures in the painting, set in the misty, veiled atmosphere of the natural landscape, contributes further to the sense of the harmony and well-being of this family. This image of the Holy Family, as did others of the period, such as those by Raphael, clearly departed from the flat and/or stiff images of the Madonna and Child of earlier years. The image of Madonna and Child, which became so human in the Renaissance, was to become secularized in future generations. By the twentieth century, one sees an image such as Dorothea Lange's *Migrant Mother* in a configuration similar to some Renaissance images.

Although the seeds of personality and psychology were sown during the Renaissance, it was in the seventeenth century that European portraiture rose to a height it had not reached since the

6. Leonardo da Vinci, *The Virgin and Child with St. Anne*, c. 1508–10. Louvre, Paris.

time of the Romans. René Descartes's famous statement, "I think therefore I am" (*"Cogito ergo sum"*) set the stage for the pursuit of rationality and the notion that concepts and knowledge of self were to be gained from empirical evidence.

In Dutch art one finds an emphasis on observation and great attention to the details of home and domestic life. With the rise of Protestantism, the Virgin Mary was no longer the primary female model. Instead the image of the domestic interior, frequently with a woman engaged in some kind of needlework or lacemaking, was a symbol of a well-ordered Dutch world and domestication of the senses. Depictions of the home and attention to objects and textures or fabrics served as manifestations of the increasing affluence of the Dutch Republic brought about by the growth in trade and commerce.

The domestic interior also was a reflection of Christian principles in an ordered setting and the roles of women in the home. One finds frequent images, such as Judith Leyster's *A Woman Sewing by Candlelight*, 1633 (National Gallery of Ireland), with young children looking on. It should be noted, though, that needlework was not simply a leisure task, but a task of labor, depending on the financial circumstances of the woman portrayed. Erasmus, the Dutch humanist, in his *Christiani matrimoni institutio*, satirized the emphasis on needlework in the education of young women of the nobility, rather than on formal study subjects.

More than ever before in painting, the viewer is let into the details of domestic interiors and the tasks of maintaining a household. Consider, for example, Pieter de Hooch's *Interior with Two Women at a Linen Chest*, 1663 (Rijksmuseum, Amsterdam). Folding and putting away laundry, what for many has become a task of drudgery and boredom, is portrayed here with dignity and significance, with a young child looking on. As housewives and Christians, these women were thought of as "stewards" of God. The young child is depicted gently playing *colf* (similar to golf) with a club in hand. The linen chest in the painting is beautifully decorated with graceful arches on its full-length doors that protectively embrace one of the women. The paintings on the wall; the expansive quality of the home, suggested by the opening into other parts of the house that are partially in view; and the elegant classical pilasters on the leaded glass window and door, indicate a home of comfort and order, a home of a newly evolving bourgeois or middle class. The notion of comfort and of a comfortable home became significant as comfort came to involve more than ease of the body, but also the fact of feeling reassured that contemplation of various objects within a setting could be comforting.[6]

Some seventeenth-century family images, such as Jacob Jordaens's series of paintings *As the Old Sing, So the Young Pipe* [7], have a pedagogical, moralistic intent, admonishing parents and elders to set good examples for children. Beyond the moralistic tone of the popular saying, which had its origins in biblical passages, though, is a sense of merriment and playful celebration. One of Jordaens's paintings of this series, about 1640–45 (National Gallery of Canada, Ottawa), contains seven figures representing three generations, who are seated around a table laden with food and drink. Some are singing and playing flutes. A mother holds up a glass to drink in one hand and a baby with a rattle in her other hand. An owl is perched on the wicker chair of an old woman who is singing, while a parrot is perched on a chair laden with fruit in the foreground. The owl is traditionally related to wisdom, while the parrot, known for its ability to imitate speech uncritically, stands as a symbol of a student who may imitate everything, both good and bad. Thus, the artist inserted symbolic reminders related to education and to the saying. In the background a laughing jester holds up a cage with a bird and her babies, another family unit to be "educated." A dog, the symbol of fidelity, peers out from under the table. Traditional still-life objects typical of various paintings— a glass vase filled with flowers that will fade in time, a snuffed candle, a book, and some documents—are in a niche in the upper left of the painting. Such objects tended to emphasize the notion of human mortality and transience. The inscription on the sheet of paper that the older woman is singing from has been translated to read, "A New Song of Callou, The Beggars," referring to a victory of the Cardinal Infante Ferdinand of Spain over the forces of Frederick Hendrick of Orange at Callou, near Antwerp, in 1638. The references to death and defeat point again to notions of mortality, indicating that a family's sons may well die in battle. The painting, while moralizing, though, is equally a celebration of fam-

7. Jacob Jordaens, *As the Old Sing, So the Young Pipe*, c. 1640. National Gallery of Canada, Ottawa.

ily merriment and a family making music together.

The middle class was also depicted in the poignant portraits of Rembrandt van Rijn. In his late portraits, Rembrandt's use of a heavier impasto than in earlier work caused his work to become increasingly expressive. Frequently, his subjects were dressed in highly textured, brocade or jeweled costumes, augmented by the thick pigmentation of the paint. One of his late paintings, *The Jewish Bride* [8], depicts an unidentified couple who are clearly in love with each other. The figures shimmer in the spotlight of Rembrandt's subtle lighting, their dress and faces radiating forth. Their hands tenderly touch. He stands with one protective arm across her shoulder and the other around her waist. The painting seems to assert, in secular terms, the sacredness of marriage and the strength and support that love can bring. Gone are the symbolic objects of the Van Eyck wedding portrait. More important is the bond of affection between the two figures that Rembrandt so eloquently depicted. When Rembrandt painted this piece, his son Titus was dead, as was the young woman of peasant origin, Hendrickje Stoffels, with whom he had lived after his wife Saskia's

8. Rembrandt, *Isaac and Rebecca* (*"The Jewish Bride"*), c. 1665–1668. Rijksmuseum, Amsterdam.

death. Alone, Rembrandt seemed to recall the power of compassion and tenderness in this piece.

Rembrandt's depiction of the Holy Family (the Hermitage, Saint Petersburg) is that of an ordinary middle- or lower-class family. No one would know that this was the Holy Family except for the angels hovering above the child.

Although portrayals of the growing middle class in the seventeenth century were significant, the virtuosity of Peter Paul Rubens, Anthony Van Dyck, and Diego Velázquez established an elaborate style of court painting, of individual and group portraits. Rubens's great cycle of twenty-one paintings, executed for Marie de Medici, to decorate the Luxembourg Palace, was a complex, composite portrait of her family and a glorification of her past.

Rubens's protégé, Anthony Van Dyck, was more strictly a portrait painter than was Rubens. His portraits, primarily of the nobility and upper class, idealize and ennoble his subjects. His long residence in Genoa, Italy, where he was the portraitist of patrician families, such as the Grimaldis, and the time he spent at the court of St. James, where he became the painter to Charles I (and was eventually knighted), resulted in portraits of grandeur for those who commissioned them. In his works, women are beautiful and never look old, while young men appear attractive and proud. Van Dyck, even more than Rubens, appears to help create the public image of these figures. As painter for the doomed Charles I, Van Dyck painted numerous images of the king and of Cavalier society. The volume of the work is significant. We see Charles with his family, with his horse, in armor, in coronation garments, and so on. Replicas of these portraits were taken out of British closets after the civil war to prove loyalty to the Stuart reign. The individual personalities painted are always enhanced by magnificent pictorial compositions, and Van Dyck, as the fashionable portraitist of the day, was commissioned frequently.

Van Dyck painted a number of images of Charles I's children. These group portraits, although formal, reflect a sense of well-being in a society of elegance and grace. *The Five Eldest Children of Charles I*, circa 1637 (Windsor Castle, collection of H. M. Queen Elizabeth II), depicts the five children, with the older boy standing with his head on a large dog that is standing in the middle of the scene. Van Dyck's fashionable portraits, both individual and group images, were to influence future generations of portrait painters, such as Thomas Gainsborough and John Singer Sargent.

The rise of Puritanism in England in the middle of the seventeenth century clearly had an impact on the family, and images of the family that were produced were far different from the virtuosity of a Rubens or Van Dyck. With the Puritan beliefs, following John Calvin's teachings that there was an "Elect," predestined to enter heaven, self-consciousness increased. Who was destined for heaven? Who was destined for hell? The Puritans moved away from the structure and "trappings" of the Catholic Church toward a privacy of the individual mind. Child-rearing practices were based on the belief that children's wills needed to be broken to teach them to be subservient and obedient to their parents. An isolated nuclear family was favored over an extended family or a number of servants, since it was thought that children could be overindulged if people other than parents were in the household. And one sees the beginnings of the Protestant work ethic, which stressed the importance of hard work as a means of spiritual improvement. Extra hard work was praised, for success in one's work was viewed as a possible sign that one was among God's Elect. Thus self-discipline, self-reliance, reason, and diligence were considered virtues. In many ways, the family was seen as an extension of, or surrogate for, the church. William Dobson's group portrait, probably of the Streatfield family (Paul Mellon Collection, Yale Center for British Art, New Haven, Connecticut) reflects a stern family with little sense of joy. The skulls and cracked masonry in the upper-left-hand corner of the painting, reflect the *vanitas* sensibilities of Dutch paintings and seem to point to a preoccupation with death and what might follow.

Some Puritans fled to America, and it is interesting to note that there was little portraiture in seventeenth-century America. Because idols and portraits were considered to be in vain and not a part of the Puritan aesthetic, there were severe restrictions on painting and sculpture in Protestant America. If there was any painting, the dominant form of the seventeenth century was portrait painting. Limners, anonymous artisans with no formal training, were the primary artists. Children were portrayed as miniature adults, with stiff postures, solemn expressions, and adultlike clothing. There were no distinctive signs of toys, children's furniture, or schoolbooks related to what we now consider a child's world.

Thus, in its diverse depictions of family scenes, the seventeenth century brought large painterly public images, as well as small, intimate private images. In general, an increased interest in the phenomena of the natural world influenced observation and the depiction of realms of domesticity. And with Descartes, reason became a dominant force in seventeenth-century thought.

Eighteenth-century Europe marked the decline of Christianity as a major factor in shaping the daily lives and identities of many and an increased emphasis on the role of reason. The term *Enlightenment* is frequently used to describe this period. Two well-known critics of Christianity were Voltaire in France and Thomas Paine in America. There was not a complete rejection of religion but, rather, an emphasis on the role of reason. For example, deism came to play a significant role in the lives of some. According to deism, God or a Supreme Being created the universe according to natural laws, but then left men and women to run their own lives. Thus, the pursuit of knowledge, scientific observation, and philosophical analysis came to play a larger role in daily lives than did prayer and faith in God. Political revolutions in France and the United States also affected people's sense of themselves. No longer were citizens bound in allegiance to a given state and accepting of their political, economic, and social status as a static given. American colonists considered it "self-evident" that "all men are created equal," although it is unclear whether this assertion included women and nonwhite men. The French revolutionists cried "Liberty, Equality, and Fraternity." In contrast, the medieval world considered it a given that all men were created unequal, that aristocrats were inherently better people than were peasants. Social rank was no longer to be defined and determined by a combination of wealth, power, lineage, title, and social connections. The middle class could become wealthy. A person's potential was thus not to be solely assigned by society or by God. A person could have some sense of choice; therefore, a variable related to the "unknown" became part of establishing a sense of self.

The eighteenth century gave birth to several major thinkers who were to influence concepts of the self. David Hume (1711–76) emphasized powers of observation. Because he understood the self to be a mental construct, the mind and what went on in the mind, he believed that any change in experience, knowledge, or perception would mean a change in the self.

Immanuel Kant (1724–1804) agreed with Hume that one could not perceive oneself directly, but that one could perceive events, other people, objects, and so forth, as well as oneself, in connection with the outside world. The self thus could not be known in isolation; it could be known only in relation to the world. Kant believed that a real self did exist but could not be known directly alone; rather, a phenomenal self was to be implied from other perceptions. Momentary glimpses of self-awareness, such as the self in some activity, would, when taken together, create some sense of a unified self established over time, almost in a collage fashion. The self is thus made, and does not arise automatically or immediately. The implications of Kant's thinking on portraiture may include the increased significance of the placement and depiction of family life related to some activity or "props" that suggest relations to the outside world as well. And the very painting itself could offer a glimpse of self-awareness, illuminated by the artwork, which is more a lamp than a mirror, as was the case in earlier periods.

By the eighteenth century, the house in much of northern Europe was becoming a home. Domesticity, privacy, and comfort, following the Dutch, became more important.

During the eighteenth century, the finest portraits seemed to emanate from England and France. Recovered from the civil war, the upper-class British were devoted to applied art and domestic architecture, and many portraits were commissioned to adorn interiors. Following in the footsteps of Van Dyck, a number of artists approached the portrait in a formula fashion.

Sir Joshua Reynolds at his height of popularity had six sitters a day. Like other eighteenth-century portraitists, he did not necessarily paint what he saw, but had a general appealing tone for flesh. Certain conventions, such as a touch of carmine color in the nostrils or in the corner of the eye, were frequently employed to flatter the sitter.

For the portrayed, the process was often a social one. It was not uncommon for a sitter's friends to come and go during the process of painting and to interrupt and even criticize the painter. Some artists set up mirrors for the sitters to watch the process as well. Indeed, the process became a kind of "performance art." It is unlikely that any in-depth relationship developed between the painter and sitter. Any in-depth interest in personality would have been restrained by a code of manners and decorum. There could be issues of power between the artist and sitter, depending on their genders and ages, as well as on their financial and social statuses and need. In some instances, the painter could be perceived as more "powerful" because of his reputation. Some commissions were clearly for political and social purposes, such as a mother commissioning a piece of a son or a daughter to be used in the arrangement of a marriage, for the appropriate parties to view, if a child, particularly a son, was not immediately available. Portraits might initially be "matched" in the process of negotiation. There were numerous portraits of children and family groups.

With increased interest in the concept of childhood, there was greater interest in portraits of children, particularly because many children died young. The commissioning of portraits of children frequently had multiple meanings. As Marcia Pointon wrote, "Children do not commission portraits, and their presence in them is the result of negotiated relationships in the adult world designed, consciously and unconsciously, to produce a set of explicit and implicit meanings. . . . On account of the centrality of the child to traditions of moral narrative, it was extremely easy for portraits of children to become bearers of the values society held most dear while denoting the particular offspring of particular parents."[7] Some portraits of children, such as Reynolds's portrait of the young Lady Charlotte Spencer and Lord Henry Spencer, 1755 (Henry E. Huntington Library and Art Gallery, San Marino, California), were sentimental and suggestive of narrative. In this portrait, the children stand with their hands entwined, in elegant

9. Sir Joshua Reynolds, *The Van der Gucht Children*, c. 1785. Huntington Library, San Marino, California.

dress, in an idyllic landscape setting that appears to have some reminders of an Italian setting, in the distant buildings and trees. Or there is Reynolds's portrait of *The Van der Gucht Children* [9], in which the children look at each other adoringly, accompanied by a robin to whom one child is holding out bread. Such images could well be illustrations in a storybook.

Somewhat different from the fashionable portraitists, such as Gainsborough and Reynolds, was William Hogarth (1697–1764). Hogarth criticized the mechanical aspects of much of British eighteenth-century portraiture, as well as the tendency for the painter to flatter and idealize his subjects. For Hogarth, as reflected in his treatise on aesthetics, *The Analysis of Beauty* (1753), the character of a given individual could be reflected on his or her face, and the changes over time in the human face were not to be discounted. Hogarth also pointed to what might lie undisclosed beneath the physical characteristics.

Two of Hogarth's portraits of children, *The Mackinen Children* (1747; National Gallery of Ireland) and *The Graham Children* [10], contained a sense of informality, a sense of spontaneity and vitality, that endears the children to almost any viewer and marks a sense of childhood that is perhaps unique to the eighteenth century. The children in these portraits were not royalty. The Graham children were the children of Daniel Graham, an apothecary at Chelsea Hospital. William (1733–1809) and Elizabeth Mackinen (1730–1780) are the grandchildren of Daniel Mackinen (1658–1720), the younger son of the clan chief of the Island of Skye, who moved from Scotland to the West Indies, where his son William (circa 1697–1767) became a wealthy landowner. Hogarth most likely painted the Mackinen children when they came to England to go to school, as was the custom for affluent British families who lived abroad. Ages seventeen and fourteen, the young Mackinens are portrayed on a lovely terrace with buildings in the background. They both are attracted by a butterfly on a sunflower that occupies the central part of the canvas. There are overtones of Adam and Eve in the Garden of Eden. The sunflower may be seen as an emblem of transient beauty, similar to the imagery in earlier Dutch paintings.

The Graham children are portrayed inside, in a well-appointed

10. William Hogarth, *The Graham Children*, 1742. National Gallery, London.

room, enthusiastic and content, with toys and an abundance of fruit in an ornate silver basket in the lower corner of the painting. The older daughter holds symbolic cherries in her left hand. A reminder of the inevitable passage of time, in contrast to the moment being captured, is found in the image of Time's scythe in a sculpture in the background. The reality of the wider world, sometimes in conflict, through the portrayal of a predator-victim relationship, is seen in the image of the greedy cat on the back of the young boy's chair. The cat appears ready to pounce on the songbird in the cage hanging above. Despite his depiction of some sense of informality and spontaneity, Hogarth was still caught in the conventions of his age, for the children are still somewhat idealized.

In France a variety of family images could be found in the second half of the century. Jean-Baptiste Greuze, breaking away from the Academic Salon, specialized in scenes of family life. As Jean-Jacques Rousseau and other philosophers were doing, Greuze began to idealize a seemingly simpler, more natural, way of life of more modest households than those of the upper class. Inspired initially by images of the seventeenth-century Dutch middle class, Greuze went further in more dramatic portrayals of family groupings. In his paintings, the father is frequently the center of attention, dramatizing patriarchal authority that reflected French law and custom that gave fathers of every class, as heads of families, almost absolute power over all household members and property. Disobedient children or wives could be imprisoned by order of the fathers at the state's expense. The so-called good mother was portrayed as happy in tending to the needs of her family. In Greuze's pieces, familial conflict may be portrayed, but his titles, such as *The Father's Curse*, 1778, or *The Son Punished*, 1779 (both in the Louvre, Paris), imply an accepted social and emotional system, in which there is a clear-cut understanding of who is in power and in control. These eighteenth-century stage sets, containing rhetorical poses of the "characters," suggest the miseries brought forth by any disruption of the family unit. They carefully fit Denis Diderot's didactic prescription that the purpose of painting at that time was to make virtue look attractive and any vices look unappealing. These two paintings by Greuze tell the story of an ungrateful elder son, who is cursed for abandoning his family and going off to the army. In the second piece, the son returns a number of years later, disabled and disillusioned, only to learn that his father died just a few moments before his arrival. Thus, he cannot be forgiven or reunited with his father. In both paintings, it is the women who appear to deal with the emotional "heat" of the moment, trying to calm both father and son, in the first piece, and expressing grief around the father's deathbed, in the second piece.

A gentler depiction of French family life at this time is to be found in the work of Jean-Baptiste Chardin, in such pieces as his *Governess*, 1738 (National Gallery of Canada), or *Grace Before a Meal* [11]. A young mother waits for her youngest child to finish saying grace before she serves the meal. There are no men and no conflicts in this scene. The emphasis is on the quiet moment of

11. Jean-Baptiste Chardin, *Grace Before a Meal*, 1740. Louvre, Paris.

domestic tranquillity and the spirituality that is part of that moment, which was potentially part of a peaceful family unit.

As the century progressed, and the average family size in France dropped from the 6.5 children of the seventeenth century to two children in the eighteenth century, owing to the first widespread use of birth control, children were seen as more and more precious, and it was thought that the future wealth of the country lay, in part, in its population of children. In an attempt to revive her image, Marie Antoinette commissioned Elisabeth-Louise Vigée-Lebrun to paint a portrait of her with her children, emphasizing the mother-child bond. The large-scale portrait (Musée de Versailles), painted in 1787 shortly before the French Revolution, is a masterful piece of propaganda painting. Depicted in the Salon de la Paix at Versailles, the queen sits elegantly and peacefully with her baby on her lap. Her older daughter clutches her right arm, while her young son stands at her feet, gesturing toward the baby and holding the sumptuous drapes of the cradle open. The rich red of the queen's dress and the slightly darker tone of the older daughter's dress, juxtaposed with the dark forest green of the drapery, as well as the pyramid structure of the figures, reminding one of Renaissance Madonnas, makes a strong statement. Vigée-Lebrun had painted numerous portraits of the queen, whose marriage represented a political alliance between the royal families of France and Austria. In many of the portraits, including the one with her children, Marie Antoinette is transformed from a rather unattractive woman to a beautiful woman and mother, who would touch the country via the painting by her maternal devotion; in addition, the children would emphasize the alliance between France and Austria. However, by the time the painting was completed for the 1787 Salon, the political situation had deteriorated further, so the piece could not be hung until after the official opening.

Vigée-Lebrun was well accepted as a portraitist of her day, and she stands out as one of the few women to be so well established.

12. Elisabeth Vigée-Lebrun, *Self-Portrait with Julie*, 1789. Louvre, Paris.

Besides painting others, she is also noted for her self-portraits, particularly those with her daughter, Julie. Two self-portraits are dated from 1789. In one, she is in a Greek togalike dress, which she favored over the stiff, corseted, ornate fashions of the day [12]. Her loose-fitting dress helps to emphasize the spontaneous, relaxed embrace of mother and daughter. In the other painting, she is more elegantly dressed, with a turban on her head, and is holding her young daughter tightly in her lap. The mother-daughter relationship is strongly and beautifully portrayed with nothing in the background to distract from the relationship of the two figures, except the drapery material on which Vigée-Lebrun is seated.

With the spirit of revolution came increased attention to the revolutionary cause, consuming interest and energy that might have been directed to family relations. Jacques-Louis David's allegorical prerevolutionary paintings based on stories of antiquity— *The Oath of the Horatii*, 1785 (the Louvre, Paris) and *The Lictors Bring to Brutus the Bodies of His Sons* [13]—point to issues of the sacrifice of family loyalties for the state's well-being. In these works the authority of the father has been replaced by a new allegiance to a cause outside the family and the self. Through his paintings, David sent allegorical messages to the French people to believe in and sacrifice themselves for the revolutionary cause. With clear, neoclassical forms, he delivered a message without a lot of emotion, excess ornamentation, or detail. In both paintings, men and women are also clearly separated in their roles and in their placement in the paintings. Hence, the power of the family patriarch was coming to an end, in both art and in reality, although privileged men would still hold the offices of the new French state following the French Revolution. Thus, we see once again the role of art as a kind of propaganda, this time teaching through a story of a past culture that was looked up to in many ways.

In America in the eighteenth century, there was a widening cultural gap between merchants and planters, who were growing in affluence, and urban workers and rural farmers. Those with greater wealth turned increasingly to commissioning or collecting paintings as status symbols and as ego enhancements. This elite wanted images to mirror "their materialistic interests, their pragmatic outlook, their egalitarian spirit, and their quiet self-confidence, which

13. Jacques-Louis David, *The Lictors Bring to Brutus the Bodies of His Sons*, 1789. Louvre, Paris.

came in part from the good life and the prosperity they had gained through their own labor. Such were the components defining the social being known as the colonial American . . . and it would be unthinkable that they should not appear as salient characteristics in the portraits of the upper-middle-class mercantile aristocracy."[8] For example, a man garbed in a dressing gown or a nightcap was a sign not of informality or impropriety, but rather of a man of letters or artistic talent. The cut of a wig or coat could identify a man's profession or social status. A typical eighteenth-century man's wig was parted in the center with curls to the shoulder, whereas a doctor's wig had no curls, but a fluffy teased effect known as a thatched bob. For children, the presence of buttons or the shape of their collars indicated their sex.

By 1750 there appeared to be some intermediary stage of dress for boys between childhood and maturity. Childhood did not simply end at age seven with the adoption of breeches, as had been the case earlier in the century. Artists also began to portray children with clothes that were less constricting than the fashionable, formal clothes of adults. During the last part of the eighteenth century, perceptions of childhood changed and were reflected in the portraits. Greater social and geographic mobility and reliance on the family allowed for the development of closer relationships within the family. Increased life expectancy and decreased infant mortality rates, particularly in the South, made emotional investment in family life possible. Greater affluence resulted in children being more indulged and enjoyed.

After 1770, the image of the nuclear family became more common. Nuclear family portraits "increasingly became the composition of choice as families became more private and insular. . . . Very rarely do portraits of this period include members of the extended family; one catches few anticipatory glimpses of the large multi-generational groups so characteristic of Victorian paintings."⁹ A 1790 painting of the Angus Nickelson family, attributed to Ralph Earl (Museum of Fine Arts, Springfield, Massachusetts) shows a middle-class family spread in a curved line in a comfortable parlor or library. The placement of the mother next to the young child and the youngest son next to the father was typical. The portrayal of the father in a paternal role was different from his portrayal in earlier paintings, which would have emphasized the father as the provider within the family group. However, a certain hierarchy of sex and status is suggested by the dress and "props"; for example, the baby and youngest daughter, dressed in sexless white dresses, are placed closest to the mother, and the boys are placed closest to the father, one with a toy train and one with a book, both associated with the male.

More elaborate and fluid family images were also created by artists who spent time studying or working in Europe, such as John Singleton Copley, Benjamin West, and Charles Willson Peale. Copley's famous portrait of his family, *The Copley Family* [14], reflects the artist's travels to London and to Italy. The warmth of feeling and color in the painting is quite different from the feeling and color of many colonial portraits completed in America, and one gets a glimpse of an extended family. Copley's family had fled the United States shortly after the first skirmishes of the American Revolution and followed Copley to London, where he hoped his art would be fully appreciated. The portrait communicates optimism and a sense of security in the family grouping. Copley himself stands in the background with papers in hand, perhaps indicative of plans or sketches for future artistic work. In front of him is his father-in-law, Richard Clarke, holding his granddaughter, Susanna, who was to die of scarlet fever just a few years later. In the center stands Elizabeth, who ultimately married a wealthy Bostonian and returned to the United States. Embracing his young mother is John Singleton Copley, Jr., who grew up to be a well-known lawyer and served as Lord High Chancellor under Queen Victoria. At the far right is the baby Mary, clutching her mother's arm. Mary remained with her father all his life and died a spinster at age ninety-five in London. A blue feathered hat balances the rich blue of Mrs. Copley's dress, and a doll dressed like the children lies on the floral carpet to the left.

14. J. S. Copley, *The Copley Family*, c. 1776–77. National Gallery, Washington, D. C.

The luxurious draperies and sofa upon which the family is seated are set before an idyllic river landscape. The juxtaposition of the complementary colors of blue and orange tones and of the black dress of the two men with the white dresses of the children adds strength to this visual statement. The painting does not tell us that Copley's youngest son had to be left behind in Boston, since he was too weak to sail with the rest of his family to join their father in London. The child died shortly after his family left Boston. Copley, his father-in-law, and the young Elizabeth gaze out to the viewer, to a wider public world. Copley seems to have painted himself between public and private worlds, since only he stands, protectively, behind his family.

In general, many portraits of the eighteenth century can be seen as part of a conserving tradition filled with social conventions to present and help maintain a state of affluence by those commissioning the pieces.

Although the eighteenth century, in general, accepted a separation of public and private life, there was still more emphasis on public life and public image. Public life was linked to a civilizing culture, while private life was linked more to nature and everyday functions, such as eating and sleeping. It is significant that the identity of self and family was still strongly bound to society, and most portraits or scenes of the family served to maintain that connection.

3

The Nineteenth Century

With the rise of Romanticism in the early nineteenth century, the supremacy of reason during the Enlightenment was challenged. There was an increased interest in nature and the role of the individual, as Romantics sought new secular models for human fulfillment. The older Christian model, in which human fulfillment was reached primarily through salvation in heaven, was no longer viable. Two revolutions in the latter part of the eighteenth century had brought about the beginning of increased conflict between the individual and society. The notion of Bohemianism, of being separate from mainstream society, also came into play.

A greater emphasis was placed on the roles of emotion, intuition, and creative expression. The concept of love, of what we now call romantic love, became the subject of artistic expression. There were further attempts to explore an inner self, perhaps to find a special talent or gift that could then be expressed. It is in this era that the cult of genius came into existence. Assertion of the individual self also brought increased emphasis on the role of freedom. Jean-Jacques Rousseau's philosophy, which emphasized the innate goodness of human beings, who were corrupted only by difficult social conditions, reflected much of the Romantic ideals. The Romantic view of the self was also a call for an active, not passive, existence. The artist Eugène Delacroix was to write, on exploring the inner depths of one's soul, "When we surrender ourselves entirely to the soul it unfolds itself completely to us, and it is then that this capricious spirit grants us the greatest happiness of all. . . . I mean the joy of expressing the soul in a hundred different ways, of revealing it to others, of learning to know ourselves, and of continually displaying it in our works."[10] Thus, the Romantic view of the self believed there was a basic human core that could include passion, soul, and moral character. Reality, then, was to be portrayed as something beyond the empirical knowledge of the human senses. The mysterious, the exotic, the far away or beyond, were frequently the subjects of artistic expression. Imagination was the most important. The Romantic drama within the individual was part of the journey to a personal depth that was to lead the way to the work of Sigmund Freud, who went further in his attempts to find objective evidence for the unconscious and subconscious. In this turn inward, however, the individual was not totally independent of society, but was more on the fringe of society. The Romantic portrait frequently depicted "the sitter not as a member of society, not yet as an individual personality, but as receptor or conductor of natural forces beyond the reach of nature, potentially destructive of the self and disruptive of the social fabric. Needless to say, the commissioned portrait is not the preferred genre of Romanticism. Characteristic subjects of Romantic portraits are the military hero, the madman, the child, and arch-threat to social stability, the artist."[11]

A German Romantic artist, particularly noted for his depiction of children, was Phillip Otto Runge. An early drawing, *Parents with Child on Table*, 1800 (Kupferstichkabinett, Kunsthalle, Hamburg), suggests an informality not frequently seen in past eras. The father sits somewhat slouched in his chair, leaning his head on his elbow on the table, watching his young baby seated on the tabletop. The mother sits, leaning forward, in her chair opposite her husband, also gazing intently at her child. The child, the object of the parents' and spectator's eye-level gaze, is clearly the center of attention on both the physical and psychic levels. Rousseau's ideas on child rearing, which advocated mothers' nursing their own children and the need for tender, parental affection, had a great impact on a number of artists' depictions of children. In Runge's work, the discovery and value of children seems to be particularly strong. One of his most famous portraits of childhood is *The Hulsenbeck Children* [15] in which he depicts the children of his friend and merchant, Friedrich August Hulsenbeck (his brother Daniel's partner). The children do not gaze at a sunflower from the world of society, as the Graham children do in Hogarth's painting, but, rather, are a part of this world of the sunflowers that bloom strong and tall, framing the painting on the left. Friedrich, the two-year-old, clings to a leaf. The elder son and daughter, August and Maria, aged four and five, stand tall, healthy, and protective of their little brother. The scale of the fence, which the children stand outside of and are not enclosed by, is oddly small, and the horizon of the city of Hamburg is distant. What would normally loom large in a child's perspective, the fence and the city, are diminished, emphasizing the freedom and mystery of a child's world. The children seem to become part of the mysteries and cycles of nature, since they are lit with a solar light.

15. Phillip Otto Runge, *The Hulsenbeck Children*, c. 1805–6. Kunsthalle, Hamburg.

Romanticism's emphasis on the individual, on nature, and on creativity could, on the one hand, cause some cracks in a family structure, but it also emphasized the image of the child growing like a flower, needing nourishment, and ultimately blossoming. This image was to influence artists later in the nineteenth century, such as Renoir and Van Gogh. Romanticism was an idealistic state of mind, the belief that a better world was possible through its principles.

The basic optimism of Romanticism was somewhat marred by growing Victorian attitudes. (The Victorian era is usually considered to be approximately 1830 to 1900. Queen Victoria reigned from 1837 to 1901.) The growth of industry and increased urbanization forced individuals and families to relook at their relationship to society and to be less optimistic about the perfectibility of society.

In the Victorian era, the Romantic tenet of individual freedom within society was expanded to the more extreme belief in a utopia outside mainstream society. Utopian experiments in communities, such as Brook Farm, rose and fell. Theories of anarchism became more prevalent. Transcendental thinkers, such as Henry David Thoreau, advocated the search for identity and self outside society in the world of nature. As society became more complex, the problems of urban life increased. The home was considered more and more as a refuge from society, rather than as an integral part of society. In homes that could afford to, there were attempts to improve domestic comfort through the use of new technology—use of gas and better ventilation—and by the late nineteenth century, Thomas Alva Edison and Joseph Swan, working independently in the United States and England, produced the first inexpensive carbon-filament lightbulbs. By the turn of the century, electric lights had become an accepted fact of urban life.

The home as a haven and the notion that domestic virtue was one of the desirable goals of life became prevalent. Concepts of domesticity frequently carried with them notions of harmony, peace, well-being, security, and cleanliness. Seeking refuge from a world that contained disorder, many families sought order within the home. Many believed that the development of children was enhanced by an "orderly" presentation of parents and children. In his popular book, *Hints for the Improvement of Early Education and Nursery Discipline* (the 16th edition appeared in 1853), T. G. Hatchard set forth the familiar axioms current at that time: "Little children should be seen and not heard," "a place for everything and everything in its place," "fortitude is built by early rising," and so forth. There was no room for spontaneous behavior. There was little sense of a natural sympathy between parent and child. A stable personality was sought after and to be reached through orderly appearance. By the 1860s, the so-called broken home was considered to be the culprit in any manifestation of deviant behavior.

Indeed, a man's success was related to his home life. As J. F. C. Harrison noted in his "Victorian Gospel of Success": "The Victorians looked on woman as the fostering, refining, civilizing influence in society; it was in the home that her influence was predominant; hence the emphasis upon the home as a bastion of morality and respectability against the tides which threatened to submerge them—tides from the vast underworld of poverty, infidelity, prostitution, and violent crime. The ideal of a happy home was geared in to the general complex of success; the business man could not afford not to have a happy home; it was part of his success. The aim of the wife should be to promote domestic efficiency, to make home so attractive that it surpassed the charms of its rivals, the club and the public house. Her literature of success was a series of home hints and manuals of etiquette."[12]

The year 1839 was an important one; it marked the beginning of photography, which allowed for increased portrayals of family groups and gave lower-class families the opportunity to record family groups because it was affordable. In that year, discoveries by two men were to have a profound impact on the history of art and visual recording in general. Louis Jacques Mandé Daguerre, a French painter with little scientific training, introduced in Paris what came to be called the daguerreotype, an image produced on a silver plate or a silver-covered copper plate. On the other side of the English Channel, the Englishman, William Henry Fox Talbot, an artist and a gentleman with a good amount of scientific knowledge, invented the process he referred to as "photogenic drawing" in his manual *The Pencil of Nature* (1844), where he noted that "when a group of persons has been artistically arranged and trained by patience to maintain an absolute immobility for a few seconds of time, very delightful pictures are easily obtained."[13] Talbot's use of the terms *artistically arranged* and *absolute immobility*, emphasizing order and appearance and the role of the photographer in that arrangement, were significant. Queen Victoria was an avid supporter of photography. In 1844, the first calotype portrait of her posed with the Prince of Wales appeared.

The invention of albumen printing paper led the way to the *carte de visite*, a paper picture mounted on a heavy piece of cardboard that could be sent through the mail or distributed as a calling card. The invention of the Frenchman, André Adolphe-Eugène Disdéri, in 1859, the card became fashionable among both the rich and the less affluent and spurred the spread of photography. The *carte de visite* images, photographed in the studio, were frequently set against dramatic landscapes and elegant interiors that were "scenery" in the photographer's studio. Upper- and lower-class people alike could be portrayed in a similar fashion. Children were frequently in adultlike stiff poses and were seen as the little "Lord Fauntleroys" or "Little Princesses" of Frances Burnett's novels. (It was not until the 1880s that candid photography was developed.)

Women of the upper class, who had a good deal of leisure time, frequently spent long hours embellishing family photo albums with floral imagery, assembling images that seemed pertinent to a sense of social self. Women's sense of self, in particular, was understood as it affected others. Women, upper class, in particular, dwelt on presentations of themselves in any kind of social setting—a special social call or appearances at the theater, a ball, and the like. The albums became a kind of microcosm of social interactions. And they were placed in areas where women socialized—the parlor, the verandah, or the garden.

Victorian family photographs and albums became part of a social face, in which all classes wanted to appear ordered and that would be preserved for generations to come. As one may suspect, these family images, in general, hid the darker sides of Victorian life, such as the situations of child laborers; women factory workers working long hours, unable to care properly for their children; harsh nannies who sometimes resorted to sedating their young charges; and upper- and middle-class husbands and fathers who took on mistresses. Photographs did not deal with these situations, but, rather, as in much of Renaissance portraiture, attempted to project personal dignity and worth. Charles Dickens described, somewhat tongue in cheek, a visit to a photographer's studio by a "Dr. Sword" and his wife. Although the description is humorous, it also has a serious side to it.

> The lady was placed on a chair before the camera, though at some distance from it. The gentleman leaned over the back of the chair; symbolically to express the inclination that he had towards his wife: he was her leaning tower, he was her oak, and she was the nymph who sat secure under his shade. Under the point of the gentleman's sword, the *Pilgrim's Progress* by John Bunyan was placed to prop it up.[14]

The photograph was to be a model of decorum, and one that reflected gender differentiation and role as well.

Americans also turned their attention to the home, and the cult of domesticity seized many Americans' affections. In a famous Phi Beta Kappa address delivered at Harvard University in 1837, Ralph Waldo Emerson urged the new American scholar to turn away from some European subjects and seek inspiration in the familiar, the local, the daily; he suggested, too, that "the meaning of household life" was worthy of artistic exploration. Household life took on a spiritual significance as the home was viewed as a temple or sanctuary away from the outside world of trade, business, urbanization, and so forth. The nuclear and/or extended family and private home were perceived of as mainstays of society, although in reality, this was not always the case. The cult of domesticity embraced various aspects of American culture, including songs, sermons, books, decorating manuals, and architectural design guides.

With increased urban expansion, there was a greater interest in, and nostalgia for, images related to a rural way of life. The demise of farm life and rural lifestyles was described by one writer in *Harper's Weekly* in 1858 this way: "High on a bleak and barren hill . . . stands the old meeting house of North Parish. Once upon a time it was the nucleus of a flourishing country village. . . . No less than three 'stores' made it a place of commercial importance. But this Augustan age has passed forever. In the valleys about, thriving factory villages have sprung up, and business has slid down into them."[15]

The cycles of life and the depiction of multiple generations became more important in the second half of the nineteenth century in the United States. Eastman Johnson's depiction of the *Hatch Family*, 1841 (Metropolitan Museum of Art, New York), for example, depicts fifteen members of a prominent New York family in the library of their elegant Fifth Avenue residence. The family members are involved in various activities, such as reading and knitting; children are playing on the floor, and older children are gazing at a baby. The family members are depicted in a friezelike formation across the canvas, frozen in time, in a setting of affluence. It is interesting to note that four of the children, three of whom are admiring the baby, are at the center of the painting. Although their elders flank them, they appear to be the heart and future of the family.

Motherhood was exalted in the nineteenth century and was closely allied to codes of morality, religious education, and cultural advancement. There were also numerous manuals on and literature related to the duties and relationships of wives and husbands.

Godey's Lady's Book, a magazine containing all types of advice and literature for women, edited by Sarah Josepha Hale, became an unofficial messenger to carry on this cult of domesticity. Beyond the distribution of the printed word in magazines, books and pamphlets, popular songs, and poems, the advent of a cheaper technology for lithography carried the emphasis on home and family further. Currier and Ives, the lithographic firm, produced millions of reproductions in magazines, books, calendars, and advertisements. One of its most popular series was entitled *The Four Seasons of Life*, four family scenes related to the stages of life—childhood, youth, middle age, and old age. "Good" family life was depicted as being governed by nature's own wisdom and rhythms. Unusual and artificial dress, diet, or manners was viewed as unnatural. And nature was seen as complemented and nourished by love, simplicity, and virtue within the family. For everything there was a season, and the seasons suggested the appropriate family style or order.

Nature and family images were further connected in some of the paintings of Abbot Thayer, in which images of domesticity took on a transcendent air. Drawing frequently on Renaissance Madonnas, Thayer honored American motherhood, the beauty of the life cycle, and a sense of the eternal. A number of his pieces are large in scale, such as *The Virgin* [16], which emphasizes the ethereal quality of the figures. The painting may be seen as a tribute to Thayer's beloved wife, Kate, who died in 1891, and two infants who died. In this monumental painting one sees his remaining children, Mary, Gerald, Gladys, set in a classical triangular composition, walking hand in hand to greet the viewer. The wind sweeps gently through their hair; their earth-colored dresses and shawls of green, ocher, and sienna; and the field grass at their bare feet. The contours of the clouds at daughter Mary's back spread like the

16. Abbott Thayer, *The Virgin*, c. 1892–93. Freer Gallery, Washington, D. C.

wings of angels that appear in numerous Thayer paintings. A flowered tree branch above Mary's head frames her face and head in the purple-blue sky and clouds. Here is the "soul" of Motherhood. Virginity for Thayer became a metaphor for all that was good and pure and for the union of sensuality and otherworldliness. The "virgin" appears as a model figure, bonded to the physical world and to the spiritual world, denying earthly sexual pleasures.

Not only was motherhood exalted, but so, too, was childhood in many instances, as Jean-Jacques Rousseau's writings on the special nature of childhood became known in the United States and children came to be seen as distinct from adults. Children were frequently portrayed as innocent, as vulnerable, and as detached from the adult world. They were sometimes portrayed with small animals, emphasizing concepts of innocence and immaturity. Girls were often shown with their dolls in a simulated nursery environment, serving or completing household chores, conforming to an angelic ideal. A well-known portrait of four young girls is that of *The Daughters of Edward D. Boit*, by John Singer Sargent, painted in 1882 [17]. This large canvas depicts these girls in a structure similar to that of Diego Velázquez's *The Maids of Honor* (*Las Meninas*) of 1656, which depicts the Maids of Honor of the Spanish royalty. Sargent was the painter of the upper class, an expatriate whose grand painterly style was the most popular with the upper class and aristocracy, who wanted to immortalize themselves and their children in a stylish and elegant manner.

Born in Florence to American parents, Sargent had spent much of his early years in leisurely travel through Europe. He studied in Rome and entered the studio of Carolus-Duran in Paris at age eighteen. A leading society portraitist of his time, Sargent, in the end, suffered from a decline in reputation. His painterly virtuosity was seen as vapid and attentive only to surfaces. But the Boit children—Florence, fourteen; Jane, twelve; Mary, eight; and Julia, four—are portrayed with vibrancy. However, their placement in juxtaposition to the large Japanese jars, taller than they are, makes them part of a larger elegant decor, rather than the central subjects of the painting.

There is a great feeling of space and depth, with the room behind cast in shadow, interrupted by a hazy reflection in a looking

17. J. S. Sargent, *The Daughters of Edward D. Boit*, 1882. Museum of Fine Arts, Boston.

glass, and the vertical thrust of the red screen. The children appear pure and pristine in their white pinafore aprons. All but Florence meet the viewer's eye. Florence stands in shadow in profile, slouched against the sumptuous tall vase. Some interpreters have suggested that the oval vessel shape is related to womblike forms, to the notion of the female as fertile and full. Little Julia sits on the richly patterned rug, caring for her baby doll. The portrait is more than a portrait in some ways; it is a tableau—a performance—austere but alive. It caught the critics at the Salon off-guard, and they protested Sargent's unconventional portrait. Others, such as Henry James, praised the piece.

In addition to the upper- and middle classes who were depicted in family and domestic scenes in nineteenth-century American art, blacks also began to be painted. Artists, such as William Sidney Mount, Christian Mayr, George Fuller, and Eastman Johnson, began to portray blacks beyond the cruel caricatures of slavery, such as those produced by Currier and Ives in their *Darktown* series. Although a number of artists were sympathetic to the abolitionist cause, the work was more apt to be picturesque than reformist or of protest. George Fuller was to write to his fiancée in 1857, "I saw a scene today. Negroes sold at auction together *with horses* and *other cattle*. It was full of suggestions I will not pursue now. The poor children, men, women and little ones looked sad. What a fate is theirs! No one to raise a voice for them and God above us all."[16] One of the best-known paintings of black family life prior to the Civil War was Eastman Johnson's *Old Kentucky Home* (*Negro Life in the South*) [18]. The painting is a harmonious one revolving around an outdoor farm scene in front of "the home." It could offend no one in the North or South. There is no hint of dissension or mistreatment. In 1867, after the Civil War, the painting was valued as a record of contemporary history by the critic Henry Tuckerman, who wrote: "*Old Kentucky Home* is not only a masterly work of art, but it illustrates a phase in American life which the rebellion and its consequences will either uproot or essentially modify, and therefore, this picture is as valuable as a memorial as it is interesting as an art-study."[17] More fervent anti-slavery protests were to be found in literary treatises, such as Harriet Beecher Stowe's *Uncle Tom's Cabin: or Life Among the Lowly*, 1852. The novel emphasizes the separation of members of slave families at auctions or at their owners' whim, calling on the sympathies of white readers who valued family life and relationships. Later portrayals of the black family in the latter part of the nineteenth century (after the Civil War) tended to sentimentalize scenes or depict poverty as picturesque.

With such a strong emphasis on the sanctity of motherhood and on the home as a sanctuary, a temple, people could not help but become disillusioned, in some instances, with what was called for and with the reality of women's work and sense of oppression. Paintings such as Louis Lang's *Trimming the Christmas Tree*, 1865 (Allison-Shelley Collection, University Libraries, Pennsylvania

18. Eastman Johnson, *Old Kentucky Home*, 1859. New-York Historical Society.

State University), which depicts a mother and child trimming the tree, or Enoch Wood Perry's *Mother and Child*, 1881 (private collection), which shows a mother nursing her baby, are, on the one hand, peaceful portrayals of the rituals of holidays or of feeding a newborn baby, but, on the other hand, contain darkness and deep shadows. Despite the harmony of the composition and subject matter, these women are isolated and alone in darkened settings and pensive, and men are not included in such scenes.

On the Continent, Impressionist painters produced numerous portraits of their wives, families, and friends, and it is with the Impressionist generations that depictions of artists' families became increasingly significant, moving away from the more traditional portraits commissioned by the wealthy and powerful. The sense of openness and the *plein air* quality, so frequently found in Impressionist works, was to be found in Impressionist portraits, such as Jean Frédéric Bazille's large-scale portrait of his beloved family on an outdoor terrace, *Family Reunion*, 1865–69. The scene is somewhat like a peaceful stage set, emphasizing the harmonious blues and greens of the sky, the women's dresses, and the green leaves of the large tree that protects the family from the sparkling sun. The light, like a theatrical spotlight, is focused on Bazille's cousin, Thérèse, turned in her chair, with a hat, parasol, and bouquet of flowers as props behind her chair at the edge of dappled sunspots and shadows on the ground. It seems as if the viewer has stepped into an intimate and perhaps serious conversation with these family members who are frozen in time. Bazille is also there, behind his uncle on the left. He was one of the most successful Impressionist artists and helped his contemporaries morally and financially until his early, tragic death on the battlefield in the Franco-Prussian War in 1870.

A different approach to depicting members of his family was found in an earlier painting by Edgar Degas, famous for his paintings of dancers, but also known for some of his portraits. At age twenty-four, Degas began a painting of his favorite aunt, Baroness Laure Bellelli; her husband, Baron Gennaro Bellelli; and their daughters, Giovanna and Giulia. He painted the piece entitled *The Bellelli Family* [19] not to please his relations, but to gain public recognition with a large canvas. Instead of portraying nations at war, which was a popular theme at the time for some artists, Degas chose to show part of the impact of a private, personal war, a family in the process of divorce. Degas had been living for several months with the Bellelli family in Florence before he began the painting. The baroness, appearing stern and sad, is dressed entirely in black, in mourning for her dead father René-Hilaire de Gas. The girls are dressed in black with contrasting white pinafores. Laure places a strong protective hand on the shoulder of her daughter Giovanna, whose soft young hands are clasped at her waist, in contrast to her mother's hands. Giovanna stares rather unhappily at the viewer. Giulia sits on a chair in the middle of the piece, forming an extended black-and-white triangle in connection with her mother and sister. She stares off to the side, connecting with no one. The baron, partially turned, looks up from his reading, but not at his family. He is distinctly separated from the rest of his family by the leg of the table and by the drab brown of his

19. Edgar Degas, *The Bellelli Family*, 1858–60. Musée d'Orsay, Paris.

jacket. All four seem to be unable to connect psychologically with one another. The physical space of this private, silent battleground is made to appear larger through Degas's use of the mirror, the doorway, and the gold-framed delicate, red chalk drawing hanging on the blue floral wallpaper. The drawing is one by Degas himself, of his grandfather René-Hilaire de Gas, placed next to Laure's head, thereby connecting both Degas and her father more closely to her and following a long tradition of including effigies of ancestors in European portraits. Some have called this painting one of the first modern psychological portraits because Degas attempted to go beneath the surface, beyond the shimmering light and color so predominant in many of his Impressionist contemporaries' works. The honesty of the portrait, particularly in this period, is noteworthy. One wonders whether Degas's private wealth allowed him to take risks in subject matter that some of his contemporaries did not consider.

In general, most Impressionist portraits were not commissions and emphasized a sense of immediacy and individuality, or personality. The artists frequently had ongoing relationships with their models, which is suggested by the sense of warmth in many of these paintings. The development of the concept of the ideal bourgeois nuclear family most likely encouraged artists to delve into personal realms for subject matter. The portrayal of one's own and others' family members within the Impressionist aesthetic, however, was primarily an embracing of the bourgeois experience. There were few sitters from the upper classes and few images of the working class. The mothers and children in works by artists, such as Mary Cassatt, are individuals primarily from the middle class, for whom Cassatt has captured the everyday tenderness of hugs; kisses; and other short, private moments of understanding and endearment. For example, in her small pastel, *Maternal Kiss* [20], one sees a small child, once in distress, comforted in her mother's calm and strong arms. Although the mother's back is par-

20. Mary Cassatt, *Maternal Kiss*, 1896. Philadelphia Museum of Art.

tially turned toward the viewer, the voluminous sleeve of her bright yellow dress adds strength for the little red-haired child clad in a more delicate blue-and-white frock. Cassatt's work was daring in her adoption of Impressionist techniques as an American expatriate living in France, her adaptation of techniques from Japanese woodblock prints, and her refusal to idealize or oversentimentalize her subjects. It seems sadly ironic that these loving depictions of mothers and children were painted by an artist who never married or had children.

Berthe Morisot, another member of the Impressionist circle, also painted primarily domestic subjects, particularly family members. Her well-known *The Cradle* [21] is a portrait of her sister Edma Pontillon with her baby Blanche. Also an artist, Edma had given up painting when she married. This portrait depicts the leisure allowed in a middle-class home, of a mother gazing devotedly at her sleeping infant, in a cradle covered by a filmy canopy of gauze and lace. This image is not only one of wonder and devotion, but one that illustrates the new prosperity for middle-class families, in which women did not have to work, servants could be hired, and nice homes and furnishings were affordable. Mothers had more time to be involved with their children if they wished to be. Morisot chose to hire a wet nurse to breast-feed her daughter Julie Manet, so she could continue her work as an artist, although the hiring of a wet nurse was common for women of her social class. Her husband, Eugène Manet (brother of the painter, Édouard Manet), was perhaps unusual in his support of his wife's development as an artist. *The Cradle* was shown at the now famous first Impressionist exhibit in April 1874. Morisot was included in all the press, pro and con, receiving much acclaim for a female artist. Indeed, perhaps one of the reasons why Impressionism was considered to be radical and "subversive" was that it included a woman. Looking at *The Cradle* today, it is difficult to believe that the depiction of such a tranquil moment was an image that was considered radical, among all the others that were exhibited, but it is a painting of a life lived, and one senses that the artist may have gazed on her subjects in the same manner as her sister gazes at her child in the painting—a manner quite different from any a commission might bring. As the poet Paul Valéry, Berthe's cousin,

21. Berthe Morisot, *The Cradle*, 1872. Musée d'Orsay, Paris.

wrote, "Berthe Morisot lives her painting—and paints her life."[18]

The psychological underpinnings of family tensions and relationships found in Degas's *Bellelli Family* were carried further by Vincent Van Gogh and Paul Gauguin. Of particular interest are Van Gogh's images of women and family, which he did while living in The Hague in 1882 and 1883 with Clasina (Sien) Hoornik, a thirty-two-year-old prostitute and seamstress who served as Van Gogh's lover, model, and domestic partner. Van Gogh wrote to his brother Theo in May 1882: "I want to go through the joys and sorrows of domestic life in order to paint it from my own experience."[19] Van Gogh, with his characteristic sensitive intensity, depicted in approximately sixty-nine drawings and watercolors of women and family life what he saw and felt. Van Gogh was influenced by the writings of Jules Michelet, the author of histories of France and the French Revolution, as well as natural histories that included, in the nineteenth century, women and sexuality. In a book entitled *La Femme*, published in 1860, Michelet set forth the conviction that the "fallen woman," if repentant, could be redeemed, particularly in the sanctity of a loving home. A woman could carry out her essential tasks for fulfillment—to nourish, to comfort, and to construct a loving environment. This premise of redemption differed from the beliefs of a number of Michelet's contemporaries, who considered the "fallen woman" to be morally and socially ruined. Influenced by these writings, Van Gogh saw his relationship with Sien and attempts to establish a stable domestic existence as a way of rescuing her and living out his own fantasies about domestic life. Many of the drawings Van Gogh made during this period are filled with melancholy, and frequently the individual becomes a type. There is no joy in domestic tasks. In a drawing entitled *Sien Sewing and Little Girl*, 1883 (Vincent Van Gogh Foundation, Vincent Van Gogh National Museum, Amsterdam), Sien sits in profile, and the little girl sits resigned, with her head bowed. In the end, Van Gogh and Sien could not sustain their relationship and separated in fall 1883. Van Gogh's "rescue project" may not have been realizable, partly because Sien was "the fallen woman," and social and economic mobility through redemption and a new marital relationship was still a cultural fantasy at the time. But the sadness of these domestic images cannot be seen as only the sadness of Sien. The sadness is also, in part, what Van Gogh brought of himself to the work, his own sense of alienation and sadness in a world in which he frequently was uncomfortable and a "misfit." These two alienated figures could not triumph above social, economic, and personal forces to make a family "work." In a sense, these are portrayals of Vincent, too, absent yet present in spirit. Thus, the distance between subject and artist was less than in many other such works. But unlike a piece by Mary Cassatt or Berthe Morisot, there is never any real intimacy, for intimacy was difficult for Van Gogh.

In 1885 Van Gogh painted his best-known family piece, *The Potato Eaters* [22], which shows a group of peasants at a meager meal of potatoes and coffee within a sparsely furnished home or *bakhuis*, a small cottage, kept for cooking and eating, separate from a peasant family's main house. A clock, a small painted crucifix, a tool rack, and a clog filled with spoons are the wall "decorations." Van Gogh made many visits to the De Groot family, portrayed here, as well as many studies for the large canvas. The dark expressive earth tones of the painting, whose only light is the cross-shaped light of the ceiling lamp, speaks of hardship, but of honest lives. The intended audience for the painting, however, was the bourgeois public, who met it with relative indifference or criticism. Disappointed, Van Gogh moved to Antwerp and subsequently to Paris in 1886.

That Van Gogh depicted these peasants and emphasized the ritual of a family meal is significant perhaps only in retrospect, as the meaning of family rituals in all classes is eroding and, paradoxically, more carefully studied in our times. Van Gogh was to write to his brother Theo in 1890, the year of his death, about the excitement of portraiture for him. "That which excites me the most, much, much more than other things in my work—is the modern portrait. . . . I would like to make portraits that, a century later, might appear to people of the time like apparitions. Accord-

22. Vincent Van Gogh, *The Potato Eaters*, 1885. Rijksmuseum Kröller-Müller, Otterlo, The Netherlands.

ingly I don't try to do that by the way of photographic resemblance, but by the way of impassioned expression, using as means of expression and exaltation of character our science and modern taste of color."[20]

Paul Gauguin, a close friend of Van Gogh, used bold lines, forms, and colors to convey his feelings and perceptions. As part of the Symbolist aesthetic with which he is frequently associated, his work involved a world of suggestion, of dreams, of mystery, of another reality. The artist Emile Schuffenecker was a close friend of Gauguin for seventeen years, and when Gauguin could not pay his rent, he frequently lived with the Schuffeneckers. The canvas *The Schuffenecker Family* [23] depicts a family quarrel. A sharp diagonal divides the painting into two areas. Emile Schuffenecker stands in his studio, attempting to step forward, in a blue area, separated from his wife and children by his easel. He stands isolated, in front of the bars of his window. The children, dressed in brilliant red, appear unhappy and serve as a visual barrier between the two parents. One child buries her head in her sister's lap. Each family member seems lost in his or her own thoughts, remote from the others. The warm colors of the yellow floor, the orange dress of Madame Schuffenecker, and the vibrant reds of the children's dresses are in great contrast to the cool blue tones of Emile's jacket and the wall color, emphasizing the rift between husband and wife. The bars on the window indicate a sense of imprisonment for this family within their tensions, even if the tensions are short-lived. There is only a glimpse of a larger outside world through the partially open window.

Inspired by his life in Tahiti, where he thought he could escape into Polynesian spirituality, away from the materialism and colonial attitudes of western European culture, Gauguin painted in his late years what some consider his last will and testament. Having abandoned his own wife and five children years before to go to Tahiti, Gauguin, discouraged and distraught, with economic, medical, and family problems (for example, his twenty-year-old daughter Aline died in 1897), attempted to take his own life but failed. He wished to leave the giant canvas *Where Do We Come From? Who Are We?* (1897, Museum of Fine Arts, Boston) as a final statement. Although not a portrait of an individual family in the strict sense

23. Paul Gauguin, *The Schuffenecker Family*, 1889. Musée d'Orsay, Paris.

of the word, this painting contains moments of family life and is
an image of a sweeping life cycle, moving from right to left on the
canvas. This life cycle is sustained and nurtured by women; nature;
and a Maori idol, which seems to indicate the hereafter. In addition, there are symbolic animals—a dog, two cats, two birds, and a
lizard, all part of the life chain, too. A strange white bird, holding a
lizard, next to an old woman near death, represented for Gauguin
the uselessness of idle words. Gauguin's visual language was flat
and bold. His verdant greens, cerulean blues, brilliant oranges, and
chrome yellows appear in large, flat planar areas, seemingly primitive to some Europeans. But the questions he raised concerning
moments of everyday life and generations passing are eternal and
particularly poignant and meaningful at a time when the world
was about to pass into a new century. The questions raised are still
relevant today: Where do we come from? What are we? Where are
we going? Social conventions and identities were questioned then
as they are now.

Farther north, the ideals of family and home life were realized
in the work of Carl Larsson in Sweden. Larsson married an artist,
Karin Bergöo, and they had seven children. Inspired by the Arts

and Crafts Movement and by folk art, the Larsson home itself was seen as a work of art, with personal familial references on borders, doorways, and furnishings. Larsson's paintings of primarily domestic harmony were made to be included in a series of books beginning with *Ett hem (A Home)* in 1899. Rather than being moralistic or self-righteous, the text was anecdotal and light, with the visual images foremost, telling one family's story for the pleasure of others. The books were like a family album with an open invitation to step into another's family. And all was not entirely harmonious. There were images of a naughty child asked to leave the dinner table and a sick child recovering from pneumonia. But there was a resolution for difficult times. Frequently, too, guests or neighbors were portrayed, at a Christmas party or working on the house.

By the end of the nineteenth century, the importance of private life had increased significantly in both Europe and the United States since the eighteenth century, when public life had been more important. A popular late Victorian sentiment was expressed by d'Avenel: "The public life of a people is a very small thing compared to its private life."[21]

As the century came to a close, painted portraiture and domestic imagery survived, despite the growing popularity of photography and changing social mores. A number of artists became increasingly discontented with the social demands and expectations of the sitter and grew interested in conveying more than a mere physical likeness. As the artist Ignace Henri Jean Théodore Fantin-Latour noted, "One paints people like flowers in a vase, happy just to depict the exterior as it is—but what of the interior, the inner life? The soul is like music playing behind the veil of flesh, one cannot paint it, but one can make it heard . . . or at least try to show that you have thought of it."[22] The inner life was to become increasingly important.

The turn of the century, or fin de siècle culture, particularly in France, was filled with contradictions. There were progress and technological innovations—electricity, the telephone, and rapid transport—but also decadence and malaise and a sense of unease as the new century approached. One writer described turn-of-the-century portraiture as perhaps "best perceived in dialectical terms as occupying the spaces between art and society, fact and fiction, surface and underlying truth, the public and the private, close up and distant focus and innovation and tradition."[23] It is in this dialectical context that family images are perhaps best viewed as the century came to a close.

The turn of the century also carried with it legacies from philosophers and social and political scientists that were to pave the way for Modernism and diverse twentieth-century concepts about identity. Georg Hegel's dialectical theory of thesis, antithesis, and synthesis was to influence Karl Marx who, with Friedrich Engels, wrote *The Communist Manifesto*, which declared that all history had hitherto been a history of class struggles, but that these struggles would end with the coming victory of the working class. In 1867 Marx published *Das Kapital*, an analysis of the economics of capitalism. Unlike Hegel, though, Marx turned away from "the spirit" toward dialectical materialism. Arthur Schopenhauer left the world with the challenge of men and women as the helpless victims of a blind will, expounded in his chief work *The World as Will and Idea*. In his view, there was no kindly creator God or Father, only a tyrannical, unknowable First Cause. A follower of Schopenhauer, Friedrich Nietzsche, subscribed to man's helplessness in a mechanical universe under eternal law (although God was dead) but did not feel Schopenhauer's despair. He saw courage as the highest attribute of man, an attribute to be used in the face of the Unknown. He called this courage a will to power, which became the title of his well-known book, *The Will to Power*. Part of this pure will involved the creative imagination, which was freefloating, not grounded in any higher being. Indeed, for Nietzsche, imagination was the demand "to live dangerously" without recourse to any higher values, without alibis or reprieves. This will to power was to lead to a supremely developed individual, the *Übermensch*, which some have translated as "Superman," who would come to be, after several generations of evolution, a light in a world of darkness. Man's arbitrary existence would become a work of art. Nietzsche argued against the eighteenth-century Enlightenment belief that there were rational foundations for an objective morality. Rather, he contended, there was nothing to morality but expressions of will, that one's morality can only be what one's will creates. Will would replace reason and men and women would become autonomous moral subjects by some heroic act of the will. This thrust toward individualism was clearly to have an impact well into the twentieth century. Distortions of Nietzsche's ideas were to lead to a ruthless use of force in political and military fields. Nietzsche died in 1900 after ten years of insanity.

The French materialist philosopher Auguste Comte brought new emphasis to the social sciences, to the relationship of humans and society, proposing that social fact-finding could be as reliable and precise as fact-finding in the natural sciences, which since the seventeenth century had allowed man to gain further insight into and control of his world. Comte's philosophy was referred to as positivism because he declared that theology and metaphysics were dead. The notion of a positive and progressive evolution of humans as a species was carried further by the work of the British Herbert Spencer and Charles Darwin. "Survival of the fittest" and "natural selection" were to lead to the weeding out of "the unfit." When applied to larger social and political spheres, "social Darwinism" became an argument for colonialism and paternalistic domestic policies.

As these theories took a stronger hold in the twentieth century, further questions were raised about the role of art in civilized communities. What is the role of the imagination? Is art to instruct, to entertain, or to elevate men and women to a higher realm? Is art the expression of culture at its best, and who decides what is best? Is art an escape from the material world to a world of dreams, illusions, another reality? The raising of such questions more frequently by the end of the nineteenth century could only lead one further on the quest for who we are and where we are going that Gauguin had visually articulated.

P A R T   I I

The Twentieth Century

The twentieth century has been a period filled with tumultuous and rapid changes in the arts, in culture, and society in general; in the configuration and leadership of nations; and in global technologies. Two world wars and other devastating wars, such as the Vietnam War and the Korean War, have left their mark on our times. The development of weapons to annihilate the entire human race, the placement of a man on the moon and men in orbit in outer space, and the development of vaccines to prevent the spread of disease point to the tremendous abilities and achievements of men and women of this century. But despite the technological, scientific, and cultural achievements, there were and still are questions about who we are, within and outside our families and in the interior and the exterior of our beings. Definition of self and notions of "identity crises" have become very much a part of twentieth-century concerns. And, ironically, despite these questions, there has been a decline in portraiture in this century. This decline in imagery (which did not include photography) was due, in general, to the rise of abstraction, the development of photography, and issues of patronage, all of which were interconnected. Photography was cheaper, allowing more people to have their portraits done individually and in groups and to be completed more quickly and efficiently.

Photography freed the painter and sculptor from having to achieve an exact likeness, if one was desired by the subject, and made it possible to find more inner fulfillment through abstraction and for artists, such as Wassily Kandinsky, to express an "inner necessity" through abstract and nonobjective art. Fewer and fewer artists chose to develop portrait skills. The traditional alliance between patron and artist, which had been typical of other periods, or the commissioning of works by the church began to disappear, not to be revived. As this century progressed, artists of significance would be more likely to choose their subjects, particularly their family members, friends, and artistic associates, rather than to be sought out to paint specific subjects, as were such artists as Sir Joshua Reynolds and John Singer Sargent. Despite this decline, it is important to examine what was created in painting and sculpture, as well as in photography and film, in portrayals of self and family.

4

1900–1945

In England, from 1901 to the beginning of World War I, often referred to as the Edwardian period, there was a kind of golden age among the middle and upper classes, and childhood became a time of innocence and joy. Queen Victoria died on January 22, 1901, and King Edward ruled for ten years while the rich grew richer and millions still lived in poverty. The king was stylish, liked comfort and splendor, and indulged his tastes. Those who were financially well off followed suit. Because children were no longer seen as miniature adults, as they sometimes were during the Victorian age, there were some social reforms that indicated a concern for the welfare of children of all classes. The employment of minors was regulated; educational systems were improved, and medical care increased; and better housing was built, and attempts were made to clear slums. Upper-class parents chose to protect their children from the concerns and business of the adult world and created a child's world, usually with a nanny, away from the rest of the household. Children had their own meals, their own clothes (distinct from adults), their own books, new brightly colored toys, parks to go to, and other, specifically child-oriented objects and activities. Although discipline was gentle, not harsh, and children were generally not spoiled, they saw little of their parents until about age fourteen. Books and music were an important part of children's lives. One finds the delightful illustrations of Kate Greenaway, in which children frequently frolic in a lighthearted manner in idyllic settings, or the enchanting illustrations of Arthur Rackham or Walter Crane. Numerous illustrations and advertisements related to the lives of children, such as an ad for Osram lamps and electricity (instead of oil and gas lamps), which showed children at a meal with an electric light overhead (Mary Evans Picture Library). An ad for Dinneford's Magnesia, "the safest aperient for delicate constitutions, Ladies, Children and Infants," portrayed a mother in an elegant robe in a well-appointed boudoir, together with her three children. Paintings depicted everyday life and routines. One such painting, by Percy Tarrant (Fine Arts and Library, Ltd., England), shows two children bidding their parents good-bye at the breakfast table before heading off for lessons at school or in the nursery. An angelic blond-haired younger child plays on the floor with a cat and a red-and-white ball. The piece is harmonious and peaceful in form and content. There were scenes of children with nannies, such as a small watercolor by John S. Goodall (Christopher Wood Gallery, England) that depicts children seated in Kensington Gardens, or children alone, such as a brother and sister seated at a table before a book with bright, colorful illustrations to capture the imagination, by Carlton Alfred Smith (Fine Art Photographs and Library, Ltd., England). The little girl with a pure white dress embellished with lace and smocking, with a bouquet of daffodils at her elbow, sits with her arm around her younger brother with auburn hair, wearing a blue sailor suit. The children's eyes, as they look out, gently catch the eyes of the viewer, inviting him or her into their world of innocence and enchantment.

This was an age in which books were written and beautifully illustrated especially for children. Titles that many still cherish appeared: *The Secret Garden*, *At the Back of the Northwind*, *Black Beauty*, *Peter Pan*, *The Wind in the Willows*, *Alice in Wonderland*, and *The Tale of Peter Rabbit*, among others. Books were advertised by publishers, as being "for the family circle," and reading together at home with other family members was an important activity. There were also the beginnings of children's magazines, more for boys than for girls. Two popular publications were *Boys' Own Paper* and *Girls' Own Paper*. A cover illustration (Bodleian Library, John Johnson Collection, Oxford University) depicts a young girl read-

ing outside on a stone bench with flowers behind her. The *Girls'*
Own Paper was actually geared toward older girls and young wives,
for it contained love stories. Although working-class homes generally had fewer books and magazines than did middle- or upper-
class homes, many families subscribed to some kind of weekly pub-
lication, such as *The Leisure Hour, The Family Herald,* or *Pears*
Cyclopaedia. Besides reading together, upper-class families played
music together or listened to the gramophone, which was first produced by Thomas Alva Edison in 1877. Families also gathered
together to watch slide shows (magic lanterns) of Punch and Judy,
scenes at a zoo, melodramas, or comedies.

This halcyon world of enchantment ended abruptly with the
events of 1914 and the beginning of World War I. The golden
days of Edwardian children were lost, most likely forever. World
War I, the "war to end all wars," took its toll on all countries, not
only in the realignment of national and international powers, but
in its impact on family units—the loss of sons and husbands, the
return of wounded family members, and so forth.

The golden side of the Edwardian age was not without its
underside, however, which was depicted to some extent by photographers. The boundaries among the classes remained quite secure,
and some photographers attempted to depict the life of an under-
culture. John Thomson, with the writer Adolphe Smith, put
together a book entitled *Street Life in London,* with visual and verbal text, that depicted the slum dwellers of London. Although first
published in the nineteenth century, the book had some impact
into the early twentieth century, for as a reporter, Smith volunteered as an official interpreter at the series of International Trade
Union Congresses from 1886 to 1905. The preface to the work
read, "We have visited, armed with notebook and camera, those
back streets and courts where the struggle for life is none the less
bitter and intense, because less observed. . . . [It is] a vivid account
of the various means by which our unfortunate fellow-creatures
endeavor to earn, beg or steal their daily bread."[1] There is a combination of social outcry and paternalism in the book. It should be
noted that Smith and Thomson were both middle-class intellectuals, and part of their work was in protest of difficult conditions and
part was an expression of individual conscience and emotion. Not

only is there documentation of life in the slums, but there is also a sense of a depth of character in the figures portrayed.

Quite different from the images of the middle- and upper classes of the Edwardian period in England were the works of avant-garde artists on the Continent in the pre–World War I period. Pablo Picasso, although frequently associated with the distorted forms of Cubism, produced, in his Rose Period (approximately 1904–6), some moving scenes of family life. Three paintings of particular interest were painted in 1905.

The inspiration for his pieces were the traveling acrobats and performers of the circus—the *saltimbanques*. Living in the Bateau-Lavoir in Paris, from 1904 until 1909, Picasso attended the circus almost nightly and became friends with some of the performers. The Bateau-Lavoir was a dimly lit, dilapidated old building, a center of Bohemian existence, where a number of artists, writers, and street vendors lived and worked. Although none of them made much money, they met frequently and had many conversations in cafés, almost like a large extended family. It was at the Bateau-Lavoir that Picasso met one of the first women he was to love—Fernande Olivier, his companion from 1905 to 1912. Olivier served as Picasso's model and sometimes did not leave the house for days. At one point, she brought home a young girl from an orphanage. The child delighted everyone at the Bateau-Lavoir, but the story goes that Picasso was jealous of the attention she received from both Olivier and their friends, and he had the child returned to the orphanage. It is in this context that Picasso painted his three 1905 paintings—*The Harlequin's Family* (Collection of Julian Eisenstein, Washington, D.C.); *The Acrobat's Family with a Monkey* (Konstmuseum, Göteborg, Sweden); and *The Family of Saltimbanques*. A fragility and tenderness emanates from the figures in these paintings, enhanced by the ochers and pale pinks of Picasso's palette, in contrast to delicate blues and stronger reds. Picasso was inspired by these traveling acrobats, or *saltimbanques* (from *saltare*, to leap, and *banco*, bench). These performers followed in the tradition of the Italian commedia dell'arte, with its stock characters, such as the Harlequin, Pierrot, and Columbine. In Picasso's work, the Harlequin, a kind of jack-of-all-trades, dominated a number of images. In the *Harlequin's Family*, a small gouache and india ink piece, the Harlequin stands in a black-and-white checkered costume with a three-cornered hat, clasping his baby to his chest, while his nude wife stands arranging her hair. They are pictured behind a stage or in a dressing area, standing before curtains of delicate blue, rose, and beige tones. The Harlequin is pictured as lithe, thin, and sensitive. Here is a moment of private, domestic intimacy, either before or after a public appearance. The Harlequin appears again in a rose-peach colored costume in *The Acrobat's Family with a Monkey*, gazing attentively at his young wife and child. The monkey seems to be an integral part of the family as it looks fondly at the baby while sitting in a human position. The presence of the monkey seems to indicate elements of playfulness and spontaneity that Picasso emphasized and treasured in much of his work. The configuration of the figures in this painting is quite similar to the composition of classical Renaissance Madonna paintings. By using such a composition, which speaks of harmony and repose, Picasso points to a certain harmony in the lives of those who might frequently be stereotyped as nomadic or unsettled with little sense of a stable family life. Picasso identified himself with the Harlequin figure. One critic noted, "The preference that Picasso shows, particularly in early life, for Harlequin suggests that analogies must exist between him and this legendary character."[2] In his large canvas *The Family of Saltimbanques* [24], one sees Picasso's identification with the Harlequin figure even more clearly, for Picasso's own profile is clearly recognizable in the Harlequin figure. A number of critics have pointed to the autobiographical elements of the painting, that the fat clown most likely represents the poet and friend of Picasso, Apollinaire, and that the boy tumblers may well represent Picasso's friends André Salmon and Max Jacob. The little girl holding Picasso's hand has been viewed as the child who was sent back to the orphanage, while the young woman seated in isolation away from the larger group of figures has been seen as Fernande Olivier, disappointed and upset with Picasso for returning the child to the orphanage. Beyond the autobiographical elements of the painting, lines from a poem by Apollinaire give us further clues to the power, sense of magic, and childhood enchantment that these performers brought with them.

24. Picasso, *The Family of Saltimbanques*, 1905. National Gallery of Art, Washington, DC.

> *The angelic music of trees*
> *The disappearance of the child*
> *The saltimbanques lifted the great dumb-bells*
> *in their arms*
> *And juggled with the weights*
> *But each spectator looked in himself for the*
> *miraculous child.*[3]

The child does not have to be seen as a specific individual, but may also represent a spirit of wonder, of miraculousness, that could be found in us all. André Salmon referred to the acrobats as "metaphysicians." Perhaps this level of thinking and acting in a reality different from the everyday world also attracted Picasso to the Harlequin and other figures, and the power of transformation that occurred in the acrobats' costumes and acts may have been what Picasso sought in both his life and work.

Picasso's involvement with many women of different personalities and ages and his fathering of a number of children, both legitimate and illegitimate, suggest that there was an ongoing restlessness in Picasso's life and a constant search for new "muses" and women to share his life at various stages in his life and career. That he completed numerous works throughout his career on the theme of families and children suggests a continuous concern for and involvement with family relationships. One finds, for example, his 1922 *Family at the Seashore* (Musée Picasso, Paris), which depicts a family in a mood of calmness and serenity at the seashore. At the time of this painting, Picasso's first child Paulo would have been about the same age as the child in the painting. In the painting, the father is sleeping naked on the sand, which some critics have suggested is analogous to Picasso's own work habits of working through the night until dawn and sleeping until close to noon.

A well-known image of a mother and child in Picasso's 1943 painting, *First Steps* (Yale University Art Gallery, New Haven, Connecticut), in which Picasso's cubist forms dominate the canvas, a young child's first steps are depicted with a sense of drama, emotion, and a little humor. The painting is of Picasso's maid, Inez, and her son. When Picasso painted this piece, he was sixty-two years old and about to become involved in a relationship with the young Françoise Gilot. In the painting, the child faces the viewer head-on and seems to be about to walk into the viewer's arms. The mother's facial expression speaks of anxiety and concern as she bends over the child and holds his hands, sharing in this exhilarating but awkward moment as this little boy attempts to set forth upright into a larger world. The cubist forms, although distorted and abstract, serve to enhance the close relationship of the mother and child and the triumph for both in this short dramatic moment of learning to walk. The child in the painting is well beyond life size, and his steps thereby become even more monumental. Here is an affirmation of self, which Picasso seemed to understand well, as the little boy begins to separate himself from his mother. This canvas was painted during World War II, when affirmation of self and family relationships were particularly important in a world torn asunder, and people were unable to celebrate traditional family "milestones" as they had once been able to do.

A 1953 lithograph, *Games and Reading* (private collection), is a portrait of Picasso's young mistress, Françoise Gilot, and the couple's two children, Claude, age six, and Paloma, age four. Each figure is absorbed in an activity—Françoise, reading; Paloma, riding a small tricycle; and Claude, playing with a truck. In black and white, with sketchy outlines of the figures, this silent piece conveys an overall sense of pensiveness and melancholy. The lithograph was one of a group of images Picasso made of Gilot and the children shortly before the couple separated. It was as if Picasso tried to capture through art what would be lost, that the quiet presence of his family would be gone. Thus, for Picasso, "the family" served as a type of "muse" at various points in his career, in that he transferred family relations to the world of art and sometimes transformed them through artistic experimentation.

Different from Picasso, but also attempting to move beyond an urban, bourgeois world, were the German Expressionists, a number of whom dealt with images related to the family. In 1905 a group of young artists, beginning with Ernst Ludwig Kirchner, Karl Schmidt-Rotluff, Erich Heckel, and Fritz Bleyl, banded together to exhibit their work in an old chandelier factory in Dresden and called themselves *Die Brücke* ("the Bridge"), since they saw their work as being a bridge from the present to a more creative future. These artists spoke out against the materialism, decadence, increased urbanization, and hypocrisy of the old order of German society. Kirchner called for a new community, particularly of youths, and wrote, "With faith in development and in a new generation of creators and appreciators we call to all youth. As youth we carry the future and want to create for ourselves freedom of life and of movement against the long-established older forces. Everyone who with directness and authenticity conveys that which drives him to creation belongs to us."[4] These artists rebelled against academic forms, against Impressionism and Neoimpressionism, and advocated a new art that would be honest, direct, and call upon an inner spirit and emotions—the expression of an inner self. A number of artists looked to the art of Africa and Oceania, finding in those primitive forms a more intense and truthful sense of a humanity that they believed was being lost in the Western world. The medium of the woodcut, with the texture of the wood and sharp angular cuts into the image, as well as the medium of painting, served the purposes of these artists well. One of Kirchner's late Expressionist paintings, *Mother and Daughter* (*Frau und Mädchen*) [25], depicts a world of emotion and symbols. A young girl in a sailor suit sits facing the viewer in the center of the painting, her mother standing solicitously behind her. The two are surrounded by rich green tropical-like plants and two mysterious carved wooden sculptures, reminiscent of African carvings, but painted in vibrant red hues. These sculptures are believed to have been carvings of Adam and Eve, made for a portal in the artist's cabin in Switzerland. It is as if the pair is standing in a lush garden of Eden that could be tainted by the presence of a contemporary Europe.

25. E. L. Kirchner,
Mother and Daughter
(*Frau und Mädchen*),
c. 1922–23. Seattle
Art Museum.

The young girl clasps a birdlike shape protectively. Her mother wears a patterned dress, possibly designed by the artist himself. The sailor suit suggests a journey to the unknown.

Kirchner's combination of European dress, exotic foliage, and mysterious sculptures in expressive, direct colors and his juxtaposition of the strong red and green complementary colors suggests a new world of emotion and mystery, which is the destination of that journey. In the same year, Kirchner created a similarly composed sculpture of a mother and daughter (with a bird in hand) that depicted the figures nude.

It should perhaps be noted that these artists' interest in an inward journey was also influenced directly and indirectly by Sigmund Freud's *Interpretation of Dreams*, published in 1900, which explored the world of dreams and the unconscious. And discourses in other disciplines, such as on the disintegration of the atom, Einstein's theory of relativity, and quantum physics, brought an end to the belief of some that the world could be viewed as a single, concrete, unchanging reality. Now there was the possibility of multiple and varied modes or lenses through which to look at the changing world. The nonnaturalistic, expressive colors and forms of the Expressionists were one of these modes.

Besides Die Brücke, there was a group in Germany called *Der Blaue Reiter* ("The Blue Rider"), which dealt more with theory, and a number of independent Expressionists. One independent Expressionist was Max Beckmann, who was profoundly affected by his experiences in World War I as a medical orderly. Beckmann's work came to reflect the violence and inhumanity that the artists felt were a part of his era. It is strong and filled with emotion, since Beckmann used angularity, distortion, and a linear expressiveness that stemmed from Gothic art. One becomes involved in a nightmarish world as one views his *Family Picture* of 1920 (Museum of Modern Art, New York). The distorted figures and perspective suggest a chaotic world. This multiple-generation family seems filled with despair. An older woman sits at a table with her hands over her face, while a child slouches at her feet. A decadent-looking young man holding a French horn is sprawled on a piano bench, while a half-dressed young woman stands in front of him, staring vainly in a mirror. Beckmann's use of strong colors emphasizes his distorted forms and shapes. In his work, Beckmann tried to go beneath the surface of reality to find the "invisible" beneath the "visible." As he noted, "I have only tried to realize my conception of the world as intensely as possible. What I want to show in my work is the idea which hides itself behind so-called reality. I am seeking for the bridge which leads from the visible to the invisible, like the famous cabalist who once said, 'If you wish to get hold of the invisible you must penetrate as deeply as possible into the visible.'"[5]

Other independent Expressionists included two women, Paula Modersohn-Becker and Käthe Kollwitz. More than some of their male counterparts, these women dealt with the social realities of women and children. Modersohn-Becker was born in 1876 in Dresden, the child of middle-class parents who were upset at her artistic professional ambitions. As a young girl, she expressed artistic interests, and in 1897 made her first visit to the Worpswede artists' community in northern Germany. The artists in this community were influenced by and interested in a variety of artists, writers, and philosophers, including Friedrich Nietzsche, Émile Zola, Albrecht Dürer, and Rembrandt, and concepts, such as the simplicity of peasant life and the purity of youth and childhood. The young Paula settled in the village community in 1898, later marrying the painter Otto Modersohn. Her diary and letters record the tensions she experienced among her roles as a wife, mother, and practicing artist. A major theme in her paintings is that of an idealized, fertile motherhood, of which Modersohn-Becker was to write, "I kneel before it [motherhood] in humility."[6] Her paintings, such as *Mother and Child Lying Nude*, 1907 (Freie Hausestadt, Bremen), suggest an archetypal fertility, a naturalness and directness of human relating, that recall, in part, some of Gauguin's glorification of the primitive Tahitian women. Mother and child become one in this intimate moment as the two figures lie together nude. It is sadly ironic that Modersohn-Becker died in 1907, at age thirty-seven, three weeks after giving birth to her only child, a daughter. Her close friend, the poet Rainer Maria Rilke, of whom she did a portrait in 1906, published a poem in 1909, entitled "Requiem for a Friend," commemorating the young artist. "I have my dead," he began and continued,

... And as you perceived fruit so, too, did
you see women
and also children, from within
grown into the forms of their existence.
And finally you saw yourself as like a fruit,
naked before the mirror. . . . [7]

In contrast to Modersohn-Becker's work, Käthe Kollwitz's images of women and children focused on the context of class and history, of women caught in economic and social forces. Unlike some Modernists, Kollwitz believed in the social function of art and was influenced by socialist philosophies. Her first major success was a cycle of engravings and lithographs based on Gerhart Hauptmann's then controversial play, *The Weavers*, about the revolt of Silesian weavers in 1844. Her somber grays and blacks and sharp outlines, for which she was to become known, emphasized the suffering and death experienced by the weavers and their families. Kollwitz, the first woman elected to the Prussian Academy of the Arts (1919), is considered one of the best graphic artists of the early twentieth century. The intensity of her prints and posters, which could be disseminated because multiple reproductions were made, was clear evidence of her advocacy for the poor and the oppressed and sensitive understanding of the suffering of others. Her interest in the theme of mother and child was also influenced by her personal life. She lost a son, Peter, in World War I and a grandson, Peter, in World War II. Images such as *Death, Mother and Child*, a charcoal drawing of 1910 [26], and *The Mothers*, a 1921 woodcut (study for final print, Museum of Fine Arts, Boston), portray a tenderness and protectiveness that are powerful and overwhelming. The velvet blacks, grays, and whites of the drawing depict primarily the heads of the mother and child in a final embrace, sinking in a sea of blacks and grays. Other versions of this subject in which more of the child's body is visible suggest the motif of Christ's descent from the cross and the theme of sacrifice. *The Mothers*, huddled together with their children in a protective, solid group, peer out, wide-eyed, at a dangerous world. One woman, seemingly pregnant, holds her hands over her unborn child as if to "stop" any intrusive force from the outside. This woodcut was part of a larger cycle of

26. Käthe Kollwitz, *Death, Mother and Child*, 1910. National Gallery of Art, Washington, DC.

prints, entitled *War*, which were completed in 1922–23 and publicly issued in three editions in 1924. The sheets in the cycle were printed in a large format and intended to serve as posters. Writing to the novelist Romain Rolland, Kollwitz spoke of her accomplishment:

> I have repeatedly attempted to give form to the war. I could never grasp it. Now finally I have finished a series of woodcuts, which *in some measure* say what I wanted to say. There are seven sheets, entitled: the Sacrifice—the Volunteers—the Parents—the Mothers—the Widows—the People. These sheets should travel throughout the entire world and should tell all human beings comprehensively: that is how it was—we have all endured that throughout these unspeakable difficult years.[8]

The sculptural elements of some of her woodcuts led Kollwitz to rework some of her motifs in three dimensions. For example, her *Tower of Mothers*, 1937–38 (Baltimore Museum of Art), contains the same huddled cluster as her woodcut, *Mothers*, done fifteen years earlier. After her son Peter's death, Kollwitz struggled for seventeen years to design and sculpt a monument to her beloved child. What she came up with is a powerfully moving tribute to her son and all sons who died in the horrors of war and to the grieving parents who prayed and cried for their children. The completed piece, entitled *Mourning Parents*, installed at the military cemetery at Dixmuiden, Belgium, shows a life-size father and mother carved in granite, kneeling at the edge of the cemetery. The figures, modeled after Kollwitz and her husband, Karl, kneel with folded arms. The woman, head bowed, is dressed in a flowing robe, in tribute to a lost child. One might ask whether the kind of works done by Modersohn-Becker and Kollwitz could have been done by men or whether a woman's sensibility was necessary to produce them, particularly at that time. Current discussions about the politics of gender, parenting, and caregiving may produce a different response for contemporary artists.

The Norwegian artist Edvard Munch also dealt with death and sickness in family life, but in a much more personal and less social context than did Kollwitz. Much of Munch's work was influenced by incidents of sickness and death in his own life. Munch appeared to have a strong perception of the psychological beneath the surface of the figures he portrayed. He sought to find the essence of people he knew and met. Character and aspects of individuality intrigued him. "When I meet a new face, I constantly ask myself: What sort of person is this? I have no peace until I have painted him."[9] Munch rarely accepted portrait commissions but chose his subjects himself. His graphic art was powerful, as was Kollwitz's. Works such as his woodcut *The Sick Room*, 1920 (Schiefler catalogue, 492, Berlin), the lithograph *Death of the Bohemian*, 1927 (Munch Museum, Oslo), or the lithograph *Family Scene*, 1920 (from Ibsen's *Ghosts*; Schiefler catalogue, 487, Berlin) articulate the power of sickness and death in the lives of families. In *The Sick Room*, one sees despairing figures hovering about the sick one. Ancestral portraits appear to hang on the back wall. Sickness seems to pervade the entire room.

The Death of the Bohemian refers to a close friend of Munch, Hans Jager, who had died in 1910. Jager was a seaman, writer, philosopher, and shorthand writer in the legislative assembly of Norway, as well as a spokesman for the Bohemians of Christiania, where Munch lived, and greatly influenced Munch. Jager's novel *Christiania-Bohème* (1885), which gave a realistic impression of the group's ideas on antibourgeois protests, free love, the emancipation of women, and so on, was banned. In this tribute to Jager, one sees the men and women gathered around his deathbed. It is interesting to note that the women appear more emotionally connected to the scene, while the men appear stalwart in the background.

The *Family Scene* from *Ghosts* was one of a number of images that Munch did for the play. In 1906 he collaborated with the playwright Henrik Ibsen and painted the scenic designs for the performance. The few figures were placed isolated in a room, emphasizing the dramatic fate of the characters. The play used the problem of hereditary venereal disease as a symbol for moral diseases inherited from previous generations that seemed to be killing the living. Munch's later lithographs, made in 1919–20, are based on the earlier designs. In the 1920 lithograph, the shadows of the family figures dominate the black-and-white piece and almost become overwhelming as they loom, larger than life. The threatening shadows allude to the human problems presented in the play. The final scene with the mother and her dying son looking toward the sunrise is powerful.

The Expressionists thus sought to portray a world of emotions and feelings. Details of physical features or clothing were not necessarily depicted true to the "natural" world. More important was the inner world, which might entail elements of mysticism, or contemplation of the otherworldly and infinite. If the viewer is at all sympathetic to the artist's deliberate antinaturalism and powerful individual expression, then the piece could also provide a personal justification for the viewer and a partial means of overcoming a materialistic, antagonistic world.

In 1923 Picasso stated: "We all know that Art is not truth. Art is a lie that makes us realize truth, at least the truth that is given us to understand. The artist must know the manner whereby to convince others of the truthfulness of his lies."[10] His statement, although not directly related to portraiture or any one of his pieces, seems to touch on some of the essential characteristics of portraying an "other," of the inevitable questions that are raised: What is true? What is false? Picasso believed in the transformative powers of the artist, not only as a kind of "magician" who could convince others of the truthfulness of his lies, but as one who has the power to "make us realize truth."

The work of the German Dada artist Hannah Höch is anti-bourgeois in a different manner. Along with Raoul Hausmann, also a member of the Berlin Dada group, she helped pioneer experiments with photomontage and emphasized its role in ideology. In a 1919 photomontage, *Bürgerliches Brautpaar—Streit* (*Bourgeois Bridal Couple—Quarrel*) (private collection), Höch parodied conventional marriage. In the background are colored illustrations of household items used for cleaning and cooking. In the foreground are male and female figures in sports outfits. The woman, who has spindly legs and the head of a child with no neck, appears distressed. The man carries a large ribboned hat on his head and back, as if it were a tremendous burden. He seems dwarfed and somewhat effeminate by the oversized hat. Höch created other works that parodied bourgeois marriages, such as a 1920 watercolor, *Bürgerliches Brautpaar* (*Bourgeois Bridal Couple*), in which a groom, dressed in formal clothing, stands holding the arm of his bride, a headless mannequin wearing a bridal veil. Some of Höch's work reflects her own struggles as a young woman in Weimar, Germany. Was she a New Woman with new freedoms, new possibilities, and new pleasures?

Born in 1878 into a bourgeois family, with an authoritarian father, as a young woman Höch frequently questioned her identity. As did a number of young leftist intellectuals, she supported communism, as is evidenced by her participation in the 1920 November Group letter that called for artists' involvement in politics. Höch was romantically involved with Raoul Hausmann for a while, particularly in the late teens and early twenties, corresponding with him as well. Although the two were considered a couple in public and had friends in common, Hausmann remained with his wife, Elfriede Hausmann-Schaeffer, with whom he had a daughter in 1907. Höch had two abortions, in 1916 and 1918, apparently refusing to have children with Hausmann unless he ended his marriage.

A scrapbook (Berlinische Galerie, Berlin) Höch put together in 1933, using mass media images in a montage format, further reflects her continuing questions about the identity of women. The placement of images and of pages served to jar previous perceptions about women and their relationships through the creation of new realities resulting from the fragments and images lifted from one reality, juxtaposed with other realities, to create new realities. For example, pages 10 and 11 combined photographic shots of nudity, nature, procreation, and women. On page 10 one finds a baby suckling the breast of its mother, a photo by Tina Modotti; a handsomely tanned nude couple holding a blond nude child in the air, captioned "The Hardy Family"; a group of babies awaiting baptism before leaving the clinic, captioned "The baby parade: Babies baptized before leaving the clinic"; and a small boy asking, "May I come in now?" The latter image, by the photographer Hedda Walther, was part of a sentimental Christmas photostory by Walther for *Die Woche*, a weekly paper.

In the middle of the page, touching the "seams" of the four photographs, is a tiny cutout on which is printed the words "Foto: Tina Modotti," referring to her photograph and a larger context. Modotti was particularly noted for the photographs she took in Mexico City in the late twenties, in which she joined art and politics. Modotti, from a working-class Italian background, had begun her career as a film actress, frequently playing the fiery Latin "vamp" in Hollywood westerns, and as a model, noted for her beauty. She later worked with Edward Weston as a model, but went on to combine her formal, aesthetic interests with the revolutionary politics of communism in Mexico. Modotti looked to the exterior world and photographed streets, women and children on the streets, and men at public meetings. She had gone from being an object, frequently photographed from above by Weston and the object of men's gazes, to a photographer, who chose to photograph the nature of women's interactions with their children or women at work, rather than the bodies of women or women as "beauties." For example, her *Mother and Child* from Tehuantepec, Oaxaca, Mexico, of 1929 (Museum of Modern Art, New York), shows the profile of a pregnant woman balancing her naked child on her hip. We do not see the woman's head. More important is the embrace of the child, whose arm is wrapped around her mother's shoulder. Höch's inclusion of Modotti is clearly a tribute and an allusion to Modotti's work that brings another level of meaning to this scrapbook page.

On page eleven one finds a nude woman; a group of nude men, seemingly involved in some form of ritual dance; and photographs of flowers—lilies, which are frequently associated with purity and innocence. Under two of the stalks of flowers are written the words *Dürer* (the Renaissance artist noted for his Madonnas and for his images of nature and landscape) and *Kirchen fenster,* which could be translated as "church window." Thus, one quickly sees Höch's attempt to interrelate elements of nature, women and families, and Christian images of purity and baptism.

On a number of pages, Höch employs an ethnographic theme. On pages 22 and 23, for example, she includes photographs that mainly concern the daily life of African women, young girls, and children. The nudity and naturalness of these figures is striking. Unlike these women, women in the Weimar Republic were frequently encouraged through advertising to aspire to the status of mannequins—beautiful, rational, in control, efficient, precise, and well put together—in short "modern." Such a state, according to advertisers, could be achieved through such products as new cosmetics, shampoo, and labor-saving devices for the home. The ethnographic photographs that Höch tended to use were highly romantic, suggesting a nostalgia for the "premodern." (Germany had lost all its colonies in 1918 as a result of the Treaty of Versailles.)

Höch's inclusion of physically fit bodies, along with sports photographs, also reflected a general cultural interest in physical fitness and athletics in the Weimar Republic. A popular documentary *Kulturfilm* (a visual "travelogue" that provided enthusiastic views of new worlds to the German public through cinematography and montage), *Wege zu Kraft und Schönheit* (*Ways to Strength and Beauty*), 1925, praised the Greeks' emphasis on fitness and athletics, spoke of the unfitness of modern men and women because of modern city life, and promoted exercise as a way to achieve and maintain health and beauty.

Throughout the scrapbook, one finds a complex approach to women and children with few shots of husbands with wives and children. Although Höch was a modernist and a leftist, she also shared with figures such as Hedda Walther a reverence for the natural, the primitive, the rural, and the sentimental. Her own experiences with Hausmann, with whom she wanted to have children, could not have helped but influence her work. But significant, too, was the concern by many people in Germany at that time about the falling birthrate during the Weimar Republic, which they perceived to be the "suicide" of the German *Volk*. Motherhood became a rallying cry, particularly for those who wanted women out of politics and the workplace. In 1931, Höch contributed work to an exhibit entitled *Frauen in Not* (*Women in Need*), organized to protest illegal abortions. Her scrapbook does contain numerous images of women and children, not of men with children, which seems to accept the "naturalness" of women's roles as mothers. And one finds few images of difficult labor or poverty in the scrapbook.

Although the photographs Höch chose to include in her montages were of individuals, her placement of individual images together allowed her to make visual statements that related to "types" and to ideology. This interest in "types" related to groups in society was also to be found in the work of another German, the photographer August Sander, whose approach to his work was different from Höch's. In 1929 he published a portfolio of photographs of German "types" from various aspects of German society, representing a broad social spectrum, entitled *Antlitz der Zeit* (*Face of the Time*). In the introduction to the work, the writer Alfred Döblin referred to Sander's approach as a kind of "pictorial sociology." The work was perhaps the best known of a number of collections of portraits, usually specific types, that became particularly popular in Germany between 1928 and 1933. These collections included *People of the Time: One Hundred and One Photos from Present-Day Germany*, 1930, primarily male portraits; *Female Faces of the Present*, 1930; *Everyday Heads*, 1931, concentrating on beggars and unemployed, lower-class urban dwellers; *German Folk Faces*, 1930, representing figures from remote country areas; *Men at Work*, 1930, depicting industrial workers; and *The Face of Age*, 1930, depicting the elderly. These collections were published in part as a way to cope with a Germany that was still faced with a national identity crisis after World War I. Questions about the nature of society, particularly of the old social order in which everyone had a specific place, had arisen. But there was no agreement as to what structure society should have. The philosopher Karl Jaspers, in his 1933 book *The Intellectual State of the Time*, spoke of the general "anthropological" obsession of the time: "Things are measured, but what is actually seen eludes all measurement and numerical fixation."[11]

Questions about identity and being had also been raised by the philosopher Martin Heidegger in his 1927 book *Sein und Zeit* (*Being and Time*). Heidegger's fundamental question was "What is the meaning of Being?," a question that he believed lay behind all aspects of everyday life and behind the empirical questions of natural science. Heidegger hoped to have all men and women ask this question. To him, a crisis had arisen in Western thought's emphasis on the seemingly one-sided technological development, resulting in "inauthentic" ways of being. Heidegger saw "man" as distinct from "things," but nevertheless nothing without "things." However, there was a danger of being submerged by "things." "Man's" freedom to choose resulted in anxiety or "Angst," but such Angst opened "Man" up to true, authentic being and finding one's true "home." In a state of anxiety, being was nowhere at home— "*Unheimlichkeit, Unzuhause.*" Heidegger offered no concrete answers to the problems and questions raised in his *Sein und Zeit*. His use of a home metaphor was appealing to some, for it was something one could relate to. Indeed, the National Socialists allowed Heidegger to become rector of the University of Freiburg when an anti-Nazi scientist resigned in protest. (Heidegger's sympathy for the Nazi party was brief, lasting until 1934 when he resigned his post as rector.)

Sander could not help but have been affected to some extent by the temper of these times. His images of families "at home" may seem part of that search for a sense of "authentic" being. For Sander, the total "unmasking" of the impact of an ideology is the task of the viewer. Sander's portraits are not necessarily directly ideological; rather, they are a survey of "types" from different classes with hints of individuality staring forth from some of the photographs. In a larger set of photographs, *Citizens of the Twenti-eth Century: Portrait Photographs*, 1892–1952, Sander included a section on "families," which is incorporated into a larger section entitled "Women." (The other titles in this larger section were "Men and Women," "Mothers and Children," "Children," "Fami-lies," "Society Ladies," and "Working Women.") Under "Family" there are seven plates, representing different types of families from different social strata. All the families were clearly aware they were posing for the camera. In the photographs, all are well dressed, their clothes reflecting their relative degrees of affluence.

The settings and furniture of the middle-class families reflect some material wealth and play prominent roles in their portraits. The poses are stiff, set either by the photographer or the subjects. The figures are stalwart, showing little emotion and seeming to accept their station and given identity and status in German soci-ety. Although there is no direct judgment by the photographer, there is an intended space for comparison in the arrangement of the photographs. It is this comparison and the questions such a comparison may raise that make Sander's photographs more than a marvelous documentation of different German characters and social types in a society that once had specific, accepted niches for its individuals, but was now in the throes of social and economic chaos, which was to become the breeding ground for the rise of National Socialism. (Sander's photographs were finally banned as "undesirable" by the Nazis, in part because Sander's son, Erich, had become a Communist.)

National Socialism had a gradual impact on the German nation before Hitler actually seized power in 1933. The National Socialists proclaimed early on that art and life should be brought together. Homage to the family, the youth movement, glorification of the human form, the cult of the heroic, a return to nature, mass meetings, and the like were all to find expression in the visual arts under National Socialism. New homes, new factories, new roads, new sports arenas, and new public buildings were constructed. In 1927, the architect Alfred Rosenberg, who also formulated a num-ber of the ideas on which the National Socialist ideology was based, formed the National Socialist Society for German Culture, which, in 1928–29, became the Kampbund für deutsche Kultur

(League for the Defense of German Culture). The goals of this organization were to make sure there was no corruption of art and to educate the people about the relationship between race and artistic values. And art was to be brought to the *Volk*, the people. Music was played in factories; numerous cultural events and outings brought people together as never before. There was no longer to be an intellectual or artistic elite. The radio was also a powerful tool for the communication of government values. A painting by Paul Mathias Padua, entitled *The Führer Speaks*, depicts a multiple-generation family sitting comfortably together listening to the radio. A photograph of Hitler hangs in a prominent spot on the wall near the radio. The painting was exhibited at the Great German Art Exhibition in 1940.

The family became an important subject in the art of National Socialism, particularly the family of the farmer. The German nation was viewed as the intertwining of all German families of the same race. Paul Hermann, an expert on racial purity, wrote, "The eugenic concept of family in its deepest essence is synonymous with the Christian concept of a 'religious-moral family,' which rests upon the twin pillars of 'premarital chastity' and 'conjugal fidelity.'"[12] A woman was considered to be "morally good" if she had several children. A childless married woman was considered inferior, as was the woman who had several miscarriages or who bore deformed or sickly children. The family was seen as the salvation and future of the state. The concept and image of "homeland" were significant.

The ideal family was similar to the one depicted by Adolf Wissel in *Farm Family from Kahlenberg*, 1939 (Ernst Reinhold/Artothek, Peissenberg, Germany). In this painting, a family of three generations is seated around a table outside, with the farm fields stretching into the background. All are fair-skinned and fair-haired. The youngest daughter sits on her mother's lap near the center of the painting in a Madonna-like pose. This pose was clearly intended to have symbolic significance, for the "woman," preordained by nature to bear children, was frequently considered sacred. Madonna-like depictions of mother and child became quite popular. Hitler also saw the woman who bore pure children as a soldier of the Third Reich. In a speech to the National Socialist

Women's Congress in 1935, he firmly stated, "The woman has her own battlefield. With any child she brings to the world, she fights her battle for the nation. The man stands up for the '*Volk*,' exactly as the woman stands up for the family."[13] The little boy sits close to his father with a toy horse in his hand. The oldest daughter is drawing, a doll and basket are to her right. The grandmother sits knitting to the right of the mother. A finely decorated coffee cup with a pair of glasses next to it are in front of the grandmother. All is harmonious. All is still. There is no conflict. The details of the painting are meticulously rendered. The self and family appear healthy and whole. But, in the final analysis, these frozen figures are lifeless. However, the peaceful and symmetrical compositions and the frozen figures were supposed to evoke a sense of unchanging universal truth and salvation to be found in the family of pure Aryan descent. The visual arts—films, paintings, posters, and so on, together with the books and music, were clearly part of the masterful propaganda program carried out by Hitler and his ministers. On the surface, the works, though frequently listless and lifeless, are innocuous. What could be "wrong" with harmony and glorification of the human form and the family? It is only in retrospect, as one views this art as propaganda, through the lenses of the horror of the Holocaust, and compares it to the art that was banned as degenerate—all that was abstract, expressionist, and concerned with the inner spirit—that one sees that the healthy, peaceful idyllic depictions of family life, of women and youths, have a dark underside of meaning. To this day, questions are still raised: How much did people in general know? Could the German non-Jewish populace have seen more than the surface of these paintings? How would the general public today, with the power of the mass media, deal with a similar widespread infiltration of imagery and events that seem to be so appealing? Are we willing to reach beneath the surface, particularly if it involves some sense of risk for ourselves and our families? How do we deal with the more subtle propaganda of advertising and television in today's culture? How do our senses of ourselves and our families evolve in relation to propaganda of any type? The questions can go on and on.

As the National Socialists took power in France, the work of the French philosopher Jean-Paul Sartre, the leading French exponent of existentialism, cannot be discounted for its impact on the time period. In his autobiography *Les Mots* (*The Words*), Sartre tells a tale of his childhood, when he and his mother would wander through the Luxembourg Gardens in search of playmates who would accept him—a child small in stature and cross-eyed. No one did. He and his mother retreated to the sixth floor of their apartment, where words and writing saved him from a world that would not accept him. In 1938, Sartre published *La Nausée* (*Nausea*), a novel that explores the feelings of revulsion and nausea of the protagonist, Roquentin, as he confronts the world, other people, and even his own body. When World War II broke out, Sartre was drafted and served on the Maginot line. He was taken prisoner, and after the institution of the Vichy government, returned to Paris, where he worked in the Resistance. In his personal life, Sartre resisted the concept of "bourgeois marriage." Instead, he and Simone de Beauvoir formed their now famous relationship.

In 1943 Sartre published *L'Être et le néant* (*Being and Nothingness*), which was an attempt to describe basic categories for understanding the world through the experience of being alone as an individual, since there was no God. Existence precedes essence, rather than the traditional view that essence precedes existence. Because there is no essence to which an individual must conform, he or she is free. Furthermore, the individual is responsible for all of his or her actions and becomes authentic in the exercise of those choices or actions. Sartre emphasized the power of the individual's consciousness as a way to respond to objects and to situations in a chaotic world. Existentialism included active involvement and "engagement." It came to be an accepted philosophy in a Europe that was experiencing the rise of fascism, in which the hero-leader, Il Duce, Der Führer, the Superman, and the nonthinking follower were part of fascist thinking. Existentialism called the individual to action, to take responsibility for shaping his or her own essence. Death was not the death of the body; it was the loss of freedom in an absurd world. In the post–World War II period, existentialism also provided a certain type of guidance for those who felt alienated and uprooted after the war.

Sartre's central themes, related to the authenticity and moral choices of the individual in a hostile world, seemed to reflect a mood of the times for many. These themes were to have an impact on the arts as well, as artists themselves made choices and took actions and isolated individuals, rather than family groups, appeared more frequently in artistic representations. As an example, one might cite the sculpture or drawings of the Swiss artist Alberto Giacometti, whose elongated thin figures frequently stand alone or with absolutely no connection with one another. In his *City Square* [27], one sees the depiction of a "city square," which is normally associated with numerous figures, some interacting, some not. In this piece, there is no interaction among the five solitary figures, only isolation. The surfaces of the thin figures are rough and blank, expressionless, standing in a large void, and remote from each other and from the viewer.

World War II ended in Europe with death, destruction, and the development of the atomic bomb, which would change lives forever because of the knowledge that most of the earth's population could be destroyed. Until World War II, the artistic centers of the world had been in Europe. Experiments in the context of Modernism had brought forth Fauvism, Cubism, Expressionism, Surrealism, Futurism, Dadaism, Constructivism, Bauhaus art, and other experiments. These experiments concentrated on innovative changes in the articulation of form, space, color, and line, as well as

27. Alberto Giacometti, *City Square*, 1948. Museum of Modern Art, New York.

new content images, depending on the movement. Artists explored the world of dreams in Surrealism, the world of the machine and speed in Futurism, inner feelings and emotions in Expressionism, and the rejection of all previous traditional art forms in Dadaism. Although there was a decline in portraiture and family images, the various movements just mentioned should not be discounted, nor should the avant-garde experiments in abstraction, collage, montage, and exploring the subconscious. Although these experiments did not frequently depict family groups, they were to become variables in later conceptions and images of who we are or were in the exploration of post–World War II identities.

Having explored some images related to the family in Europe in the first part of the twentieth century, I now turn to the United States during the same period. By 1900, the average life expectancy for American children was forty-seven years, compared to about thirty-five years in 1800. (By 1980, it had risen to seventy-four years for men and women together.) Thus by 1910, millions of family members began to live longer. In 1910 the total population of the country was about 100 million. With the coming of the Industrial Revolution and the growth of factories, men no longer worked at home, and the workplace and home were separate spheres. Women and children of lower-class families worked on their family farms or in factories. Cities grew, particularly as immigrants from other countries flooded onto American shores. In the quarter century following 1890, 18 million immigrants came to the United States. Americans were faced with fears of an overwhelming growth in the population, on the one hand, and advances in technology that allowed for communication and mobility, on the other hand. The term *family planning* also began to be used by the early part of the century as contraception (primarily in the middle- and upper classes) and more frequent washing came to be part of everyday life. After 1880, children had to attend school for a minimum time and to be inoculated against certain diseases. Social reform became a popular cry. As early as 1903, Charlotte Perkins Gilman published her book, *The Home, Its Work and Influence*, which demanded domestic reform. She wrote:

Set the woman on her feet, as a free, intelligent, able human being, quite capable of putting into the world more than she takes out, of being a producer as well as a consumer. Put these poor antiquated "domestic industries" into the archives of past history; and let efficient modern industries take their place. . . . The man relieved of two thirds of his expenses, provided with double supplies, properly fed and more comfortable at home than he ever dreamed of being, and associated with a strong, free stimulating companion all through life, will be able to work to far better purpose in the social service, and with far greater power, pride, and enjoyment.[14]

The Century of the Child (1913), by the Swedish sociologist Ellen Key, also became popular in the United States. As the title suggests, the book dealt with the possibility of raising happier and healthier children, as well as issues related to women at work and their role as mothers.

Women, such as the social worker Jane Addams, responded to the call to young middle-class women to do more than be part of an empty marriage and to became involved in settlement house work among the urban poor. As it did in Europe, World War I took its toll on American family life and perceptions of the self and family.

Some of the traditional ideas of marriage involving patriarchy and monogamy were challenged by unorthodox writers as "Bohemian" lifestyles were taken up. There also was a growing diversity of family types—the families of "ghetto" immigrants, frequently living in poorly kept tenement houses; middle-class families, living in tidy houses with tidy yards; and the families of farmers, migrant farmworkers, blacks, and American Indians. In general, though, the turn-of-the-century family, particularly the middle-class family, was in a state of flux and stress. The rising divorce rate, the sexual revolution, and the increased number of women in the workforce brought about changes in the Victorian ideal of the family. As one writer noted, "Many Americans believed that the family was being destroyed, but in fact a new kind of family was emerging from these demographic and cultural revolutions: It was the 'companionate family,' a new model and ideal of family function and behavior which remains with us today.[15] The "companionate family," instead of following the Victorian ideal of the family as a sacred haven in a corrupt and chaotic world, with patriarchal authority, viewed wives and husbands as friends and lovers. Parents and children would be "pals." Sexual gratification, rather than sexual repression, was now emphasized in marriage. The "new woman" of the 1920s and the post–World War I era was characterized by the "flapper," who wore short skirts and had short hair, as a new sense of independence evolved.

Working farther and farther from their homes, men began to distance themselves from their roles as domestic patriarchs and as shapers of the characters of their children. The father was no longer seen as a moral force, and the wife became responsible for most of the running of the household. In their famous study of the town of Muncie, Indiana, during the 1920s, the sociologists Robert and Helen Lynd found that there was a growing psychological gap between husbands and wives. Men were preoccupied with earning an income and a few practical matters, such as car maintenance, while their wives were responsible for household matters, such as educating and caring for the children or arranging social engagements. The Lynds also noted the development of a distinct youth subculture, different from the world of adults. Unlike children in nineteenth-century families, children in the 1920s were also given more opportunities to express their feelings, and affection between parents and children was demonstrated more frequently.

Increasingly, middle-class Americans seemed to be more aware of books, newspapers, the radio, movies, schools, and churches—those institutions or methods of communication that transmitted culture. People began to talk about "culture" and ideas more frequently. The organized feminist movement became more articulate as women sought more rights and voting privileges. Women were not allowed to vote until 1920.

In a growing consumer economy, necessary for economic growth, there was increased consumption and increased advertising. Numerous ads contained various images related to family life and exerted a greater and greater influence on one's sense of identity. For example, a 1915 *Saturday Evening Post* advertisement for

Ivory Soap pictured a grandmother about to bathe two young children. The text of the ad begins, "With youngsters growing bigger every minute and flannels shrinking smaller every washday, woolen undergarments soon feel anything but comfortable to the tender skins and active bodies. These garments, however, can be kept to their original size and shape if washed according to the following instructions." A 1925 *Saturday Evening Post* ad for P and G Naptha laundry soap included an interview with a young Mrs. Marshall, who lived in a "friendly" house, "with bright chintzes, glistening white woodwork, and welcoming, comfortable chairs." Mrs. Marshall is pictured in a low-cut dress in a cameo oval inset above the text, while her two young boys are pictured above, wrestling playfully with the family dog in front of an immaculately kept house.[16] As advertising increased, the Protestant ethic of earning and saving appeared to decrease and the age of consumerism began.

In 1914 Mother's Day was made an official holiday, when Congress and President Woodrow Wilson signed a joint resolution designating the second Sunday in May as Mother's Day. In 1921, the first Miss America contest was held, telling us more about Americans' interest in beauty and the notion that beauty was what women needed for any kind of success. The "production" of beauty was to become a big business—soaps, cosmetics, shampoos, beauty parlors, and the like. The image of wife and mother was increasingly linked to beauty as well.

The so-called avant-garde visual artists of early twentieth-century America did not, however, concentrate on images of middle-class motherhood or beauty. Artists, such as the early American Modernists—Arthur Dove, Marsden Hartley, Charles Demuth, Charles Sheeler, Georgia O'Keeffe, and John Marin—were part of the inner circle surrounding the photographer and supporter of modern art, Alfred Stieglitz. They turned to abstraction, primarily related to the rhythms of nature or to the urban landscape. As did the philosopher Henri Bergson, a number of artists believed that the role of individual intuition was significant. For some critics, Georgia O'Keeffe's flower paintings, rather than figurative works, became an expression of female and maternal sensibilities. Herbert Seligmann, a contemporary of the culture critic, Lewis Mumford, and Stieglitz's friend, wrote in 1923: "O'Keeffe has made the ocean, wave, or sky, flower for fruit herself. She has added to America's chronicle hitherto unattempted truths of a woman's sensibility. It is in terms of the identity in her statement that all her works are related to each other and to life."[17] And the critic Louis Kalonyme associated the soil and earth with sexual and maternal forces: "The world she [O'Keeffe] paints is maternal, its swelling hills and reclining valleys are pregnant with a beauty born of a primeval sun. The sun's rays points, piercing the human forms of the earth give birth through her to singing flowers which are fragrant chalices of a golden radiance. . . . She reveals woman as an elementary being, closer to the earth than man, suffering pain with passionate ecstasy, enjoying love with beyond good and evil delight."[18]

Important for the literary and artistic avant-garde were numerous "salons" held in the living rooms of advocates and supporters of new ways of thinking, seeing, and writing. It was in these settings that both artistic and intellectual ideas and ideas of political and social reform were exchanged and discussed. Mabel Dodge Luhan, the Arensbergs, and the Stettheimers were prominent hosts of these salons. The Stettheimers were a wealthy family with five children. Florine, one of the daughters, was an artist who had studied at the Art Students League and briefly in Berlin. With her mother and two unmarried sisters, she ran their celebrated salon. One sister, Ettie, had earned a Ph.D. in philosophy and published two novels. Florine's sister Carrie spent twenty-five years creating an elaborate dollhouse that included an art gallery with real miniature paintings created by well-known Modernist painters. Florine's paintings both parodied and celebrated Manhattan's high society. Her subjects included the ostentatious marriage of two New Yorkers, with diamonds from the elegant Tiffany's swinging from a banner in the sky and a Rolls-Royce with a dollar sign on its grille, or images of her social and artistic circle that included Maurice Sterne, Gaston and Isabelle Lachaise, Albert Gleizes, Leo Stein, and her sisters. Her paintings are filled with fantasy—brightly colored and calligraphy-like, with lithe figures integrated with her personal symbolism. This sensibility is seen in her 1919 painting, *Heat* (Brooklyn Museum, Brooklyn, New York), in which she depicts a party celebrating her mother's birthday, on July 22. In the painting, Florine's mother sits in a black corseted dress in the rear center of the fanciful, brightly colored setting, inspired by the family's rental of Rupert Hughes's farm in Bedford, New York, for the summer. Indoors and outdoors are interchangeable in that large willowlike trees stand close to comfortable, well-stuffed living room interior furniture. The four Stettheimer daughters languish in chairs in front of their mother. A large birthday cake, with "Mother, July 22, 1918" inscribed on it, stares up at the viewer on a table in the lower center of the painting. There is considerable distance among the figures and no sense of connection among them except through the occasion commemorated by the cake. Yet the overall ambience of the painting, with Stettheimer's naive and decorative style, is one of enjoyment, and the figures are a significant integral part of the total scene.

Stettheimer's personal symbolism is further seen in her *Family Portrait II* [28], in which members of her family sit in a stylish stagelike tearoom, with a transparent ghostly version of the Chrysler Building in the background. Enormous floating flowers dominate the center of this family stage set. On the floor is a kind of patchwork rug made with pennant shapes, on which are written family names—Ettie, Florine, and so on. The figures are dressed in modish clothes. This is not the typical American family but the expression of an individual fantasy. The painting seems quite telling of the imaginative and intellectual forces that were part of the wealthy Stettheimer family constellation. Because of her family's affluence, Florine was freed from any economic pressures to exhibit or sell her work. At her insistence, any gallery that did show her work had to redecorate the gallery like Stettheimer's home, indicating Stettheimer's strong attachment to her family and home.

More traditional images of family life in the early part of the century may be seen in a 1923 painting by Charles Hopkinson, *The Hopkinson Family Portrait* [29], depicting a seemingly harmonious family scene in a living room. The mother and youngest daughter are seated on a chair, their hands entwined around the mother's shoulder, while the others stand somewhat informally around them. The father, with only his head and shoulders visible,

28. Florine Stettheimer, *Family Portrait II*, 1933. Museum of Modern Art, New York.

stands behind the group, preoccupied by the book he holds. The emphasis is on the mother and children, dressed primarily in bright pastel colors. The family members are surrounded by four bouquets of flowers, connecting them with the world of nature and adding fragrance to the painting. The white walls and receding arches of the room contribute to a sense of openness and lightness that dominates this peaceful portrait of a family at home, at ease with each other.

Hopkinson did a number of paintings of his wife, Elinor Curtis, and his five daughters, Elinor (Elly), Isabella (Ibby), Mary (Maly), Harriet (Happy), and Joan, frequently experimenting with techniques and theories with his family as the subject. In addition to his 1923 portrait, there is, for example, his large 1926 canvas *Five in the Afternoon* of his five daughters, painted on the terraces of the Hopkinson house. Here, Hopkinson combined his admiration of nature's beauty and plenty with the youthful grace and beauty of his daughters, who are an integral part of the idyllic scene. The painting won a silver medal at the Sesquicentennial International Exhibition in Philadelphia in 1926.

29. Charles Hopkinson, *The Hopkinson Family Portrait*, 1923. Museum of Fine Arts, Boston.

Hopkinson's paintings of his family record his children's growth and evolution over time. A much later painting, of 1952, for instance, depicts his granddaughters, Mary, Alice, and Marjorie Gibbon, the daughters of his daughter Mary. The background of this painting shows the lower portion and frame of Hopkinson's 1923 painting, thereby pulling together several family generations through the medium of the visual arts.

Another painting done in 1923 was *Emma and Her Children*, by George Bellows [30]. This painting, though, contains the darker, more somber palette that Bellows used in his paintings associated with the Ashcan school, such as *The Wrestlers*, 1905 (Museum of Fine Arts, Boston), and *The Cliff Dwellers*, 1913 (Los Angeles County Museum of Art). Unlike many of the Ashcan school paintings, which explored the "guts" of urban living, particularly for the lower class, this painting clearly indicates that Emma and her children are well-off. Emma is dressed in black. Her younger daughter, in a frilly white party dress, is seated on her lap,

30. George Bellows, *Emma and Her Children*, 1923. Museum of Fine Arts, Boston.

while the older daughter, dressed in a frothy dress with small red-orange dots, holds an elegant fan, as does her mother. They all sit on a black couch in a dark room with the shades drawn. Two small glints of light appear from the outside world. No father is present, and the figures appear somber and saddened, in contrast to the Hopkinson portrait.

This is a portrait of the artist's wife Emma and daughters, Anne (the older child) and Jean (the younger). It is the only finished family portrait of his wife and daughters. Bellows had used his wife Emma as a model in a number of canvases. He had also done a complex oil painting of his entire household, including Emma's mother, the family maid, and himself at the easel, in *The Studio* (1919). Emma, Anne, and Jean also appeared in *My Family*, a lithograph of 1921, in which Bellows leans protectively over the sofa where his family is sitting. In 1923 Bellows also depicted himself with Emma and Anne in the guise of Maine fishermen and women, in *Fisherman's Family*. In *Emma and Her Children*, Bellows appears to emphasize Emma's role as a mother as she approaches forty and the role of maternity, in general, and does not depict himself in a protective role.

Although posed or formal family portraits were far from the focus of the Ashcan school, it is perhaps important to note that in the painting of this school, there were numerous depictions of children and families in the street scenes. Bellows's *The Cliff Dwellers*, for example, depicts a crowded New York tenement area on a hot summer day, with men, women, and children standing or sitting outside on stoops, steps, and balconies. Lines of laundry blow in the wind while a trolley car attempts to make its way through the throngs of people in the street. The figures appear pleasant and earthy, and human energy fills the canvas. Unlike the literature and art of the late nineteenth century Gilded Age, which had sentimentalized the poor as harmless or ignored the poor completely, a number of artists associated with the Ashcan school chose to depict the poor faithfully, capturing their humanity. As Robert Henri, an artist and teacher, wrote in his 1923 book, *The Art Spirit*, "Because we are saturated with life, because we are human, our strongest motive is Life, humanity: and the stronger the motive back of a line, the stronger, and therefore more beautiful the line will be."[19] It was this sense of humanity, rather than direct social protest, that inspired Henri and his contemporaries.

The year 1929 brought despair to all social classes in the United States, when the stock market crashed and the Great Depression began. Families were confronted with economic crisis and insecurity. Nine million families lost their savings, when a fifth of the nation's banks closed their doors. Poverty spread beyond the traditional poor—the tenant farmers, the urban immigrants, disabled people, members of single-parent families, and the elderly—to former middle-class and working-class families. For some families, the Great Depression encouraged family members to turn to each other, to become a stronger unit. For other families, though, the economic downswing tore up family life with unemployment, reduced living standards, relatives' demands, and lower self-esteem, particularly for men. Children suffered from malnutrition and caught more diseases. In many instances, they were expected to find some sort of job. Midwestern and southern farm families, especially sharecropping families, were in particularly difficult straits. When Franklin Delano Roosevelt took office as president in March 1933, many families in the United States were in need of help. It was clear that private charity and local governments could not provide the kind of assistance they needed. Roosevelt's New Deal marked the first time that the federal government became a major guarantor of family welfare. For example, the new administration created the Civilian Conservation Corps, to reduce unemployment among the young; the Federal Emergency Relief Administration, to fund state-run welfare programs; the Civil Works Administration, to provide jobs for 4 million jobless families; the Works Progress Administration (WPA); and the social security system as we know it today, established by the Social Security Act of 1935. Part of the WPA's funds were for the employment of visual artists—for example, for artists to paint murals in public buildings, of rural, local, or regional scenes, particularly of frontier days, which helped the American people regain a sense of positive identity. The Farm Security Administration (FSA) hired notable photographers, such as Arthur Rothstein, Walker Evans, and Dorothea Lange, and gave them good equipment to travel to stricken areas and visually record conditions. The term *documentary*, rather than *artistic*, became the guiding focus of these photographers. After viewing some of these images at the Grand Central Palace exhibit in 1938, the art critic Elizabeth McCausland wrote:

> After the usual diet of the art world—cream puffs, eclairs, and such—the hard, bitter reality of these photographs is the tonic the soul needs. They are like a sharp wind, sweeping away the weariness. . . . In them we see the faces of the American people. The American people which lives under the threat of unemployment, hunger and eviction. We see the farmers, the sharecroppers, the homeless migrant agricultural workers, the children who suffer from malnutrition, the whole families whose homes are part of that dreadful sub-standard "one-third of a nation."[20]

Walker Evans traveled to the South, documenting American farms and faces—the conditions of the land, the sharecroppers, their houses, their belongings, schools, churches, stores, and the like. Despite the impoverished living conditions of those he photographed, there was always a dignity inherent in the figures he photographed. In 1941, Evans collaborated with the writer James Agee to produce their well-known book, *Let Us Now Praise Famous Men*. Evans grouped thirty-one photographs at the front of the book, before the title page, without a single word of explanation. The photographs were to stand alone, as equal to the written text. The photographs, clear and sharply focused, recorded the life and milieu of these tenant farmers. There is a mother with a bandaged foot, holding and consoling her baby, each in worn and spotted clothes. There is a family of mixed generations posed on and next to an old, peeling iron bed. The little boy has a shirt on; the others' clothes are pinned and tattered. Their slumped postures are evidence of a chronic fatigue and of the burden of subsistence survival. There is a photograph of photographs pinned on the wall— one of four young children and one of an older woman. And there is a mother photographed with eight children. Besides the dignity of the photographs, there is evidence of Evans's and Agee's respect for these people, whom they visited and lived with during July and August 1936 while on assignment for *Fortune* magazine. (The negatives were to belong to the FSA, where Evans was employed.) The two collaborators wrote at the beginning of the book, "To those of whom the record is made. In gratefulness and in love, J.A., W.E." Agee's words, with strong visual elements, balance the spare beauty of Evans's photographs. The last page contains a eulogy commemorating these little-known men and women. It starts with "Let us now praise famous men, and our fathers that begat us" and continues with "And some there be which have no memorial, who perished, as though they had never been, and are become as though they had never been born, and their children after them. But these were merciful men, whose righteousness hath not been forgotten. . . . Their bodies are buried in peace, but their name liveth for evermore."[21]

Dorothea Lange specialized in the difficulties of migratory workers. Her famous 1936 photograph, *Migrant Mother* [31], has been reproduced frequently and stands as an icon of the period. Lange's field notes accompanying the photograph read, "Camped on the edge of a pea field where the crop had failed in a freeze. The tires had just been sold from the car to buy food. She was 32 years old with seven children."[22] The migrant mother, with two children, their heads bent on her shoulders, is a Madonna of hard times. With her torn dress, worried brow, and worn hands, she faces the viewer. There is no glamour, but a dignity and deep-seated humanity, a sense of universal suffering and perseverance, which is perhaps why this photograph has been so frequently reproduced. Social and economic forces seem to have overcome this young mother. The photograph was also noted for its direct-ness and honesty.

This image of a young migrant Cherokee woman, whose actual

31. Dorothea Lange, *Migrant Mother*, 1936. Museum of Modern Art, New York.

name was Florence Thompson, as well as one of Allie Mae Burroughs, from *Let Us Now Praise Famous Men*, became somewhat
politicized in the late 1970s and early 1980s, when the press ran
stories related to the ongoing impoverished lifestyles of these
women, one of whom was the subject of what became the world's
most reproduced photograph.[23] (In 1991, the *Migrant Mother* sold
at Swann's auction house for $44,000.) Questions thus arise:
Should the photograph be seen as representative of something
independent of the life of the subject? What happens when cultural appropriation of a work removes it from any specific original
context? Are unknown subjects of what become famous photographs often vulnerable to economic exploitation?

The subject of the *Migrant Mother* was transformed in 1990 by
the photographer Kathy Grove to that of a young beautiful cover
girl (*The Other Series*), *After Lange*, 1990 (Pace McGill Gallery,
New York). Although still dressed in torn clothes with two hungry
children at her sides, the woman's skin is unwrinkled and clean,
and her nails are filed and healthy looking. Gone are the years of
worry and hard work stamped on the wrinkled face of the original
photograph. The migrant worker is made into a young woman
from the world of magazine glamour. The straightforward, honest
statement of her identity and situation in the initial image has
become a commentary on the politics and power of the forces of
photographic reproduction. What does this 1990 photograph say
about the manipulation and deconstruction of one identity
through mechanical means to a totally different identity that is
shaped, in part, by the mass media and world of advertising? Or
had the original photograph lost its power nearly sixty years later,
and is it appropriate to add a new level of meaning through transformation by the lens and perceptions of contemporary culture? Is
this new version how the photograph may actually be perceived by
some contemporary eyes? Does the relation of mother and child
become subservient to the "beauty" of the young woman in the
1990 version?

Lange and other FSA photographers also photographed a
number of billboards that had been commissioned by the National
Association of Manufacturers (NAM) in the 1930s to promote
various businesses and a general image that American economic

life could still flourish. The FSA photographers deliberately placed these billboards in contexts that would present the middle-class families who were frequently portrayed on them in a new ironic context, as families smug and indifferent to much of their environment. One of the most famous NAM billboard photographs was taken by Margaret Bourke-White, a documentary photographer of industry and an associate editor of *Fortune* and *Life* magazines. Bourke-White, together with her husband Erskine Caldwell, a writer, also produced a photographic survey of the South, *You Have Seen Their Faces*, in 1937. Her photographic essay for *Life*, of Muncie, Indiana, the city the Lynds had chosen for their study, *Middletown*, 1927, showed a graphic cross section of the people and cityscape. The billboard photograph for which she is noted, *At the Time of the Louisville Flood* [32], shows a line of poor black people waiting for relief food in front of an NAM billboard of a prosperous, middle-class white family riding in their car. The billboard slogans read "World's Highest Standard of Living" and "There's no way like the American Way." As in other NAM billboards, the family figures are painted in the cheerful style of the "Dick and Jane" readers used in elementary schools. The antithesis of this smiling family, complete with a cute pet dog and a car, is the world of the migrant workers and sharecroppers, photographed by the FSA. In this image, whites literally stand over blacks, and the shiny technology of the automobile seems to dominate the image as it "shelters" this white middle-class nuclear family. The billboard image reinforces the image of the father as being in control, as was the case in most middle-class families. The father, at the wheel of the car, is larger and at the center of the piece. Bourke-White's photograph, taken outside a relief agency in Louisville, Kentucky, appeared in the February 15, 1937, issue of *Life* as part of a story about a flood in the Ohio River valley, where the black people were flood victims. The same NAM billboard appeared in another photograph, one by Edwin Locke, who photographed the billboard near Kingwood, West Virginia, at the foot of a hill of rubble below three rundown houses, in 1937 (Library of Congress photo). The irony of the "all-American family" with the "world's highest standard of living," in juxtaposition to destitute living conditions, is clear.

32. Margaret Bourke-White, *At the Time of the Louisville Flood*, 1937. Museum of Modern Art, New York.

In general, the FSA photographers contributed much to the development of documentary photography as an important visual medium. Not only did newspapers and magazines publish the photographs, but authors and editors also used them in books, such as Archibald MacLeish's *Land of the Free*, Sherwood Anderson's *Home Town*, or Edwin Rosskam and Richard Wright's *Twelve Million Black Voices*. John Steinbeck's novel *The Grapes of Wrath* actually grew out of an assignment for *Life*, during which the photographer Horace Bristol and Steinbeck toured "Oakie" camps for material for a book of photographs and stories for the magazine in 1938. *Life* ran the story in its February 19, 1940, issue. The idea for the book of photographs was dropped to make way for the novel *The Grapes of Wrath*.

Specifically, the FSA photographers had documented the difficult realities of the depression era, including family life and living conditions. The visual statements were not clichés, but honest, direct, sharply focused images that genuinely disturbed a number of people. But by the autumn of 1940, the head of the FSA, Roy Stryker, was asking for a different kind of picture of American life, one of abundance and lush landscapes. Hitler had arrived at the world's doorstep. In contrast to the 1938 Grand Central Palace exhibit, which consisted of images of hard times to contrast with the NAM's claims that the country was prospering, the 1941 FSA exhibit at Rockefeller Center in New York was entitled *The Way of a People*, a title similar to the NAM's texts. The show consisted of images of healthy, strong, and prosperous Americans. A February 1942 memorandum by Stryker read, in part: "People—we must have at once: Pictures of men, women, and children who appear as if they really believed in the U.S. Get people with a little spirit. . . . We particularly need men and women who work in our factories, the young men who build our bridges, roads, dams, and large factories. . . . More contented-looking old couples—woman sewing, man reading . . . coming from church, at picnics, at meetings."[24] In 1942 an FSA exhibit, mounted by Edward Steichen, the photographer and a lieutenant commander in the navy, was held at the Museum of Modern Art. The aim of the exhibit, entitled *Road to Victory*, was to instill and inspire patriotism through combinations of enlarged positive FSA images of the American people and navy publicity pictures of warships and fighter planes. The FSA photographers were not always happy making these types of propaganda pictures. Dorothea Lange, when assigned to photograph the Japanese Americans interned in camps in the West in 1942, took photographs that were sympathetic to the Japanese people.

While photographers worked for the FSA, a number of painters, such as Grant Wood, Thomas Hart Benton, and Ben Shahn, worked for the Federal Arts Project of the WPA, which lasted from 1934 until World War II. More than five thousand artists were employed in almost every state, and more than a million works of art came to adorn public buildings. By the mid–1930s, Regionalism and Realism thrived, with emphasis on social-content painting. Regionalism, an art that developed from local or regional experiences, grew as the United States attempted to look more closely at itself and to document itself after the stock market crash of 1929. The Midwest, which had not really been affected by European artistic currents, was seen as an important resource for the emergence of a truly American art.

One of the best-known images from this period is Grant Wood's *American Gothic* [33]. Although the painting was not directly a "family portrait" (the models were Wood's sister and his dentist), the image has become a symbol of the midwestern Regionalist program, with the stalwart expressions of this couple. Ironically, the painting was intended as a satire on American "repression." The Gothic Revival house, with its allusions to religion, and the crosslike lines on the farmer's overalls, repeated again in the pitchfork, speak of severity, sacrifice, and death. The clarity of design and detail and the stiff poses of the pair are reminiscent of the Renaissance Flemish painters whom Wood admired. There

33. Grant Wood, *American Gothic*, 1930. Art Institute of Chicago.

is a coldness in their faces and in the precise clean lines that dominate the painting that suggests there is a criticism implicit in the painting, that this man and woman were spiritually dead, caught in a culture that was losing its social and economic anchor.

Although Wood was a New Deal Democrat, he continued to believe in the power of the local, of the individual. His *American Gothic* image has been parodied and appropriated in numerous formats in the years since it was painted. It has become the caricature for the White House "First Couple," or the figures have worn gas masks to point to environmental pollution. An August 8, 1994, issue of *Time* pictured the couple as representing two young "hip" figures, who represented the "mass production" of "hippiedom" that occurred when the twenty-fifth anniversary of the historic Woodstock concert was celebrated. In that parody, the woman appears with multiple pierced earrings, short cropped hair, and Rollerblades in one hand. The man appears with a pierced ear, beard, and John Lennon glasses. Two dalmatians stand in front of the Gothic Revival house, which now included a carport with a red van in partial view. Why has this image become such an icon and point of departure for later imagery? As both a "critical" and a straightforward image, it is clearly "accessible" to the viewer, who is confronted head-on with the couple. The pitchfork in the center of the painting becomes a kind of stop sign. Who are these people? Do we see part of ourselves, individually or culturally, past or present, in these figures? Does part of the Protestant work ethic, in which some Americans still pride themselves and others criticize, inherent in this painting of hardworking individuals, dressed in somber, practical clothes, still speak strongly? Is there a sense of nostalgia for this rural lifestyle and straightforward existence that was dependent on the land? Or are the recent caricatures more telling of what the image was meant to be? Ironically, a number of Regionalist paintings show prosperous farms with fields of crops representing a nostalgia for what was lost during the depression years. The grim, industrialized city and the world of abstraction was not a part of the Regionalist aesthetic.

A sense of loneliness and isolation in the American city was captured by the artist Edward Hopper, who had studied with Robert Henri and been influenced by John Sloan, both of the Ash-

34. Edward Hopper, *Nighthawks*, 1942. Art Institute of Chicago.

can school. Although Hopper did not depict specific family groups, his evocation of a haunting loneliness and the dilemmas of human communication in a number of his works, frequently set in hotel rooms, trains, restaurants, or movie theaters, was significant. For example, in his well-known *Nighthawks* [34], one sees the isolation of four people in a stark, fluorescent-lit café at night. Even the man and woman seated next to each other appear unable to relate to each other as they stare into space. Hopper's paintings emphasize a self alone, sometimes alienated, in the starkness of the modern world.

A number of black artists were attracted to the Regionalist aesthetic and social-protest art during the 1930s, when there appeared to be a growing self-consciousness among black artists. Alain Locke, a black advocate of American scene painting, described the thirties as a time "when American art was rediscovering the Negro."[25] During this period, black artists, such as Horace Pippin, William Johnson, and Jacob Lawrence, emerged. A significant recorder of middle-class black family life in Harlem, and of the Harlem community in general during the 1920s and 1930s, was the black photographer James Van Der Zee. During these decades, Harlem was at its height. Jazz, the literary works of the Harlem

Renaissance, and the United Negro Improvement Association, all contributed to an individual and cultural sense of identity that gave pride to middle-class blacks. Those who came to Van Der Zee's studio were dressed in their best clothes and wanted to be remembered as part of an important culture. Van Der Zee had a real interest in the people he photographed and spent time achieving the desired effects. He had skillfully painted backdrops for the photographs and exerted considerable effort hand tinting and retouching the negatives. He made the images his own art, as well as images of the subjects he photographed. He commented on one interchange with a subject, Daisy, who came back to see him and said, "Mr. Van Der Zee, my friends tell me that's a nice picture, Daisy, but it doesn't look like you! That was my style, though. Not like other portrait photographers where all you saw was more faces that looked the same."[26]

Family portraiture was a favorite aspect of Van Der Zee's work. He himself had memories of a happy childhood in Lenox, Massachusetts, where his family gathered on many evenings in their living room, singing and playing instruments. He played the violin. Van Der Zee frequently photographed his own family, as well as clients. An early photograph of his first wife Kate and his daughter Rachel, Kate and Rachel [35], is a poignant study of a mother and daughter in a lush woods setting. The photographer appears to equate the outdoor natural environment with motherhood and the innocence of childhood. Kate and Rachel each hold a bouquet. In his studio portraits, Van Der Zee spent time studying and posing his subjects, attempting to analyze, if only briefly, the personality of the sitters. He valued motherhood, and a number of his images contain Madonna-like poses. Van Der Zee himself was reported to be a devoted father, affected deeply by the premature deaths of his young daughter, Rachel, in 1908, and his son, Emile, in 1910. He did wedding portraits and funeral pictures as well. A photograph, dated 1929, shows a large wedding party lavishly dressed, framed by two clergy. Flowers are abundant, and the bride's flowing train takes up much of the foreground of the picture. Van Der Zee's photographs are, in general, complimentary and sympathetic.

Van Der Zee's family portraits became popular for calendar companies in the 1930s and 1940s, although by the 1940s, the

35. James Van Der Zee, *Kate and Rachel*, 1906. James Van Der Zee Estate.

emergence of small, cheaper cameras brought about a decline in his and other photographers' studio businesses. His work is significant not only for the grace, beauty, and dignity he captured in his subjects, but for the kind of pride in family and culture that existed for a short time in an area that was destined to become a major urban slum, filled with despair, poverty, and crime. In Van Der Zee's photographs, blacks were momentarily freed from any feelings of inferiority, poverty, and stereotypic imagery.

The world of film also had an impact on Americans' concepts of identity and family in the pre–World War II years. By the 1930s, the image of Greta Garbo, with her glamour and maturity, became a popular one in the United States. Women were rarely shown as wives or mothers in films during the 1930s unless they were in a sophisticated, upper-class setting. More frequently, they were portrayed as career women or socialites. They were usually elegantly dressed, particularly because a 1933 production code had barred open sexuality on film. In a time of economic and social confusion and difficulty, it appeared that the image of a strong woman was needed.

In general, however, women of 1930s films did not question the fact that marriage was an appropriate goal for women and that a woman might appear subservient. The actresses who were popular in this era, such as Carole Lombard, Joan Crawford, Katharine Hepburn, and Jean Harlow, were assertive and proud. One of the most popular films of the 1930s was *Gone With the Wind*, 1939, directed by Victor Fleming and starring Vivien Leigh and Clark Gable. Set in the Old South during the Civil War, it depicts Scarlett O'Hara (Vivien Leigh) as an assertive, headstrong, determined, and intelligent young woman. But her marriage to Rhett Butler (Clark Gable) does not work out. When their daughter dies, their marriage dies, and Rhett leaves. All that remains for Scarlett is the earth of her roots, her beloved "Tara," her "home," the plantation where she had grown up and where she plans to go and to find the future, claiming that "tomorrow is another day." Scarlett's last words in the movie as she stops after wandering around the room, stunned by Rhett leaving her, are: "Oh, I can't think about that now! I'll go crazy if I do! I'll think about it tomorrow. Tara, home, I'll go home and I'll think of some way to get him back! After all, tomorrow is another day!"

For Scarlett, a sense of place, of home, was important for her sense of self and well-being when her marriage died. Films like *Gone With the Wind* questioned the possibility that independent women could find happiness in marriage.

The child actress, Shirley Temple, who was one of the most popular film stars of the decade and stole the hearts of many of her viewers, projected an image that was quite different from that of the mature, sophisticated women, such as Scarlett O'Hara. Young Shirley clearly showed the difference between women and children. Because of her innocence and lack of sophistication and because she appeared untainted by the larger world, Shirley seemed able to solve family and social problems that adults could not successfully deal with. For example, as Rebecca, in *Rebecca of Sunnybrook Farm* (1938), the endearing young actress is able to bridge the world of the home of her spinster aunts with the world of entertainment and radio that seems so foreign and inappropriate to her elderly aunts. Or we see the little girl take on political and military forces in the *Littlest Rebel* (1935), set during the Civil War, in which she attempts to save her father, a Confederate officer, from charges of espionage. Her pleas to Mr. Lincoln are successful, and the delightful child saves her father.

In general, though, it has been noted that "American films tend to picture both hero and heroine unbound by family ties. . . . The most frequent relations of heroes are in-laws and children. This reflects the American emphasis on the family you make, as against the family you come from. The fact that children, when present, almost always make some difference in the plot underscores this point." [27] For example, in the 1930s film *Stella Dallas* (1937), based on the Olive Prouty novel and directed by King Vidor, Barbara Stanwyck plays the daughter of a mill hand who marries into a wealthy family, but never escapes her lower-middle-class ways. In the end, she sacrifices everything for her daughter, so she will not be in the way of her daughter's aspirations, but she loses her husband as well. In the 1940s film, *Too Young to Know* (1945), the heroine gives birth to a son after her husband has quarreled with her and left her. She allows her child to be adopted by a childless couple.

By the 1940s, the film image of the independent or career-minded woman had been replaced by a renewed emphasis on the family and respectability as a way of helping the war effort. It is interesting to see the changes in film imagery noted by one writer in the span of twenty-some years: "Films of the 1920's first introduced the 'new' woman as the modern wife, but films of the 1930's emphasized her subordination and need to be 'tamed' by a strong man and the domesticating influence of a child." [28]

World War II brought an end to the depression as war production provided more jobs. Contrary to the thinking of some, war seemed to bring an increased emphasis on the family. There was a dramatic reversal of the declining marriage rate of the 1930s. And fertility increased; between 1940 and 1945, there was an increase in births from 19.4 to 24.5 per one thousand of the population. The average age of those entering marriage dropped, and the marriage rate increased, partly because of the possibility of draft deferments for married men in the early war years and partly because of the departure of soldiers to foreign shores. Popular magazines, films, and radio programs carried appeals for the sanctity of the home and for the support of the war effort. In one segment of a radio series sponsored by the U.S. government's Office of Facts and Figures, a young male voice talked about what the war was about—"About all young people like us. About love and gettin' hitched, and havin' a home and some kids, and breathin' fresh air out in the suburbs. . . . about livin' an' workin' *decent*, like free people."[29]

Hollywood clearly joined the war effort. One of the most popular and effective films of the early 1940s was *Mrs. Miniver*, which won the Academy Award for best picture of the year in 1942, as well as seven other Academy Awards, including Best Actress. Directed by William Wyler, based on Jan Struther's novel, and starring Greer Garson and Walter Pidgeon, the film chronicles the life of a well-off, genteel English family during the war. The film opens showing the leisurely harmonious lifestyle of the Miniver family, as the young wife buys an expensive new hat and her husband buys a new car. When war hits England, this lifestyle is changed forever. Mrs. Miniver finds a gunned-down Nazi pilot in her backyard. When much of her lovely home is destroyed, the young mother comforts her children in an air-raid shelter during relentless bombing by the Germans. She must endure the loss of family. Her son goes off to war, and her new daughter-in-law, Carol Beldon, is killed in the car as the two women seek shelter from an oncoming "blitz." Mrs. Miniver is the model for an indomitable spirit who attempts to preserve family life and at the same time supports the war. President Roosevelt used the final, stirring speech (given by the vicar in his church damaged by bombs) in a leaflet that he had air-dropped over Europe. It contained, in part, the following words:

We in this quiet corner of England have suffered the loss of friends and those very dear to us—some close to this church. . . .

The homes of many have been destroyed. . . . And why?—
Why in all conscience should these have been the ones to suffer
—children, old people, a young girl [Carol Beldon] at the height
of her loveliness? Are these our soldiers, our fighters? Why should
they be sacrificed? I shall tell you—because it is not only a war of
soldiers in uniform, to be fought only on battlefields, but in villages, factories and farms, in the homes and hearts of every man,
woman, and child who loves freedom. . . . They [the dead] will
inspire us with unbreakable determination to free ourselves and
those who come after us from the tyranny and terror that threaten
to strike us down. This is the people's war. It is our war. We are
the fighters. Fight it then. Fight it with all that is in us. May God
defend the right.

Following the vicar's stirring words, the families of the congregation rise to sing together the hymn, "Onward Christian Soldiers." Mrs. Miniver's son, whose young wife died, goes to stand
beside his wife's grandmother who stands alone. The movie ends as
the viewer and members of the congregation look upward through
the damaged church roof to the open sky, where formations of
planes in a "V" (for victory) configuration fly overhead. The
planes, from a distance, look like small religious crosses. The
church, families, homes, patriotism, and support of the world war
thus become closely entwined by the end of the movie. Prime
Minister Winston Churchill commented that the film helped
Britain more than an additional fleet of destroyers would have
done. And director William Wyler accepted his Academy Award
in absentia, for on that very evening, he was flying a bombing run
over Germany.

A 1943 war-propaganda film sponsored by the government,
This Is the Army, which starred Ronald Reagan, Joan Leslie, and
George Murphy and was directed by Michael Curtiz, also affirmed
the family and revealed a discomfort with the interrupted or
altered gender roles caused by the war operation. The movie
involved an army nurse who persuades her reluctant soldier-
boyfriend to marry her; when he goes off to the front again, she
remains at home, emphasizing the vision of what men were fighting for. In the movie, the soldiers joke about their female superior

officers and burlesque a female dance, which reveals the concern for altered gender roles underneath the comic elements.

In the same year that Hollywood produced *This Is the Army*, the illustrator Norman Rockwell created his series, *The Four Freedoms*, for the *Saturday Evening Post* [36]. This series was inspired by Franklin D. Roosevelt's 1941 speech to an anxious and troubled nation, outlining the four freedoms: "Freedom of Speech, Freedom from Want, Freedom of Worship, and Freedom from Fear." Rockwell's images brought these concepts of freedom to concrete visualization and were to inspire much of the nation. In 1942 the Office of War Information (OWI), domestic branch, had produced a pamphlet, *The United Nations Fight for the Four Freedoms*, with an intro-

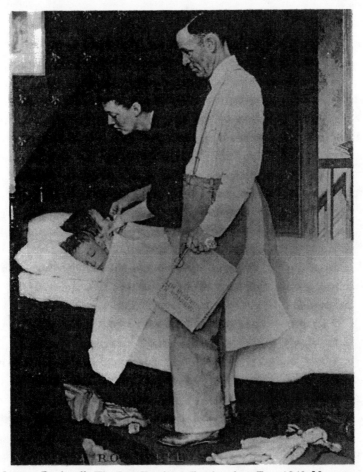

36. Norman Rockwell, *The Four Freedoms: Freedom from Fear*, 1943. Norman Rockwell Museum, Stockbridge, Massachusetts.

duction by Roosevelt that also emphasized the four freedoms. The production of the pamphlet was directed by the poet Archibald MacLeish, the Librarian of Congress. Discussion of the four freedoms appeared in 1942 in other publications, such as *Education*, *Catholic World*, and *Parents' Magazine*. The *Parents' Magazine* article, entitled "Cultivating the Four Freedoms: Children Must Learn Their Meaning at Home," by Dr. Frank Kingdon, spoke of the need to establish the inherent dignity of all humans within the home to appreciate better the four freedoms. A consortium of artists' groups, Artists for Victory, including the Society of Illustrators, of which Rockwell was an active member, took the four-freedoms ideals as a theme for its work. It organized and celebrated "Four Freedoms Days," September 12–19, 1943, and instituted a national war-poster campaign. Various artists interpreted the four freedoms. For example, Hugo Ballin painted a large mural for the Burbank, California, city hall, using images that ranged from Moses and the Ten Commandments to women and children shopping for food.

Rockwell's interpretation of the four freedoms consisted of four separate paintings executed in 1943, each of which was an attempt to capture the feeling behind the words. In *Freedom of Speech*, the setting is a town meeting of people of diverse ages and types—the town family, democracy, at its "grass roots." In the painting, a man stands, proudly, strongly, about to speak; all eyes are turned toward him. In *Freedom of Worship*, one sees the profiles of men and women of diverse ages, with bowed heads and hands clasped in prayer, with the caption "Each According to the Dictates of His Own Conscience"—the family of God. In *Freedom from Want*, members of a multiple-generation family are seated together about to share a holiday meal; the grandparents stand at the head of the well-set family table as they lay a golden turkey on it. In *Freedom from Fear*, Rockwell deals with the subject of parents providing security for their children. A father and mother stand at the bedside of their two sleeping children. The mother gently pulls the bedcovers up to the children's chins, protecting them. The father looks on, holding a newspaper whose headlines refer to bombing. This painting, in particular, touched the hearts of many because it portrayed the domestic ritual of tucking one's children safely into bed and suggested that the children's sleep would not be interrupted by gunfire or intrusion.

In all four paintings, Rockwell celebrated the "common man." When the series of paintings appeared in the *Saturday Evening Post*, a photograph of the Rockwell family, depicted as an ordinary family, laughing together outside their Vermont home, accompanied the series. *The Four Freedoms* series was credited with helping to sell over $132 million in war bonds.

Following the war, Rockwell went on to capture the hearts and minds of many Americans in his *Saturday Evening Post* covers, many of which focused poignantly and humorously on aspects of family life. His August 30, 1947, cover, *Going and Coming*, for example, depicts a family of several generations going enthusiastically on vacation and returning exhausted but satisfied in general. The children, the dog, the boat, the sun umbrella, and the car itself, all speak of a family that has moved beyond the Depression and war years and is now able to vacation together.

Why have Norman Rockwell's images continued to appeal to so many Americans? Do they make many Americans feel that they were members of a big happy family with shared values? Whether the images are true to life or not, they have nonetheless created a myth about American life, a myth that may be seen as positive or negative. Some think the images depict what was once an actuality, whereas others see them as "the way we never were" but may want to be.

In *The True and Only Heaven: Progress and Its Critics*, Christopher Lasch distinguishes between memory and nostalgia:

> Nostalgia appeals to the feeling that the past offered delights no longer obtainable. Nostalgic representations of the past evoke a time irretrievably lost and for that reason are timeless and unchanging. Strictly speaking, nostalgia does not entail the exercise of memory at all since the past it idealizes stands outside time, frozen in unchanging perfection. Memory too may idealize the past but not in order to condemn the present ... Nostalgia evokes the past only to bury it alive. It shares with the belief in progress, to which it is only superficially opposed, an eagerness to proclaim the death of the past and to deny history's hold on the present.[30]

Do current positive responses to Norman Rockwell's work and other idyllic images have to do with memory or nostalgia? Do we wish to freeze those moments, such as the family dinner or parents tucking their children safely into bed, out of time, in condemnation of the present, which may hold moments that are too difficult and painful for our minds to bear? Or are these true memories in which there is a sense of the persistence of the past, of both the pleasant and unpleasant, the simple and the complex? And are there ways for the past to penetrate and be integrated into our lives and provide a sense of continuity? I suspect that for many, nostalgia plays a larger role than actual memory and that a carefree world, represented by the simplicity and innocence of childhood and harmonious family life—whether or not such a world was real or imagined for any given individual—is a desired subject. For Lasch, when nostalgia and a sense of progress deny the significance of the cultural past, they both make any intelligent use of the past impossible.

It is difficult to ascertain exactly how much some of the images of the mass media—film, radio, and magazines—influenced Americans' perceptions of themselves as individuals and as families. Conversely, it is difficult to ascertain exactly how much visual imagery might have reflected or built upon already existing perceptions of self, socially, economically, and politically. It is significant, though, that the interaction of "self," individually and within a family, and the mass media was to become increasingly important, particularly as movies became more popular with the general public and as the age of television began to emerge.

The year 1945 brought with it events that were to have a far-reaching effect on all spheres of society. On April 30, 1945, Hitler committed suicide. On May 8, the Allied forces celebrated VE Day, ending World War II in Europe. The Allied Control Commission divided Germany into four zones, and Berlin was occupied by three powers. On August 6, 1945, the United States dropped an atomic bomb on Hiroshima, and on August 9, it dropped a second bomb on Nagasaki. With the surrender of Japan, World War II ended on August 14; with the end of the war, a new configuration of international powers arose and the Cold War began. In the same year, Franklin D. Roosevelt died, Benito Mussolini of Italy was killed, and General Charles de Gaulle was elected president of the French provisional government. The Independent Republic of Vietnam was formed, with Ho Chi Minh as president.

World War II had brought both challenges and disruptions to family life on all levels of society. After the depression and world war, Americans hoped to build a secure and stable future and saw the home and domestic life as the center for doing so. Looking back on the days immediately following World War II, a psychologist noted, "We would achieve the serenity that had eluded the lives of our parents, the men would be secure in stable careers, the women in comfortable homes, and together they would raise perfect children. . . . It was the *Zeitgeist*, the spirit of the times."[31]

5

The Late Forties and Fifties

T he late forties and the fifties were a time to begin to rebuild
a world disrupted by world war and return to stability. But
despite the end of World War II, political conflicts continued to disturb balances of power. In 1948, Mahatma Gandhi was
assassinated, the same year that the Marshall Plan was approved by
the U.S. Congress for U.S. aid to Europe. That year the USSR
stopped road and rail traffic between Berlin and the West, and the
"Berlin airlift" began (until September 1949). In 1949 the German
Federal Republic came into being with Bonn as its capital, and the
Democratic Republic became East Germany. Also in 1949, the
Communist People's Republic of China was proclaimed under
Mao Zedong. The 1950s began and ended with political turmoil.
The Korean War broke out in 1950, and a revolution in Cuba
brought Fidel Castro to power in 1959. In between, events, such as
the death of Josef Stalin and the emergence of Nikita Khrushchev
in the USSR, the fall of Dien Bien Phu in Vietnam, the "Red
Scare" and the McCarthy trials in the United States, the execution
of Julius and Ethel Rosenberg for espionage against the United
States, the launching of Sputnik I by the USSR, and the beginning
of outer-space exploration, were to alter traditional views and perceptions. The threat of atomic and nuclear war loomed larger when
the first hydrogen bomb was exploded in 1952. The Algerian War
of Independence began in 1954. In 1956 the Suez Canal crisis

occurred and Soviet troops invaded Hungary and quickly crushed the rebellion against Soviet domination. The European Common Market was established in 1958.

In science, the xerography process was invented in 1946 and Bell Labs invented the transistor in 1947. In 1954 Jonas Salk's polio vaccine was used in a mass immunization of Pittsburgh schoolchildren. In 1958 NASA, the National Aeronautics and Space Administration, was formed in the United States. A spirit of exploration and a sense of a new frontier was firmly established.

In literature, works such as J. D. Salinger's *Catcher in the Rye*, Allen Ginsberg's *Howl*, and Jack Kerouac's *On the Road* explored and celebrated the adolescent, the individual traveler, and Ginsberg's and Kerouac's works marked the beginning of the beat generation. Samuel Beckett wrote *Waiting for Godot*, Arthur Miller wrote *Death of a Salesman* and *The Crucible*, Simone de Beauvoir wrote *The Second Sex*, and Paul Tillich wrote *The Courage to Be*. In music, the German composer Karlheinz Stockhausen experimented with electronic sounds, and John Cage wrote his well-known 4'3" (a piece of silence and random, spontaneous sounds from the environment) in 1952. Rock and roll and Elvis Presley blared as American youths found their own music.

The center for avant-garde experiments in the visual arts came to be New York City as the generation of Abstract Expressionists, such as Jackson Pollock, Mark Rothko, Robert Motherwell, Willem de Kooning, Hans Hofmann, Barnett Newman, Adolph Gottlieb, and Franz Kline, came to the forefront of the art world. Their large-scale gestural and color-field paintings were filled with emotion, intensity, and power, enveloping the viewer. The critic Robert Rosenblum referred to some of these works as evincing the "abstract sublime" and traced Abstract Expressionism back to nineteenth-century Romantic landscape painting in his 1975 book, *Modern Painting and the Northern Romantic Tradition*. The artist Barnett Newman declared in an article entitled "The Sublime Is Now":

> The question that now arises is how, if we are living in a time without a legend or myths that can be called sublime, if we refuse to live in the abstract, how can we be creating a sublime art? We

are reasserting man's natural desire for the exalted, for a concern
with our relationships to the absolute antiquated legend. . . . We
are freeing ourselves of the impediments of memory, association,
nostalgia, legend, myth, or what have you that have been the desires
of Western Europe painting. Instead of making "cathedrals" out of
Christ, man or "life," we are making them out of ourselves, out
of our own feelings. The image we produce is the self-evident one of
revelation, real and concrete, that can be understood by anyone who
will look at it without the nostalgic glasses of history.[32]

Thus, while some may have viewed with nostalgia works such
as those of Norman Rockwell, others, including Barnett Newman
and his supporters, wished to free themselves of the "impediments"
of both nostalgia and memory.

It seems appropriate to view the imagery related to the family
and domesticity from the late 1940s and the 1950s in the context
of the historical backdrop just presented. Although the emphasis
in this section is on American art and Americans' sense of identity,
it is helpful to consider a few examples of artistic statements outside the United States as comparisons.

A close personal associate of Alberto Giacometti was the
painter Balthus (Balthasar Klossowski de Rola). The figurative
work of Balthus, who after his discharge from the French army
settled in Switzerland, combined a classical calm inherent in his
figures and comparison with a sense of anxiety and decadence.
Encouraged by the German poet Rainer Maria Rilke and influenced by the frescoes of Piero della Francesca, Balthus created
enigmatic and dreamlike situations that struck at the confused
anxieties of postwar Europe. His paintings were usually set inside
in a well-appointed living room setting. Frequently, he dealt with
the erotic potential of young adolescent girls, hardly aware of their
sexuality. The normal "props" of a comfortable domestic life, such
as a chaise lounge or couch or a family cat, became accompani-
ments to a newly awakened eroticism. In *La Semaine des quatre
jeudis*, 1949 (private collection), for example, a young girl is
sprawled suggestively on a comfortable chair, while her cat peeks at
her over the top of the chair. At the window a young woman
stands tensely, staring out the window into the wider world. The

title of the work refers to a week of holidays, since French schools formerly held no classes on Thursdays.

The figurative work of the Canadian painter Alex Colville also dealt with dreamlike forms. Influenced by Surrealism, many of Colville's works contain an apprehension of disaster or difficulty. In *Family and Rainstorm* [37], there is an impending storm, emphasized by the black, white, and gray tones that dominate the painting. Only the tawny skin tones, blonde-brown hair, and light beige of burned-out grass contrast with the black, white, and grays. The family is based on Colville's own—his wife Rhoda and his youngest and eldest children, Ann and Graham. The location is specific, too—the Minas Basin looking north toward the Blomidon Peninsula in Nova Scotia. The woman has her back to the viewer, watching the children climb into the car, whose large open door dominates the center of the painting. A family day at the beach has been curtailed by rain, but there appears to be an acceptance of it, since the family figures and car become integral parts of the landscape in color, shape, and form. Although the family and place are specific, Colville's image also speaks of a larger acceptance of reality, of a harmony with that reality through the coolness of his classical smooth forms. It has been noted that Colville has "avoided too close a personal identification with the subject matter by using timeless symbols and a cool painting style. He opened a gap between the subjective and the objective through the distancing effect of metaphor, and through a sculpturesque simplicity that echoed the past rather than substantiated the present. By these means he had tried to avoid jeopardizing the communicability of his images when expressing the private nature of his experience."[33]

In some works, done in the early fifties, Colville dealt with the issues of soldiers leaving home during the war and celebrations of their return, which also had a strong foundation in his experience of wartime separation from his wife and his longing to return. A piece, such as *Four Figures on a Wharf*, 1952 (National Gallery of Canada, Ottawa), in which four female marblelike classical figures stand—waiting, remembering—on a white wharf stretched into the sky and water, is a reflection of memory and Colville's longing to return home. In *Woman, Man and Boat*, 1952 (National Gallery of Canada, Ottawa), one sees a man and woman about to greet

37. Alex Colville, *Family and Rainstorm*, 1955. National Gallery of Canada, Ottawa.

each other. The woman stands knee-deep in the water to meet the man standing in the boat. There is no movement in the simplified reduced forms of the painting and no physical contact between the two figures, only the anticipation of meeting. *Soldier and Girl at Station*, 1953 (private collection), is more specific in its location and depicts the departure of a loved one in the eerie night light of an empty and lonely train station.

Another Canadian artist who dealt with the issue of memory was Jean Paul Lemieux. From the mid–1950s to the 1970s, Lemieux was particularly interested in the metaphor of a figure (or figures), frequently isolated in the landscape in which it lived and carrying with it elements of the anxieties of existentialism. In a number of paintings, he tried to capture moments in a fleeting world. A painting entitled *1910 Remembered*, 1962 (private collection, Quebec City), Lemieux painted himself as a child, standing between his two parents in profile. The parents appear tall, stern, and stoical and do look at each other. The child, dressed in a sailor suit, appears small, is close to but not touching his father, and faces the viewer. Although he is framed by his parents, the little boy appears isolated and alone, standing before the vast stretch of sky and ground in the distance, where two figures with parasols appear small on the horizon and faintly suggest other human presence. The colors are muted blues, off whites, and earth tones—dreamlike colors that emphasize the notion of the remembrance of things past in an attempt to recapture lost time. This dreamlike reverie seems to depict a psychological emptiness that came to be part of the modern family. Lemieux communicates a sense of solitude and a kind of abandonment, but communicates it with resigned acceptance, rather than anger and total despair. Unlike Colville's figures, Lemieux's figures do not seem to be an integral part of the landscape. For Lemieux, the solution to this state of affairs was an escape into his imagination and his artwork. Lemieux was to take the theme of *1910 Remembered* further in a series of small paintings for an album he created under the same title in 1978. These paintings are more sketchlike and contain fragments of family and friends in scenes, such as five figures seated in the bow of a yacht or two austere older woman sitting on a bench with hazy suggestions of children's figures in the background.

One finds this sense of psychological emptiness in other paintings like *Le Tapis Rouge*, 1957 (Musée de Québec, Quebec City), in which a little girl stands to the far side of the canvas, one arm cropped from the image, in a separate room from where a slender young woman plays the piano. The little girl has large haunting eyes, similar to some of Munch's figures, but there are no facial features on the woman playing the piano. Except for the red rug in the outer room, the colors are dark and somber—dark purples, blues, and greens. This somber palette is used in another painting by Lemieux, in which the sense of isolation is seen further through the eyes and feelings of a child. In *Les Grandes Personnes, The Grown-Ups*, 1960 (Montreal Museum of Fine Arts), a little girl with dark, piercing eyes stands in front of her severe-faced elders, who seem to take no joy in each other's company. The colors are limited to browns and black tonalities. Only the little girl's hair ribbon and collar stand out in their white purity. Even the plant in the lower corner of the painting appears in brown, shadowy tones.

Lemieux's paintings are about the people and world that he inhabits, but they are also about his inner search for meaning and his dealing with issues of memory, individual and collective; childhood; dreams, both day dreams and night dreams; fear; and anguish. As he noted as early as 1938, "What counts in a painting is the artist's interpretation, the personal vision and sensibility; the subject is only a starting point, a basis on which to build, a motif to be used to express one's emotions, one's state of mind."[34] But Lemieux's expressive and poignant works allow the viewer to face his or her own inner origins and anxieties, to examine the notion of lost childhood and of time's passing.

On the other side of the Atlantic, working in three dimensions, was the British artist Henry Moore. For a number of years, Moore had depicted the theme of mother and child frequently in his abstract figurative images. Although he was interested in the archetypal image of mother and mother with child, the catalyst for his ongoing interest in the theme was the birth of his daughter, Mary. Following World War II, Moore, for the first time, added the figure of the father to his sculpture in his *The Family Group* [38], originally designed for the Barclay School, Stevenage, that was intended to be the center of social life for the surrounding villages. *The Family Group* was the first major piece by Moore to be cast in bronze. There was an edition of four—for the collections of the Museum of Modern Art, New York; the Tate Gallery, London; and the Nelson D. Rockefeller Collection, New York, as well as the Barclay School. The sculpture was based on Moore's *Shelter Drawings,* which were done during World War II, when Moore traveled through the Underground, observing men, women, and children huddled together in underground tunnels. Moore used monumental, simplified forms that evoke qualities from primitive and medieval sculpture. The figures are entwined; the arms of the mother and the father each embracing the child form a knot, tying the three into a unified family group. In 1954–55 Moore created the *Harlow Family Group,* out of hadene stone for Harlow New Town, which was rehousing families from the East End of London. The sculpture is more dense and solid than the 1948–49 piece. It depicts a child sitting on the mother's lap with the father's protective presence at his side. In a number of Moore's pieces, the negative space, "the holes," are as significant as the positive sculptural material. Moore said that "the hole connects one side to the other, making it immediately more three dimensional. A hole can itself have as much shape—meaning—as a solid mass. The mystery of the hole—the mysterious fascination of caves in hillsides and cliffs."[35] Moore's mothers and children and his family groups are universal and timeless in many ways. Their beauty and power lie not only in their specific harmony of shape and form for the given piece, but in the celebration of the continuity of human life and the potential, positive parent-child relationship that may be possible.

In the United States the 1950s is sometimes viewed as an uncreative and unidealistic period in which conformity reigned. One often conjures up images of carbon-copy suburbs, of *Leave It to Beaver* and *Father Knows Best* [39] families, of TV dinners (by

38. Henry Moore, *The Family Group*, c. 1948–49. Metropolitan Museum of Art, New York.

1954, 29 million U.S. homes had television sets), and poodle skirts. In certain circles of the arts, however, such as the Abstract Expressionists, there was a growing distance between the artist and the larger mainstream society. Americans' perceptions of themselves came to be reflected, influenced, or even shaped by both avant-garde and popular culture, both fine arts and the mass media.

An American artist and art critic who never received widespread recognition but who was friends with artists, such as Willem and Elaine de Kooning, Jane Freilicher, and Larry Rivers, and poets, such as John Ashbery and Kenneth Koch, was Fairfield Porter. (His brother was the well-known nature photographer Eliot Porter; T. S. Eliot was his cousin.) Porter, with his brilliant sense of color, created intimate sun-drenched paintings that recall

39. *Father Knows Best*: "No Apron Strings" episode. Photofest.

the Post-Impressionism of the French painters Édouard Vuillard and Pierre Bonnard, but the subjects are thoroughly American. A number of Porter's paintings are devoted to his family—his wife Anne and his five children, individually and in groups, at various stages in their lives. For instance, in *Anne and Katie*, 1949 (Parrish Art Museum, Southampton, New York), painted shortly after Katie's birth, Anne rocks peacefully in a rocking chair nursing her new baby. A 1955 painting, *Katie and Anne* (Hirshhorn Museum and Sculpture Garden, Smithsonian Institution, Washington, D.C.), shows Katie at about age six, posing for her father's painting on a rug while her mother reads to her. (One recalls the youngest Boit daughter in John Singer Sargent's painting in a similar position.) The painting, with its impressionistic brushwork, is alive with color—purple, yellow, blue, green, red, ocher, white, and black. In *October Interior*, 1963 (private collection), one sees Katie, now a teenager, sitting at the end of a sun-filled interior, with plants and flowers at the large windows that look onto the October foliage of a suburban world. Katie's sister, Lizzie, is on a swing outside, framed in the left window. A red-and-white rocking horse, which Kenneth and Janice Koch had given to Katie when she was a little girl, sits in the center of the painting, serving as a bridge between the two girls and as a symbol of the idylls of childhood. The painting is not simply a domestic interior; it is also a statement of Porter's emotional attachment to the subjects. In a 1964 painting, *The Screened Porch* [40], Porter painted his friend, the poet Jimmy Schuyler, who spent much time with the family; his daughters Katie and Lizzie; and his wife Anne on his screened painting porch. One sees his can of brush cleaner, his palette knife, and tubes of paint at the edge of the painting. This work, nicknamed in secret "Four Ugly People" by Anne, was Porter's largest work to date. It was the first in a series of square-format and life-size scaled pieces, the square format being seen as unusual for figurative works. Anne stands outside the screen porch at the edge of the canvas, framed by the screen panel. She and Porter's table of paints, on the other edge of the canvas, representing his presence, in a sense protectively frame the other three figures. Jimmy is reading and Lizzie's hand is on his chair, while Katie stands alone, looking at the viewer or the painter. Porter's show at the Tibor de

Nagy Gallery in 1964 was quite successful. By 1959, Abstract Expressionism was on the wane and the Museum of Modern Art had mounted an exhibit entitled *The Images of Man*, which emphasized the vitality of figurative painting, although the focus was on expressionist work. In 1960 Porter had been represented in a traveling show, *The Figure in Contemporary American Painting*, organized by the American Federation of Arts.

Porter's paintings were of a world at ease, of family and friends comfortable with one another and with themselves. His paintings are not sentimental, but, rather, concentrate on the particulars of light, time, and place and emphasize his emotional attachment to the subjects. Some criticized Porter's paintings as being inexpressive. James Schuyler countered this argument in a review in *Art-*

40. Fairfield Porter, *The Screened Porch*, 1964. Whitney Museum of American Art, New York.

news by noting that the work "accepts the expression a person posing wears as just as personal as any other, an uninsistent perception that one can scarcely not be oneself."[36] Porter included himself in a 1966 painting *The Mirror* (Nelson Atkins Museum of Art, Kansas City, Missouri). In this large canvas, one sees his young daughter Lizzie sitting on a stool in Porter's Southampton, Long Island, studio. Borrowing from Diego Velázquez's *The Maids of Honor* (*Las Meninas*), Porter painted himself into a large mirror placed behind Lizzie's stool. The mirror reflects the back of Lizzie, her bright red-orange sweater, and the bright light from the large studio window opposite. If the mirror was not painted, the viewer would see himself or herself in it. In the mirror, Porter stands full bodied with a brush in hand. He is the sole observer here, and Lizzie watches him intently. Theirs is a private dialogue between a father and a daughter, who poses good-naturedly. The colors of the painting are somewhat different from those of the other pieces, for the only vivid colors are Lizzie's red-orange sweater, her red socks, Porter's mustard color shirt, and a small bright yellow pillow on the sofa at the edge of the canvas that balances the colors of the figures' shirts. Otherwise, the colors are limited to muted grays, browns, black, and white. The blocks of bright color serve to draw the figures closer to one another.

Porter portrayed his family and friends over the years as they changed and grew up, a kind of family album in large-scale painting. One critic pointed to the poignancy of his portrayal of the passage of time, "Theirs is a spirit of stoical sadness. Their very charm implies that the passage of time changes everything, that the sun will set over Penobscot Bay, the children grow up, and the trees cast longer and longer shadows."[37]

While Porter depicted a seemingly untroubled existence in family life, photographers, particularly those working for *Life* and *Look* magazines, chose to depict images of the American "national character" as friendly, decent, and kind. The photographers made visits to private homes in pursuit of the "perfect" picture of family life. In some instances, they persuaded subjects to dress in their best clothes or even to alter their interior furniture arrangements or exterior landscaping for a better picture. *Life* produced photo-essays to dramatize the nation's "new economy" and postwar prosperity. One, entitled "Dreams of 1946," included pictures of a new dream car; a display of about $1 million worth of gowns, mink coats, jeweled necklaces, and the like; and a centerfold of a family of three children standing by their new house in the country with a Chrysler convertible, new appliances, a television set, lawn furniture and mower, pots and pans, and a $48,500 helicopter flying overhead. The emphasis was on progress and change. And the essays implied that all Americans seemed to be enjoying the nation's prosperity, buying new appliances, watching television, sharing the same values, and so on. The notion that the United States was heterogeneous in population and values was not portrayed at this point in time. Photographs for *Life*, *Look*, the United States Information Agency, and other organizations should be noted for emphasizing homogeneity. Americans were portrayed as being white, middle class, and members of a small nuclear family. The fathers held full-time jobs that could support their entire families. The mothers were housewives and, at the most, worked part time. The children were cute and well mannered. Their homes were usually pictured as new, in the suburbs or small towns, and there was usually at least one fairly new car. These happy family images were similar to those that had appeared in advertisements since the 1920s, on the NAM (National Association of Manufacturers) billboards, or in elementary school textbooks, but they were photographs, not drawings, and thus were considered "real" by many and therefore more convincing.

An expanding industrial economy was depicted as important to family life. For example, a brochure produced by the Board of Community Relations of Buffalo, New York, stated that "safety on the job and security for the breadwinner are essential parts of the security of the family." An illustration that appeared in the brochure pictured a man in work clothes with a wife and three children facing a Ford company billboard.

Owning one's home was seen as a significant part of the American Dream. Thus, a number of photo-essays emphasized families and their homes. In particular, the kitchen, with its new appliances and labor-saving devices, was seen as a symbol of American technology's progress and an indication of American capitalistic corporations' devotion to the happiness of middle-class families, especially to the contentment of women, who were the major consumers. William Levitt, the developer of Levittown, New York, commented, "No man who owns his own house and lot can be a Communist. He has too much to do."[38]

On his visit to Moscow in July 1959, Vice President Richard Nixon compared American superiority to the suburban home, an example of which had been sent as an exhibit to Moscow, and especially pointed out the kitchen to Soviet Premier Nikita Khrushchev. Nixon emphasized the availability of such a suburban home to all Americans. His frame of reference was always the family. "There are 44 million families in the United States. Twenty-five million of [them] live in houses or apartments that have as much or more floor space than the one you see in this exhibit. Thirty-one million families own their own homes and the land on which they are built. America's 44 million families own a total of 56 million cars, 50 million television sets, and 143 million radio sets. And they buy an average of nine dresses and suits and 14 pairs of shoes."[39]

This emphasis on the technical, on the quantitative numbers related to family life, may be seen as a growing modernist view of the self based on rationality and reason, which had arisen in the early twentieth century, in opposition to a romantic view of the self in which there was a basic human core that had the capacity for personal depth, including passion, soul, and moral character. A number of modernists believed in *systems*—of education, of work, of a stable family life, of moral training, and of rational dialogues between family members. In short, for some, the modernist home became less a sanctuary from the industrialized world than a laboratory for its values. The capacity for soul and passion was being eroded in many instances, although these emotions were expressed, to some extent, abstractly in the heroic gestural brushstrokes of the Abstract Expressionists. For example, Willem de Kooning's large-scale series of women evoked both brutality and a passionate energy. And Mark Rothko's and Barnett Newman's color-field paintings called for contemplation and allowed "the self" to experience a sense of oneness with a larger mythological world.

A growing influence of the rational and mechanical, as well as of popular culture, is seen in the well-known 1956 collage by the

British artist Richard Hamilton, *Just What Is It That Makes Today's Homes So Different, So Appealing?* (collection of Edwin Janss, Jr.). Here one sees a photograph of a muscle man holding a large lollipop with the word "Pop" inscribed on it and a pin-up girl wearing only a hat, in a modern living room. The room is filled with images of a consumer world—a tape recorder, a canned ham, a television set, a comic book cover, a Ford advertisement, and a vacuum cleaner. The view through the window shows a movie marquee displaying Al Jolson in *The Jazz Singer* (the legendary first talking film of 1927). This apartment scene appears to reflect an admiration for American material prosperity and technological progress. The piece was originally done for an exhibit at the Whitechapel Art Gallery in London, called *This Is Tomorrow*, which displayed a series of contemporary environments developed from photographs of architecture and imagery of the advertising world.

In 1955, to expand the concept of the family to include world families and to promote the notion of one vast world family that shared similar experiences of birth, work, worship, and death, Edward Steichen mounted an exhibition of photographs, the well-known *Family of Man*, at the Museum of Modern Art in New York. The exhibit was very popular and seen by hundreds of thousands of Americans and millions of foreigners. Following its opening in New York, the show traveled to forty-one foreign countries in various versions. It included 508 photographs by photographers from sixty-eight countries. A book accompanied the exhibit. It is interesting to note that the exhibit and book contained fewer than one in ten photographs that were unmistakenly made in the home. There was some criticism of the exhibit at the time, as well as later, for its editorial superficialities. One writer asserted: "The human experience is universalized, and thereby trivialized, into a series of simplistic and woolly minded—though undoubtedly liberal—platitudes. The real complexities of life, rooted in the social order, are overlooked."[40]

The stereotypical image of the American family and of families being part of a larger network of supermarkets, towns, corporations, and so forth, of belonging to "something," and images of a prosperous American economy were countered, to some extent, by actual events of the decade. In 1954 and again in 1955, the U.S. Supreme Court ruled that segregated schools were illegal. Many white Americans in both the South and the North saw this ruling as a threat to their established way of life. The implementation of the Court's ruling was met with protests, demonstrations, and violence. For example, in 1957 the state of Arkansas tried to prevent the integration of Little Rock Central High School, and President Dwight D. Eisenhower had to send in U.S. paratroopers to prevent riots. Roland Barthes asked sarcastically, "Why not ask the parents of Emmett Till, the young Negro assassinated by the Whites[,] what they think of *The Family of Man* exhibit?"[41]

It is perhaps important to note the interaction of actual events, so-called reality; the viewer; and the photographer, with his camera, with his perceptions. As the photographer Gilles Peress noted, "In any given picture, there are something like four authors. There's me—I make the decisions. I push the button. But there's also reality. Reality is incredibly forceful and talkative and says alot of things. It always has a chance for revenge. The camera . . . does something very specific as well: It changes what it sees. And then there's the viewer, the people who look at the pictures. It's a collaborative venture."[42] With events such as those revolving around segregation-integration issues, the stereotype of the happy and friendly American family began to be contradicted by mass media news stories and images.

There were also some photographers, such as Robert Frank and William Klein, who had begun to look at American life through a different lens, exposing its darker side. During 1954 and 1955, Klein photographed in New York City, and in 1956, his photographs were published (in France) in a book entitled *Life Is Good and Good for You in New York*. His photographs show a contempt for the American way of life. Klein brought with him his own experiences of having grown up in New York, of having studied painting with Fernand Léger in Paris, and of having lived for six years in Europe after marrying a Belgian woman. Klein entitled the first section of the book "Family Album." This section contains few pictures of the nuclear middle-class family, but attempts to express the concept of the city as a civic "family" and parodies the myth of the melting pot. When he inserts the image of three grinning Mr. Peanut mannequins wearing black top hats beneath two businessmen wearing suits and ties, he implies that the concept of the city as an extended family is some kind of joke.

While Klein was photographing New York and Steichen was mounting the *Family of Man* exhibit, a Swiss fashion photographer-turned-photojournalist, Robert Frank, was roaming the American countryside, documenting American life, much of which he did not like, on a Guggenheim fellowship. The result was his powerful set of photographs in his book, *The Americans*, published in 1958 in Paris and in 1959 in New York. Frank's images were often irreverent, exposing the glut of a consumer society and subtle racial attitudes that perhaps only an outsider could have captured in the 1950s. In *Trolley, New Orleans* [41], which appears in the book, one sees Frank's abilities to capture complex psychological and social issues without resorting to verbal rhetoric. The windows of the trolley become structural boxes on the continuum of a grid, whose structure separates the people on the trolley literally and figuratively. There is no contact among the figures in the images or with the world outside the trolley, except for blank stares. The trolley and its windows become a metaphor for entrapment, of alienated figures in the "social landscape" (a term coined by photographer Nathan Lyons in the 1960s). Here, we see part of a family— the two small, well-dressed white children, most likely a brother and a sister, framed by the trolley window, not at home, but out in the world, unaware of the great social conflict inherent in the grim faces of the white woman and black man on either side of them. Some of the images in the book were blurred or unevenly framed, reflecting Frank's rebellion against established print techniques. Many Americans did not want to deal with Frank's style or content, and he was widely criticized. Frank's America was similar to Jack Kerouac's America in *On the Road*, an invisible America, at the side of the road.

Photographers depicted not only the general middle-class population and the darker side of American life, but also celebrities portrayed in their own nests of domesticity. For these celebrity figures, normalcy was important, too. During the 1950s, the photographer Sid Avery photographed a number of Hollywood celebrities at home. The photographs represent Hollywood as it wanted to see

41. Robert Frank, *Trolley, New Orleans*, c. 1959. Art Institute of Chicago.

itself and as it wanted others to see it—as a normal, stable, well-functioning, prosperous community. The images became an extension of the American Dream, with its happy families, privately owned homes, boats, pools, and other luxuries. In these photographs, celebrities such as Debbie Reynolds, Rock Hudson, Humphrey Bogart, Audrey Hepburn, Paul Newman, and Kirk Douglas were depicted with their families in relaxed, comfortable settings that reinforced the values of a middle- and upper-class society, which was both formed and reflected by the impact of the mass media. One sees, for instance, the *Bogarts Saying Good-bye to Their Son*, 1952, as Lauren Bacall and Humphrey Bogart sit in their sleek Jaguar XK120 in front of a large brick Georgian house. Bo-gart reaches out to hug his young son Steven as Bacall looks on. Or one sees Audrey Hepburn seated outside on a bed of leaves, nestled against her husband Mel Ferrer, who is playing with their small dog in a 1957 photograph. Mel holds a book on the American icon, Abraham Lincoln, open in one hand. The smiling couple is completely surrounded by foliage. Or one sees Debbie Reynolds sitting happily in her living room in 1960 with her two young children, who are playing on a toy merry-go-round. The three are photographed in a distinct triangular composition that recalls the traditional composition of Renaissance Madonna-and-Child images. In the photograph, Reynolds appears in a different setting and persona from the kind of roles she frequently played in films—that of an immature, adolescent beauty, who was frequently intent on securing a husband.

Besides looking at still photographs, particularly those in magazines, Americans also went to the movies, although the advent of television networking in 1948 caused a number of movie theaters to close. (In 1949, 1 million television sets were sold; in 1950, 4 million; and in 1954, 32 million.) A number of significant films in the late 1940s and 1950s dealt with issues related to the family. In 1946, when the war was finally over, films and magazines began to deal, to some extent, with the needs of returning veterans to domestic settings. One of the hits of the year was *The Best Years of Our Lives*, directed by William Wyler and starring Fredric March, Myrna Loy, Teresa Wright, Dana Andrews, Virginia Mayo, Hoagy Carmichael, Gladys George, and Harold Russell. The film collected seven Oscars, including Best Picture. Russell, an actual veteran who had lost his hands, took home a second Oscar, given as a special award for bringing hope and courage to other veterans. The film involves the return of three veterans, Homer Parish (Harold Russell), who had a serious girlfriend at home and lost his hands in the war; Fred Derry (Dana Andrews), who had hastily married a rather shallow nightclub girl before going to war twenty days later; and Al Stephenson (Fredric March), who left a stable family life with a wife and two children. The veterans' lives become intertwined after they return, and each tries to come to terms with reentering civilian life. Unlike the stories that evolved from reentry after the Vietnam War, this film has a happy ending. Homer Parish comes to terms with his disability and marries his girl friend, who remains kind and faithful to him throughout the film. Derry realizes that his marriage is a sham and, in the end, falls in love with Stephenson's older daughter Peggy.

Between 1948 and 1956, the film director George Stevens did four major films dealing with various issues related to the family. His 1948 *I Remember Mama* [42] was based on the 1943 collection of short stories, *Mama's Bank Account,* by Kathryn Forbes and the subsequent 1944 play by John van Druten. The book, the play, and the movie revolved around a Norwegian family living in San Francisco with a stalwart and kind mother who does everything she can to preserve her home and family in the face of illness, prejudice, strikes, and a generally difficult life as an immigrant family. In the family's struggles, there is always a sense of love and respect. Written originally during the war years, the book and play provided a model of stability and sincerity in a chaotic world. The appearance of the movie in 1948, starring Irene Dunne, Barbara Bel Geddes, Philip Dorn, and Cedric Hardwicke, provided a model, too, for postwar domesticity, with life revolving around the family; that the family was an immigrant family seemed secondary. More important were the family values of hard work, education, honesty, and respect that were portrayed in such poignant scenes as Mama finding a way to send her son to high school or helping her uncle to die in peace.

Between 1951 and 1956, Stevens directed three films that were meant to be seen as a trilogy: *A Place in the Sun* (1951), *Shane*

42. *I Remember Mama*, 1948. RKO Radio Pictures. Photofest.

(1953), and *Giant* (1956). *A Place in the Sun*, based on Theodore Dreiser's novel *An American Tragedy*, starred Montgomery Clift, Elizabeth Taylor, Shelley Winters, Raymond Burr, Anne Revere, and Keefe Brasselle. The film won six Oscars, including Best Direction. Winters plays the lowly production line worker, Alice Tripp, who falls in love with George Eastman (Montgomery Clift), the nephew of the owner of the company, by whom she ultimately becomes pregnant. But the young Eastman is lured by the wealthy socialite, Angela Vickers (Elizabeth Taylor), who loves him as well. Eastman dreams and seriously considers staging a drowning "accident" for the pregnant, unmarried Alice, but in the end, according to his testimony, cannot do it. However, out in a boat on a shimmering silver lake with George Eastman, Alice stands and tips the boat over. Unable to swim, she drowns. Raymond Burr, as the fiery district attorney, succeeds in convicting Eastman for murder, and Eastman is sentenced to death. An appeal by Eastman's mother is unsuccessful. Angela's father, with his power and money, keeps his daughter out of the courtroom proceedings. The movie ends with Eastman walking through the prison to his execution. This is a movie about the power of wealthy families and American morals of the time, as well as the difficulty of crossing class lines. Abortion was clearly not a consideration. Eastman's own parents, missionaries—his father dead, his mother with a modest income—have little influence in the end. It is indeed an American tragedy in that a young pregnant woman dies, a basically decent young man is executed, and another young woman in love is left alone to deal with the consequences of social and moral forces that are stronger than she is.

Based on the novel by Jack Schaefer, *Shane* returns to an early time, focusing on a family in the days of the developing American frontier in the late nineteenth century. Starring Alan Ladd, Jean Arthur, Van Heflin, Jack Palance, and Brandon de Wilde, the film is, in many ways, a classic western, but makes some comments about family life. Shane (Alan Ladd), a gunman who wishes to settle down, comes to a town to defend some homesteaders who are being harassed by cattlemen, who object to the fences/homes these settlers have built. In particular, Shane becomes involved with one farm couple—Joe Starrett (Van Heflin) and Marion Starrett (Jean Arthur)—and their young son, Joey (Brandon de

Wilde). Shane inspires Joe to stand up for himself, is disturbingly attracted to Marion, and is greatly admired by Joey. Marion is also attracted to Shane, but remains faithful to her family. To save this family and the other settlers' families from one of the cattlemen's hired guns, Jack Wilson (Jack Palance), Shane, although tired of violence, participates in the inevitable "showdown" that is part of the Western movie. Protection of the family prevails, and good triumphs over evil, as the notion of one's own land safely delineated by fence and cultivated by man predominates—the roots of the American Dream of the fifties. But Shane, the savior, has no roots and continues to travel onward. The film ends as Shane is leaving the family homestead. "Bye, little Joe," he says. Joey, beginning to cry, replies, "Pa's got a lot of things for you to do, and Mother wants you. I know she does. . . . Shane! Shane!" Joey cries for Shane to come back as we see Shane ride over the mountain. Stevens thus raises questions about the nature of certain heroic figures: Can they consistently be a part of family life? Or is there a need for "tall storybook figures," out of the myths of the American West in this instance, for Americans to look up to, to inspire both children and adults? Did or does part of a sense of self lie in the stories and myths of the settling of America by strong, stalwart, and heroic figures?

Giant, based on Edna Ferber's novel, brought Stevens an Oscar for Best Direction in 1956. A film about two generations of Texans, starring Elizabeth Taylor, Rock Hudson, James Dean, Dennis Hopper, Sal Mineo, Mercedes McCambridge, and Chill Wills, it spans the time of the height of large Texas cattle ranches to the discovery of oil and the impact of that discovery on a family's way of life. The story revolves around the family of Texan Jordan Benedict, into which Leslie (Elizabeth Taylor) marries. Not a Texan, Leslie has a mind of her own and does not fit the stereotype of the "southern belle" wife. We see her weather the storms of ranch and family life and what happens when a poor, disgruntled ranch hand (James Dean), who is attracted to her, strikes oil and becomes a millionaire on a piece of land bequeathed to him on the death of one of Jordan's sisters. When Jordan, Jr., Jordan and Leslie's son, marries a Hispanic woman and has children of mixed lineage, it is Leslie who first embraces her new daughter-in-law. Here, one begins to see some acceptance of nonwhite figures within white homogeneity. Although headstrong, Leslie always focuses on her family and her relationship with family members.

The three films together are powerful statements of a contained family life. In some ways, they, particularly *Giant*, reflect the ideology of domestic containment that was seen as part of the larger containment policy of the beginning of the Cold War era, even though the films do not deal directly with Cold War issues. During the 1950s, it was believed that women who were married to strong men who assumed their rightful economic and sexual dominance in the home would channel their sexual energy appropriately in the marriage and not be frustrated wives and mothers.

In 1942, Philip Wylie had written *Generation of Vipers* and coined the term *Momism*, which referred to frustrated women who smothered their children with overprotection and overaffection, making their sons, in particular, passive and weak. As a loyal patriot during the war and an ardent anti-Communist after the war, Wylie argued that the negative impact of Momism could weaken the United States and make it vulnerable to enemy attack and takeover. Wylie later wrote *Smoke Across the Moon*, a novel in which a sexually liberated left-wing woman encourages Communist infiltration and destroys men. In 1954 Wylie wrote *Tomorrow*, in which he presented civil defense as a protection against Communism and Momism and suggested that rearmament and nuclear war were ways to combat Momism.

One of several films and books to deal directly with the issue of Momism was the 1952 film, *My Son John*, directed by Leo McCarey and starring Helen Hayes, Robert Walker, Dean Jagger, Van Heflin, Frank McHugh, and Richard Jaeckel. In the film, John's brothers are off to war in Korea. John, a Washington intellectual, played by Robert Walker (who died during the making of the film), is portrayed as quite close to his mother (Helen Hayes). The mother appears to be somewhat flaky, but independent and sympathetic. Through the eyes of John, one views the American family with some discredit and contempt. John's father's American Legion costume and his simplistic patriotic slogans are observed with some ridicule by his son. During the course of the film, one learns that John is not only a Communist, but a spy, who betrays his mother for a female spy. His mother has a nervous breakdown, and his father is unable to help her. This family has a sexually unsatisfied mother; a weak father; and a cold, isolated son. Thus, Communists were not necessarily foreigners, but could easily be Americans. Furthermore, the American family with these kind of members was seen as a source of Communism and something to be guarded against.

By the mid-fifties, a number of critics had expressed doubts about the conformity and homogeneity of American middle-class life. In 1956 John Keats wrote *A Crack in the Picture Window*, with suburbanite characters, such as John and Mary Drone, whose lives are spent deciding how to buy washing machines and to avoid their busy-body neighbors. The 1955 film, *Rebel Without a Cause*, became a voice of an active generation, speaking of youthful alienation and rebellion. Directed by Nicholas Ray, it starred James Dean, as the alienated Jim Stark, searching for a "niche" and some sense of identity; Natalie Wood as Judy; and Sal Mineo as Plato, along with Jim Backus, Ann Deran, Dennis Hopper, and Nick Adams. A newcomer to town, the teenager Jim Stark tries to find some type of self-esteem. Scenes, such as the one in which Stark and some peers bet who can drive a car closest to a dangerous cliff, from which a fall would be fatal, before jumping out of the car, show the power of the peer culture and teenagers' need for acceptance. There are communication problems between parents and children, and Jim, Judy, and Plato try to make a surrogate family for themselves through their friendships. The film remains painfully powerful today because it sensitively portrays the distance between parents and children and youthful alienation.

Another film made that year, which also starred James Dean, dealt with rivalries within a family constellation. *East of Eden* [43], directed by Elia Kazan and starring Julie Harris, Raymond Massey, Jo Van Fleet, Burl Ives, and Richard Davalos, as well as James Dean, was based on the John Steinbeck novel about the rivalry of two brothers—Caleb (Dean) and Aaron (Davalos), for their father's (Raymond Massey) attention. The story is rooted in the biblical story of Cain and Abel, in which one brother sells his birthright and kills the other. Cal (Caleb) appears to be alienated,

43. *East of Eden*, 1955. Photofest.

and Aaron appears as the "model" brother, whom, along with his girlfriend, his father approves of.

Cal, on the other hand, seems to be able to please no one, but deep down desperately wants his father's love and attention. Their mother (Jo Van Fleet, who won an Oscar for her role), whom the brothers are told is dead, left home and became the head of a house of prostitution. Cal eventually learns the truth about his mother. As the film comes to a close, Aaron goes off to war; the father has a stroke; and Cal, still wanting to please his father, tries once again to do so as his father lies bedridden. Telling the nurse that his father dislikes leaving the room, he sits close to his father, whereupon a faint smile comes to his father's face. Finally, there is some recognition and reconciliation. This is not an "all-American" harmonious family nestled safely in the suburbs. Here, on film, is a dysfunctional family whose problems, particularly those of the brothers, were and are not unlike the difficulties faced by many families on various levels.

Thus, the medium of film, as well as still photography, raised some questions about the "all-American family" and the nature of family life. It also raised new questions about a sense of self and the identity of the family.

National esteem was called into question on October 4, 1957, when the Soviet Union launched Sputnik into orbit, beating the United States into space. It was thought that national security might be jeopardized if Americans could not dominate the field of technology. Some claimed that American science had put too much money and faith in developing consumer items, rather than in concentrating on more important goals of national security. In books, such as John Kenneth Galbraith's *The Affluent Society* (1958), various aspects of the consumer culture came under attack, and the recession in 1957–58 created further doubts about the consumer economy. The United States did attempt to match the Russian Sputnik launch in December 1957, with its Vanguard I. Unfortunately, the rocket sank sadly to the ground in front of television and newspaper reporters after rising a mere four feet into the air.

44. *The Adventures of Ozzie and Harriet.* Photofest.

Although there were clearly anxieties and questions about both public and private life by the end of the decade, it should be noted that on television, the middle-class suburban sitcom had become the primary form for representing family life. Programs such as *The Adventure of Ozzie and Harriet* [44] and *The Donna Reed Show*, depicted the lives of nuclear families in suburbia with humor. In these sitcoms, the parents appeared contented, the modest number of children seemed reasonably satisfied, and the neighbors were friendly. In general, the mother attended to the home-related tasks, and the father worked outside the home, although he still had a say in family affairs. In *The Donna Reed Show*, for example, Donna lived in the pristine suburban town of Hilldale with her husband, Alex, a doctor, and their two children. Her next-door neighbor, Midge Kelsey, was also married to a doctor. Although these programs were out of sync with the growing critique of suburban life, they stayed on the air into the early 1960s, thus remaining a pervasive image in many American homes. But the "cracks in the picture window" by the end of the 1950s clearly had an impact on images of self, family, and nation that were to lead to the upheavals of the 1960s.

6

The Sixties

The sixties was a decade of tremendous upheaval and tumultuous change, evident in many facets of society throughout the world. There was great violence and there were miraculous achievements. The decade began with headlines in 1960, such as "U–2 Reconnaissance Jet with Pilot Gary Powers Is Shot Down over Russia"; "South African Police Kill 92 Blacks during Demonstration at Sharpeville"; "Khrushchev at UN Pounds Shoe in Anger"; "Blacks Sit In at Greensboro, North Carolina, Lunch Counter"; and "Kennedy Wins Narrow Victory."

The youthful John F. Kennedy, the first Catholic to be elected president of the United States, brought with him the spirit and vision of a "new frontier." His 1961 inaugural words rang clear and spoke of a time of "Camelot."

> Let the word go forth from this time and place . . . that the torch has been passed passed to a new generation of Americans. . . . So let us begin anew. . . . Together let us explore the stars, conquer the deserts, eradicate disease, tap the ocean depths, and encourage the arts and commerce. . . . All this will not be finished in the first one hundred days. . . . The energy, the faith, the devotion which we bring to this endeavor will light our country and all who serve it—and the glow from that fire can truly light the world.[43]

Kennedy established the Peace Corps, for which approximately ten thousand volunteered in its first three months. He proposed civil rights legislation, cut taxes, and pushed space exploration. But he faltered during the disastrous Bay of Pigs invasion in 1961. A year later, nuclear war threatened during the Cuban missile crisis. But, in general, Kennedy and his family brought a sense of hope and style to the White House. The Kennedys became American royalty.

All that quickly changed, however, on a clear November day in 1963 in Dallas, when Lee Harvey Oswald raised his gun and assassinated Kennedy, and along with him the dreams of many. It was a tragic day that few who lived then can forget. It was a bitter omen of what was yet to come in the decade.

The same year that Kennedy was shot, Martin Luther King, Jr., gave his famous speech, highlighted by the well-known words:

> I have a dream that one day this nation will rise up, live out the true meaning of its creed: "We hold these truths to be self-evident, that all men are created equal." I have a dream that one day on the red hills of Georgia the sons of former slaves and the sons of former slave-owners will be able to sit down together at the table of brotherhood. I have a dream that one day even the State of Mississippi, a state sweltering with the heat of oppression, will be transformed into an oasis of freedom and justice. I have a dream that my four little children will one day live in a nation where they will not be judged by the color of their skin but by the content of their character.[44]

Yet the words, so strong that day, were hollow echoes five years later, in 1968, when King himself was tragically assassinated. As if one assassination was not enough in 1968, Robert F. Kennedy, who was running for president, was also killed that year. (The militant Black Muslim leader, Malcolm X, was assassinated in 1965.)

Following King's death, protest riots broke out, and the militant Black Panthers emerged. Kennedy's successor, Lyndon B. Johnson, called for "the Great Society," and a "war on poverty." But the Great Society became secondary to the issue of the Vietnam

War, which left lasting scars on the United States, so torn over its validity.

American culture of the 1960s was heightened by a new activist spirit. There were civil rights activists, and Eldridge Cleaver wrote *Soul on Ice*. Feminism was reborn; the National Organization for Women was founded in 1966, led by women such as Betty Friedan, who wrote *The Feminine Mystique* in 1963, and Gloria Steinem. Rebellious youths became part of the Free Speech Movement and were "hippies" and "flower children." They marched to the 1968 Chicago Democratic convention to protest the Vietnam War, only to be beaten down by Mayor Richard Daley's police, all seen on national television. The music of the Beatles and such groups as Jefferson Airplane were inspiring. The rock festivals at Woodstock and Altamont were like giant Happenings. But the spirit of Altamont was subdued by the bloody violence that followed. American youths and students were not the only ones to rebel. French, German, and Mexican students clashed with established forces in the late sixties.

And beyond Vietnam there was turmoil elsewhere. In 1965 there was the Indian-Pakistani War. In the same year, Mao Zedong announced his Cultural Revolution in China, against all established power, and the Red Guards struck at any attempts to revive the old culture of China. In the Mideast, a third war broke out between Israel and its Arab neighbors in 1967. Although the war was won by Israel in six days, there were marks of continuing problems in the area. The year 1967 also brought a military coup in Greece and the killing of the revolutionary leader Che Guevara by Bolivian troops. In 1968 Prague Spring ended with the Russian invasion of Czechoslovakia.

Space exploration was firmly established when the Russians put the first man in space in 1961. In the same year, Alan Shepard was the first American to fly in space. In 1962 U.S. astronaut John Glenn orbited the Earth three times. And in 1969 Neil Armstrong and Edwin Aldrin landed on the moon and walked, leaving behind their plaque that read, "We came in peace for all mankind." Scientific discoveries also brought the first heart transplant and the beginnings of the computer age.

The literature of the decade was a mixture of reflections of tension and anxiety about the times and visions for a different world. James Baldwin wrote *Another Country*, Ken Kesey wrote *One Flew Over the Cuckoo's Nest*, Peter Weiss wrote *Marat/Sade*, and Aleksandr Solzhenitsyn wrote *The Cancer Ward*. Marshall McLuhan, whose prophecies of a "global village" were to ring true, wrote *Understanding Media: The Extensions of Man*.

The movies *Bonnie and Clyde* and *Easy Rider* captured the bravado spirit of the decade. Stanley Kubrick envisioned new and different worlds in *Dr. Strangelove* and *2001: A Space Odyssey*.

The radical politics and violence of the world at large did not permeate the art world of the 1960s as much as one might think. But the rate and amount of change, as art movements tumbled one after the other, from Pop art to Op art to Hard Edge to Minimal, and so forth, were indicative of the vast changes going on in the rest of society. With the arrival of Andy Warhol, artists became celebrities and art became an industry that more and more people talked about.

The language of Op, Hard Edge, and Minimal art was clearly abstract, while the imagery of Pop art concentrated frequently on a world of commodities, celebrity figures, and popular culture. Warhol glorified the Campbell soup can, the Coke bottle, and the dollar bill, as well as the faces of those, such as Jackie Kennedy and Marilyn Monroe, in his paintings and silk-screen prints, which could be reproduced in large editions, widely marketed, and distributed as desired. Warhol's aesthetic celebrated the image of the celebrity: that everyone could be equally famous, if only for a few minutes. His portraits were "products," slick, clean, polished, and largely superficial. There was no sense of an inner self. Rather, there was a cool detachment inherent in his images, a distancing that was to influence how Americans saw themselves and others.

As the artists Andy Warhol; Roy Lichtenstein, with his blown-up comic strip paintings; Tom Wesselmann, in his billboard-like images that drew on images from advertising and American home scenes, such as his *Bathtub Collage #3* that employed actual home furnishings; and James Rosenquist, in his large *F–111* (10 feet by 86 feet) drawing of American consumer images, many Americans were highly influenced by the actual imagery of popular culture related to family life. The vocabulary of the New Frontier and the perceived need to pursue space exploration called on traditional moral foundations of family life to be coupled with the new goals of public life. Domestic space and outer space began to have connections. *Life* magazine, for instance, ran biographical pictorial essays depicting family scenes and the life histories of the astronauts. In the May 18, 1962, issue, the astronaut Scott Carpenter appeared on the cover of *Life* with his wife René. Inside were photos of Scott's family life as a child and his own children. The Carpenters were depicted as the ideal American family. Many American families took on the space-age enthusiasm and named their newborn sons after John Glenn.

On television, popular depictions of family life included those with elements of the fantastic or science fiction. Programs, such as *Bewitched, I Dream of Jeannie, The Jetsons*, and *The Munsters*, replaced shows like *Ozzie and Harriet* and *The Donna Reed Show*. In this regard, it is interesting to note that in January 1966, *Mad* magazine published a cartoon version by Mort Drucker and Stan Hart of the perfect American television family—Oozie, Harried, Divot, and Rickety Nilson—who "lived completely and hermetically sealed off from reality." One frame shows Oozie reading a newspaper that Harried has "edited" to remove all references to disturbing news, such as those related to Vietnam, Laos, and race riots. Oozie complains to his wife that "First, I pulled the wrong cord on the Venetian blind. . . . Then, Art Linkletter's House Party was preempted by a space shot. . . . It's been one thing after another."[45] *Mad*'s spoof was part of a larger shift in television representations of the family during the 1960s. Besides sitcoms that included "fantastic" elements, there were also those that began to show one parent missing and new characters who served as surrogate parents, for example, Uncle Charlie in *My Three Sons* and Aunt Bee in *The Andy Griffith Show*. Despite the rising divorce rate during the 1960s, missing parents were depicted as having died and divorce was not depicted on television because of network censorship.

Although Americans watched television frequently, the movies also brought a diversity of depictions of the family. The 1965 musical *The Sound of Music*, based on the real-life story of the Austrian Von Trapp family who fled from their homeland in 1938 to escape the Nazis, was a "blockbuster" success, winning five Oscars, including Best Picture and Best Director for Robert Wise. Christopher Plummer and Julie Andrews, as well as the children, stole the hearts of many with their songs and acting. In this film, the mother of the Von Trapp children is dead and Maria from the Abbey becomes the surrogate parent, and ultimately the children's stepmother. Here, public and private life become intertwined as political events and ideals influence the course of the family's life. Maria becomes the force in the movie that helps make the individual Von Trapps once more into a family group.

Julie Andrews also appeared in the popular *Mary Poppins* the year before, directed by Robert Stevenson. Based on P. L. Travers's book about a "practically perfect" nanny who brings profound changes to the somewhat stiff Banks family of London in about 1910, the film emphasized the power of affection, imagination, song, and wit in family life. Laughter and charm pervade the film, with its "fantastic" special effects. The film won Oscars for the musical score, the song "Chim-Chim-cheree," special visual effects, and editing, and Andrews received an Oscar as well.

A father raising his children without a mother was also seen earlier in a serious film, *To Kill a Mockingbird* (1962), directed by Robert Mulligan. Adapted from the 1960 Harper Lee novel, the movie tells the powerful and poignant tale of Atticus Finch (Gregory Peck), a southern lawyer who is raising his children, Jem and Scout, alone with the help of a black woman, Calpurnia, in Maycomb, Alabama, in the early thirties. During the summer of 1933, Atticus is asked to defend a black man, Tom Robinson, accused of rape. Atticus tries to explain the proceedings to the children, since the family lives in a town that is still fighting the Civil War and is still terribly prejudiced against blacks. Tom Robinson is convicted and is shot and killed as he tries to run away. He leaves behind a wife and children. The Finch children not only are a part of these racial issues, but come to terms with their neighbor Boo Radley (Robert Duvall in his film debut), who has been labeled insane, or crazed, and dangerous by the neighborhood. Through the power of imagination, playfulness, and innocence, Boo comes out of "hiding" in the end to save the children from an assailant in the nearby woods and then gently interacts with the Finches. It is the children who are best able to deal with an "other," a "different" one in their society, which primarily wants homogeneity and the conserving of the status quo. The novel and film, which appeared just prior to the stirrings of the civil rights movement, provided an elegant statement of a small town, one-parent family dealing with the inequalities of their culture in their daily lives. Gregory Peck won an Oscar for his role, and Horton Foote won an Oscar for his screenplay.

A film of the same year but with a quite different theme was *The Manchurian Candidate*, directed by John Frankenheimer and starring Frank Sinatra, Laurence Harvey, Janet Leigh, Angela Lansbury, and Henry Silva [45]. The film was a harrowing presentation of a Richard Condon story in which the family, particularly the mother, is depicted as a negative force, rather than representing positive values. As did *My Son John*, this film depicts a weak father, a frustrated mother, and an isolated son. Playing on the theme of Momism, the film attempted to awaken Americans once again to the threats of Communism. One writer noted that *The Manchurian Candidate*, "capitalizing on its improbabilities by mixing realism with science fiction, . . . is the most sophisticated film of the cold war."[46] Laurence Harvey, the Manchurian Candidate, is captured during the Korean War and is brainwashed by the Communists to carry out political assassinations. During the brainwashing process, he and the other American soldiers who have been captured hallucinate that those who give them orders are middle-aged women who resemble their mothers. The queen of diamonds is Harvey's control card. Harvey's mother (Angela Lansbury), whom he hates but whose power he is consumed by, is trying to promote the career of her Joseph McCarthy-like husband, Harvey's stepfather. She is secretly a Communist who is trying to propel her husband into the presidency. Harvey is programmed to kill his own fiancée and thus is still stuck in his mother's power. He is also programmed to kill the man at the top of the political ticket, to allow his stepfather to become president and to put his Communist mother in control. His mother, who finally realizes her son is an instrument of sacrifice, that her feelings as a mother run stronger than her party loyalty, vows to turn against the Communists once her husband is president. Harvey's hate, however, is so powerful by the end of the film that he climbs to the top of the convention hall and shoots his mother and stepfather instead of the candidate he was programmed to kill. His intensity of feeling had, in a sense, freed him from party control. Michael Rogin commented on the role of the American family in this film: "Domestic ideology promised that the American family would triumph over Communism. *The Manchurian Candidate*, by subordinating Communist to maternal influence, showed what that promise entailed. The family defeats Communism only by first generating Communism and then self-destructively replacing it.[47]

Near the end of the decade, racial and family issues were further explored in *Guess Who's Coming to Dinner?* (1967), directed by Stanley Kramer and starring Sidney Poitier, Katharine Hepburn, Katharine Houghton (Hepburn's niece), and Spencer Tracy (in his last film). In the film, Houghton attempts to convince her parents

45. *The Manchurian Candidate*, 1962. Photofest.

(Tracy and Hepburn) that her fiancé, Poitier, is worthy of dinner, and marriage. This is a genteel story, but one that attempts to raise social consciousness.

By the end of the decade a film such as *Bob & Carol & Ted & Alice* (1969), directed by Paul Mazursky, took a look at possible changing family lifestyles. Natalie Wood and Robert Culp play an ultrasophisticated couple who try to "modernize" the thinking of their best friends, a couple played by Dyan Cannon and Elliott Gould, about sexual freedom. The couples decide to swap partners, but, upon finding they cannot, they leave their hotel room and mingle with a Las Vegas crowd as the soundtrack plays "What the World Needs Now Is Love, Love, Love."

In the area of still photography, the civil rights movement inspired Bruce Davidson and other photographers to record the street and family life of poor people and blacks. In 1966 Davidson brought a large-format view camera, flash, and tripod onto East 100th Street, one of the worst blocks in New York City. There, he photographed for two years, his work culminating in an exhibition at the Museum of Modern Art [46]. Davidson invited his subjects to the show. Photographers, such as Davidson, Leonard Freed, and Danny Lyon, were known as "concerned photographers" because they were particularly concerned about social issues. The terms *social landscape* and *concerned photographer* came to be used because the volatile events of the 1960s led photographers to search out and record images of fear, loneliness, affection, and alienation that were major aspects of the domestic lives of the poor and nonmainstream, or minority, groups.

The viewpoint of Diane Arbus, although different from the more sympathetic viewpoints of the concerned photographers, still focused on elements of American culture. Hers was a photography of confrontation, photographing the underside, the "darker" side, of life, using images of freaks, social misfits, and the physically deformed. She asked viewers to face unpleasantness and their own "freakishness" head-on. Even her images of "ordinary" subjects have a haunting, otherworldly quality.

Born in 1923, Arbus started as a fashion photographer, but by the 1960s had also turned to more personal imagery. Breaking the barriers often surrounding suburbia and the suburban image, she

46. Bruce Davidson, *East 100th Street*, 1966–68. Museum of Modern Art, New York.

frequently immersed herself in the lives of others. She alerted
viewers to the possible duplicities in the idealized nuclear family in
suburbia and introduced them to the domestic life of the fringes of
society—the freaks, the nudists, the disturbed. *A Retired Man and
His Wife at Home in a Nudist Camp One Morning, N.J.* (1963); *A
Family on Their Lawn One Sunday in Westchester* (1968); *Russian
Midget Friends* (1963); and *A Jewish Giant at Home With His Parents in the Bronx* (1970) depict other realities than that of mainstream middle-class domesticity and force viewers to face their
own "strangeness" and "freakishness." The photograph of the Jewish giant, for example, at home with his parents, becomes all the
more extraordinary because of the ordinariness of its setting. In his
nondescript living room, the giant looks down at his Lilliputian
parents. Arbus spoke of the significance of freaks for her own life

and her work, referring to freaks as aristocrats, who could help answer riddles about "self" and "reality":

> Freaks was a thing I photographed a lot. It was one of the first things I photographed and it had a terrific kind of excitement for me. I just used to adore them. I still do adore them. I don't quite mean they're my best friends but they made me feel a mixture of shame and awe. Like a person in a fairy tale who stops you and demands that you answer a riddle. Most people go through life dreading that they'll have a traumatic experience. Freaks were born with their trauma. They've already passed their test in life. They're aristocrats.[48]

Even in her magazine work, Arbus's images pointed to a dominant chaotic side in the poignant expressions of men, women, and children that may have been beneath their alluring, affluent exteriors. Some examples are her *Bill Blass Designs for Little Ones* (*Harper's Bazaar,* September 1962); *Petal Pink for Little Parties, White Over Pale for Parties* (*Harper's Bazaar,* November 1962); and the portraits of Mr. and Mrs. Howard Oxenburg and Mr. and Mrs. Armando Orsini, in the series "On Marriage" (*Harper's Bazaar,* May 1965). Although Arbus's images were frequently cold and antiseptic, they forced the viewer to look at "outsiders" and an "other," both within and outside themselves.

In painting, the cool distancing of Pop art's personalities and mechanical emphasis was further seen in the flat planar colors of Alex Katz's paintings, which depicted Katz's family and friends like billboard images, with no sentimentality or emotion. As did some photographers who had turned to the everyday environment and "snapshot aesthetic," Katz frequently painted smooth, silhouette-like forms that resembled cool, stylized snapshots. Often Katz portrayed his figures, usually his friends, family, or personalities of the art world, close up, from the shoulder up. The flat planar colors and simplified pictorial language emphasize the stiffness, complex coolness, and sense of distancing of the figures from the viewer. We may know the figures in general, but not specifically, for no detailed information is provided by the painter. The figures seem to be absorbed in their own private worlds and have no real con-

47. Alex Katz, *Supper*, 1974. Hood Museum of Art, Dartmouth College, Hanover, New Hampshire.

nection to each other or to the larger world. Consider, for example, *Ives Field II*, 1964 (Weatherspoon Art Gallery, Greensborough, NC); *Supper* [47]; or *The Ryan Sisters*, 1981 (Marlborough Gallery, New York). In *Supper* one sees three figures from the waist up, seated at a table set for four. The painting depicts Katz's wife Ada (in black) in profile, closest to the viewer, and two others, the gallery owners Brooke and Caroline Alexander, dressed in strong blue and red clothing, respectively, about to eat dinner. It is as if the artist has excused himself from the table and that he and the viewer are observing the meal from close at hand—the table's edge—or are looking at it through the wide-angle lens of a camera. In this painting, the familiar ritual of sharing a meal with family and friends has been transformed into a monumental icon of late twentieth-century American life.

Like a number of other realist artists, including Alfred Leslie and William Beckman, Katz frequently included images of his wife in his work. One writer commented that "these images stand as the symbolic alter egos of the artists. In the past when paintings of this kind were made, they were generally private and intimate records of a family—in celebration of the birth of a child, for instance, or some family milestone. Their scale was generally relatively small. Today, however, they have a scale that emphasizes their public role. The family portrait has come out of the family parlor."[49]

It is interesting to note that Alfred Leslie began his career as a promising second-generation Abstract Expressionist, but following a tragic fire in his studio, turned to a striking realism in 1966. His theatrical compositions drew from Mannerist portraits, from Caravaggio, and the Spanish Baroque. In many of his paintings, such as the family scene *Birthday for Ethel Moore*, 1976 (collection of the artist), there is a heightened psychological intensity. Of particular note is the dramatic lighting on his stage-set compositions.

One finds the public scale and cool distancing of Pop art and Katz's paintings carried further in photorealist surfaces in Robert Bechtle's painting *'61 Pontiac* [48]. In this painting, one sees the

48. Robert Bechtle, *'61 Pontiac*, c. 1968–69. Whitney Museum of American Art, New York.

49. Chuck Close, *Frank*, c. 1971. Minneapolis Institute of Arts.

"all-American" family standing in front of their Pontiac station wagon in a pristine, clean suburban neighborhood that has grass, trees, sidewalks, and so on. The family of four—a father, mother, and two small blond-haired children—stand in the center of the three-part painting that could be likened to a three-part Renaissance altar piece. Here, the object of worship is the car and all that it represents in American society. Given the events of the sixties, it is difficult to ascertain whether this "portrait" is partially tongue-in-cheek, in that the cleanliness and purity it portrays is in such opposition to the chaos of the larger world. In any case, the emphasis on the reflective surfaces of the car and the car's predominant role in all three parts of the canvas are significant. In this painting, there is no emotion, no affect; rather the focus is on the mechanical, even in the process of making it.

Although he dealt primarily with individuals, Chuck Close's large-scale photorealist portraits of himself and his friends emphasized the mechanics of reproduction. The portraits, such as *Frank*

[49], were painstakingly exact in likeness, but they became, para-doxically, depersonalized abstractions. The meticulous monumen-tal images appeared to neutralize any possible emotional response to the viewer. Standing close to the paintings, the viewer can see and experience only fragments of the whole. Visual-surface infor-mation related to depth of field, focus, scale, and the like seemed to be more important than any psychological factors related to the person portrayed, the artist, and the viewer.

The lack of affect in a number of Realist portraits during the sixties and subsequent decades reflected, to some extent, a growing sense of self-effacement by both the artist and the subject. Mini-malism and Pop art praised the elimination of the artist from the artwork or the reduction of the artist's role as an interpreter of experience. Art and the cult of the artist were to be demystified. Advertising images were becoming almost more real than reality itself. Surfaces were more important, in some instances, than any-thing that might lie beneath them. Gone were the romantic "self" and any sense of passion or mood. Personal traits of the subject were to be removed. The reality of inner experience was to be denied. Here was a "minimal self."[50]

Seeking a place in a world of chaos and adversity, but afraid to risk the "pains of any self-revelation" to oneself or to others, Christopher Lasch noted, "notwithstanding its self-imposed ban on self-expression, late modernist art unmistakably expresses the 'numbed emotional aura' of the age [or] as Carter Ratcliff [put it] ... 'the stasis or numbness induced by the refusal to risk the pains of self-revelation.' "[51]

Alice Neel's approach to the figure and realism was quite dif-ferent from a number of Realists. Neel was interested in going beneath the surface. Her expressionistic portraits received little credence during the Abstract Expressionistic era, yet they provided penetrating views of her family members, fellow artists, and neigh-bors. Neel was from a wealthy Philadelphia family but rejected her background when she married a Cuban student after studying at Moore College of Art. Her life seemed to be filled with tragedy: Her first child died of diphtheria, and she was abandoned by her husband. After her release from a hospital following a nervous breakdown, she went to New York. Her somber and often expressionistic pieces of the 1940s and 1950s were not recognized at the time. It was not until the 1960s and onward, when there was renewed interest in the figure, that her portraits of people, such as Bella Abzug, Ed Koch, and Red Grooms, received recognition. Sometimes referred to as a "collector of souls," Neel often probed deeply into the psyches of her subjects in her penetrating portraits.

Neel did a number of images of her own extended family, particularly of her daughter-in-law Nancy, and Nancy's children. The earliest painting of Nancy is *Mother and Child (Nancy and Olivia)* [50]. In this painting, in which Olivia, Nancy's first child, was three months old, Neel captured the uncertainty, as well as the possessiveness, that can accompany young motherhood. Nancy anxiously hugs the baby, who is squirming in her arms. A painting of 1980, *The Family*, shows Nancy and her three younger daugh-

50. Alice Neel, *Mother and Child (Nancy and Olivia)*, 1967. Private collection. © The Estate of Alice Neel. Courtesy of Robert Miller Gallery, New York.

ters seeming to tower over her. Here, Nancy's face has become a mask, hiding internal tensions that may go with motherhood—self-sacrifice, self-denial, and so forth.

Neel also painted family relationships of others, attempting to capture an essence of her subjects. An unusual portrait was of Cindy Nemser and her husband, Chuck, painted in 1975. The couple is depicted nude, seated in the protective frame of a couch. Cindy Nemser described the self-revelations that came to her as a result of the painting having been done.

> My image disclosed an unexpected sensuosity, coupled with sad-
> ness and vulnerability, while my husband's portrait underscored
> his healthy sensuality and basic generosity of spirit. These traits
> were not only delineated by the rendering of our facial expres-
> sions, but were also to be read in the pose we had chosen for our-
> selves, which Alice then transferred to her canvas. We sat close
> together, holding hands in an attitude of mutual support. My body
> concealed Chuck's sexual parts while his hand rested on my waist
> in a gesture of affectionate protectiveness. In this double portrait,
> Alice had psyched us out as individuals and had also arrived at the
> essence of our relationship.[52]

The intensity of Neel's work serves to make the viewer's encounter with the image, and sometimes subsequently with himself or herself, more immediate and engaging. But Neel was perhaps not fully recognized until 1975, when the Whitney Museum held an exhibition devoted to her work. In 1976 Neel was elected to the National Institute of Arts and Letters.

Abroad, the British artist Lucian Freud, a native of Berlin and friend of the painter Francis Bacon, also penetrated beyond surface details in his moving, expressive portraits. The grandson of the psychoanalyst Sigmund Freud, Lucian Freud has been a figure of myth and mystery. He has kept himself from the public, giving his telephone number to no one, and does not have his name or number on his front door. He has been both severely criticized and highly praised. One critic for *Le Monde* stated that he paints "flesh like badly carved ham." Yet Robert Hughes, art critic for *Time*, called him "the greatest living realist painter," and John Russell, of the *New York Times,* called him "the only living realist painter. . . . As a witness to human nature in the second half of our century [he] has had no equal, whether in Britain or elsewhere."[53] There is a disturbing sense of anxiety about many of Freud's pieces, which are usually painted from models in his studio. "What do I ask of a painting?" Freud said, "I ask it to astonish, disturb, seduce, convince."[54] Freud's portraits have continued to be provocative over several decades. In the early seventies, he began a series of powerful portraits of his mother, Lucie Brasch, which continued into the eighties.

By the early eighties, Freud had moved from meticulously rendered paintings and drawings to larger, less exacting, images. His work became freer and less linear, more painterly, revealing the very process of painting. Frequently, Freud used his family and friends as models or subjects. Many of his compositions with more than one figure suggest relationships, whether intimate or detached, that contain some tension. A number of Freud's more recent works, such as *Ib and Her Husband*, 1992 (private collection), have been set in his studio, thereby intertwining Freud's work and self into the lives of his subjects. Some of Freud's paintings also suggest a narrative, an untold or unfinished story, to be completed by the viewer. *And the Bridegroom*, 1993 (private collection), shows a naked couple, with their touching, twisted bodies, their eyes closed, on a studio bed, draped with a drab, gray cloth. They lie exposed in front of a black screen. There is no ornamentation in the piece. The title, *And the Bridegroom*, is a quotation from an ode celebrating both marriage and death. With his painterly emphasis on these twisted human forms, Freud asks the viewer to consider who these people truly are, unclothed and unmasked, in his studio.

A somewhat different approach to Realism was found in the work of the Colombian painter, Fernando Botero. Botero's rounded, streamlined figures, sometimes obese, are frequently presented with a subversive wit. Attending the San Fernando Academy in Madrid, Botero found himself inspired by Francisco de Goya and Diego Velázquez, taking an ironic view of the human condition from Goya and a liking of solid, well-rendered forms from Velázquez. In Botero's *Presidential Family* [51], one sees a family group that includes a fat clergyman and an overweight

policeman or member of the military. The political family's identity and security are clearly connected with the church and state in
this portrayal, which seems to be a parody of early royal portraits.
The composition is similar to Goya's in *The Family of Charles IV*
(1800). As did Goya, and Velázquez (in *The Maids of Honor*, 1656),
Botero included himself in this large painting. As did Freud, the
artist has brought himself into the constellation of viewer and subject. In a later painting, *Portrait of a Family*, 1974, Botero's obese
figures are to be identified with the Latin American bourgeoisie.
This family stands somber, with a baby, a toy train, and a small dog
at their feet, while the diagonal of a ladder and partial view of a fat
leg reaching into a fruit tree in the rear jars the verticals of the
family group. The mother touches no one, while the father holds a
young child and an older daughter clings to his shoulder from

51. Fernando Botero, *The Presidential Family*, 1967. Museum of Modern
Art, New York.

behind. Stiffly posed, this family does not appear to be a happy one, despite the "trappings" and "props" of middle-class life and dress that are present.

Moving from the rounded sculptural forms of Botero to the realm of three dimensions, the Paris-born Venezuelan artist Marisol Escobar, working in New York, dealt with the subject of the family throughout much of her career. A self-taught sculptor, strongly influenced by American folk art and pre-Columbian pottery, many of her works, which are primarily in wood, are at once Pop art and like Primitive or Folk art. Many of her works have exposed the stereotype of the "happy" wife and mother. Her mother died when Marisol was eleven. A number of her sculptures from the 1960s dealt with the mother-child theme, using anonymous images with features similar to Marisol's own. In *The Family* [52], Marisol depicts a nuclear family with some degree of tension but a seemingly strong emotional attachment between the mother and her children (no father is present). This assemblage sculpture was based on an old photograph that the artist found among some trash near her studio. The names and life stories of the models were unknown, although the family is clearly not affluent. Marisol's drawing and painting on wood invite the viewer into this family's life, questioning who they are behind their somewhat somber facial expressions. The artist's use of actual doors, behind the figures, decorated with curvilinear elements, help to unify the disparate figurative elements.

Another 1962 assemblage depicted a dust-bowl farm family. Later work also focused on less fortunate families, reflecting Marisol's concern for larger social and political issues related to poverty. One such work was her 1986 *Poor Family I*, an assemblage made of wood, charcoal, stones, and a plastic doll, that confronts the viewer head-on with an array of pensive, unhappy, and defiant faces.

Marisol also depicted the plight of the working woman with children. Her 1987 *Working Woman*, in wood, charcoal and plaster, portrayed the mother as stiff and tense, imprisoned in plaster and plywood, with her child in one hand and her briefcase in the other. The child, too, appears stiff and somber, caught in the dilemma of his or her mother's situation, which is filled with the tension of

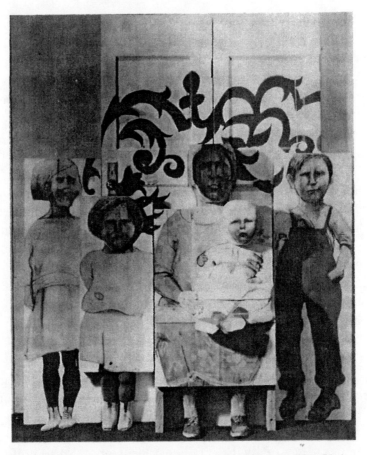

52. Marisol, *The Family*, 1962. Museum of Modern Art, New York.

juggling work and children. In this piece, Marisol captured the plight of many mothers, who must work outside the home and struggle to spend time with and care for their children. Again, there is no father in this image. It is the mother who must primarily perform the juggling act of balancing work and family life.

The 1960s, in general, were filled with days of hope and days of rage. The decade opened up whole new ways of thinking and new realities on all levels of society. Family life was no longer seen as always idyllic, wholesome, or homogeneous. The flower children of the decade sometimes abandoned the nuclear family and sought new family constellations in communes and other family groups. As has been shown, artists depicted the family in a variety of ways.

The decade probably raised as many questions as it provided answers. As one cultural historian noted, "The outcome and meaning of the movements of the sixties are not treasures to be unearthed with an exultant Aha! but sand paintings, something provisional, both created and revised in historical time. Why assume history has a single direction [or a single sense of self], posing clear answers to the question of where it is tending?"[55]

7

The Seventies

The decade of the seventies dawned with the United States' invasion of Cambodia, antiwar demonstrations, and the tragic killing of four students at Kent State University by the Ohio National Guard, all in 1970. Hannah Arendt wrote *On Violence* in the same year. Terror continued into the decade with the death of Israeli athletes at the 1972 Munich Olympics. In 1973 war again broke out between Israel and the Arab countries, and in another part of the globe, President Salvador Allende of Chile was murdered by right-wing forces. In Germany industrialists were killed by secret revolutionary organizations. In Italy Red Brigade terrorists kidnapped and killed former Prime Minister Aldo Moro in 1978.

Besides global unrest, there was a diminishing faith in U.S. government policies and officials. In 1971 the *New York Times* published the Pentagon Papers, which pointed to the government's deception of the public. This exposé was followed by the Watergate burglary in Washington, D.C., in 1972, and the ensuing scandal involving cover-ups led to the threat of the impeachment of U.S. President Richard M. Nixon in 1974. Nixon became the first president of the United States to resign when he left office in 1974, to be succeeded by Gerald Ford. Jimmy Carter was elected two years later, bringing with him older fundamentalist beliefs in religion, the family, and progress through the mind and technology. Evangelical Christianity began to sweep through the United States and had gained more than 50 million devotees by the end of the decade. Attempts to deal with the complexity and uncertainty in the world surfaced in other religious and meditative groups as well. Many turned to Eastern religions and studied Zen Buddhism. Small groups of chanting and dancing members of the Hindu Hare Krishna sect were often seen on street corners, with their shaved heads and flowing gowns. Many people turned to transcendental meditation, or TM, which is based on Indian religious beliefs. Sensitivity or therapeutic, "T," groups also became fashionable in many circles. In the Middle East there was a Muslim revival, a revolution in Iran, and the establishment of an Islamic government by the Ayatollah Khomeini in 1979. The tragic extreme for faithful believers was seen in 1978 when the Reverend Jim Jones and nine hundred of his followers from the People's Temple killed themselves and their children in a mass suicide in the jungle of Guyana. In that same year Karol Wojtyla, a Pole, became Pope John Paul II, the first non-Italian pontiff in four hundred years. A search for spiritual meaning was also reflected in the writings of one of the most prominent writers of the decade, Aleksandr Solzhenitsyn, who was awarded the Nobel Prize for literature in 1970 and whose *Gulag Archipelago* was published in 1974.

It was a decade of feminist politics and solidarity. Kate Millett wrote *Sexual Politics* (1970), and Germaine Greer wrote *The Female Eunuch* (1971). In 1973 the U.S. Supreme Court ruled that abortion was legal. The United Nations declared 1975 the International Year of the Woman, and a world conference on women was held in Mexico City. *Time* magazine's 1975 "Man of the Year" cover was "Women of the Year," with photographs of twelve women who had contributed to the larger society (Betty Ford, the First Lady; Carla Hills, secretary of the U.S. Department of Housing and Urban Development; Ella Grasso, governor of Connecticut; Barbara Jordan, a member of the House of Representatives; Susie Sharp, chief justice of the North Carolina state Supreme Court; Jill Ker Conway, president of Smith College; Billie Jean King, a tennis star; Susan Brownmiller, author of *Against Our Will: Men, Women and Rape*; Addie Wyatt, an advocate for labor; Kathleen

Byerly, a lieutenant commander in the U.S. Navy; Carol Sutton, the first woman managing editor of a major U.S. newspaper, the Louisville *Courier Journal*; and Alison Cheek, the first woman to celebrate communion at a U.S. Episcopal church). The first U.S. National Women's Conference was held in Houston in 1977. More American women joined the workforce and pressed for equal pay and job opportunities.

Blacks pressed for equal opportunities as well, and some of the ideals of the civil rights movement became realities. More blacks entered public office, from Carl Stokes in Cleveland to Thomas Bradley in Los Angeles. Alex Haley's *Roots*, which traced his black heritage, was a best-seller, and its television dramatization in a miniseries was popular.

There was also a demand for tolerance of sexual preference. The gay rights movement was formed in the early 1970s, after the Stonewall riots of 1969, demanding that the law not impinge on the private lives of gays and lesbians.

Scientific exploration continued. The People's Republic of China launched its first satellite in 1970. The United States launched Skylab, the first orbiting space laboratory, in 1973. American and Soviet astronauts met in space in 1975 with the Apollo/Soyuz docking. The U.S. Viking 1 and 2 landed on Mars and sent back photographs in 1976, and the U.S. Pioneer II photographed Saturn's moons, rings, and satellites in 1979.

The 1970s has been called "the Me decade," accentuating the need for instant gratification and a sense of well-being. It was a time of pluralism and eclecticism, in which individuals and individual groups emerged outside the mainstream. Books of this period included Jerzy Kosinski's *Being There* (1970), Frances Fitzgerald's *Fire in the Lake* (1972), Erica Jong's *Fear of Flying* (1973), and William Styron's *Sophie's Choice* (1979). In 1970, Gabriel García Márquez's family chronicle, *One Hundred Years of Solitude*, was translated into English. The engaging novel told the story of the rise and fall of the Buendia family, as love and death, war and peace, and youth and old age were strikingly juxtaposed.

The Me generation also turned to attending museum exhibitions and investing in art. Prices at art auctions soared. Blockbuster art shows, such as *The Treasures of Tutankhamen*, attracted many as the shows toured the United States. Most of these shows focused on art from the past, such as artifacts and treasures from Pompeii, ancient China, or Celtic Ireland. Contemporary artists of the decade reflected the pluralistic spirit of the 1970s, in that they explored a wide variety of materials, forms, and content, further breaking down traditional barriers and definitions of art.

Partially in response to the chaos of society and to the youth movements and drug culture of the late 1960s and early 1970s, a number of films came to deal with the child as sexual, monstrous, selfish, or even cannibalistic. The child became an alien force within the family, who threatened all adult authority. The child became an "other," invading the "normal" world. Thus, in films, such as *The Other* (1972), *The Exorcist* (1973), *The Omen* (1976), and *Audrey Rose* (1977) children ran amok, possessed by the demonic, the supernatural, and the irrational.

Science fiction films like Steven Spielberg's *Close Encounters of the Third Kind* (1977) led to people's reports of contact with alien beings. One writer noted the convergence of the horror, science fiction, and family melodrama genres in the seventies, "testing" the limits of more traditional family configurations, as the family was exposed to horrific and alienating forces, as distinctions between family members and alien others and between public and private space became less pronounced, "and the glaring contradictions which exist between the mythology of family relations and their actual social practice" become apparent.[56] George Lucas's *Star Wars* (1977), a kind of space-age western, emphasizing the heroism of the space hero as good triumphed over evil, became one of the most popular films of all time. It established the fantasy and allure of an "other," an unearthly side of man or woman, both positive and negative, that became a complement to terrestrial perceptions. There seemed to be a strange irony in the fact that the father of Luke Skywalker turned out to be the dark, evil element that was to be fought against in the figure of Darth Vader. (This fact is not learned until a sequel film to *Star Wars*.) With this film, the fantastic, the larger spatial universe, and an extraterrestrial "force" had clearly entered American homes. The Force (Luke's "guardian angel") became an inspiration for many.

Quite different from the space-age films were the epics *The*

Godfather (1972) and *The Godfather, Part II* (1974), directed by Francis Ford Coppola. *Part I*, starring Marlon Brando, Al Pacino, Robert Duvall, James Caan, and Diane Keaton, won Oscars for Best Film, Best Actor (Brando), and Best Screenplay. Although this is a gangster film, there is a deep sense of family and intense loyalty to family members. Here the Mafia take care of their families by means of organized crime. Here is the dark side of the American Dream, in which glamorous, ruthless people aspire to wealth and power. Here life and death and the rituals of family life are portrayed in an intense epic fashion. (The infant in the baptism scene was Coppola's own infant daughter.) In some ways, these epic characters are to be admired, and one cannot help but mourn with Brando and Pacino the murder of Sonny (James Caan).

In *Part II*, the corrupting impact of power is further explored in relation to family life. This film, starring Al Pacino, Robert De Niro, Diane Keaton, John Cazale, Lee Strasberg, Talia Shire, and Troy Donahue, won Oscars for Best Film, Best Director, Best Screenplay, Best Supporting Actor (De Niro), Best Art Director, and Best Original Music. Michael (Pacino) has become head of the Corleone family and ruthlessly attempts to make his family the leader in Mafia circles—at the cost of rejecting his wife (Keaton) and murdering both his brother-in-law and his own brother, Freddie (Cazale). His argument is that all he has done is for the good of the family. But in the end, Michael is alone, omnipotent, but isolated, having been corrupted by the desire to control others totally.

In 1990 Coppola directed *The Godfather, Part III*, starring Pacino, Keaton, George Hamilton, Andy Garcia, Eli Wallach, and his own daughter Sofia, as Pacino's daughter. Here, Pacino attempts to remove himself from the world of crime, but circumstances draw him and his family back into the tides of violence and corruption.

The women in these films are primarily subservient to their men. It is a male culture. But despite the extremes of violence, of the manipulation of power and wealth, these are films that, when the extremes are softened, are about family relationships that could have some bearing on other families' relationships. There may not be physical murders in most families, but there may be psychological or spiritual murders. And conversely, it may not be a powerful Mafia family that sows the seeds of violence, but a small-town, unknown, and less affluent family, in which murder strikes, in which a teenage boy murders his parents and sister.

At the end of the decade, the death of a marriage was poignantly portrayed in *Kramer vs. Kramer* [53], directed by Robert Benton. Based on Avery Corman's novel and starring Dustin Hoffman, Meryl Streep, Jane Alexander, Justin Henry, Howard Duff, and JoBeth Williams, the film won Oscars for Best Picture, Best Actor (Hoffman), Best Screenplay, Best Director, and Best Supporting Actress (Streep). In this film, the home and family life is disrupted by a wife (Streep) walking out on her upwardly mobile husband (Hoffman) and leaving him to care for their young son (Henry). Streep plays a woman who is trying to find herself beyond the walls of domesticity. And one sees the father and son begin to get to know each other in the absence of the

53. *Kramer vs. Kramer*, 1979. Photofest.

mother-wife. The film sensitively touches on some of the agonies of separation and divorce and the social problems that result for parents and children.

In the area of still photography, although many photographers rarely exhibited the strong individualistic, often defiant, visual statements of Robert Frank or William Klein in the 1950s or Diane Arbus in the 1960s, a number had a strong social orientation and had been influenced by the photographers employed by the Farm Security Administration during the Great Depression. One such photographer was Bill Owens, whose 1973 book *Suburbia* dealt with the suburban American Dream, particularly in California, which was not, in Owens's eyes, to be idealized. (Owens also did work for *Newsweek* magazine in which he felt he had less control over the images he shot.) In his book, which was originally to be entitled *Instant America*, Owens included such images as a family putting in an instant sod lawn and a young married couple posed in an empty room, next to a photograph of the couple in the room, filled with plush, new, unimpressive furniture and with an artificial Christmas tree in the corner. Compared to the photo-essays in *Life*, *Look*, or the USA pamphlets in the 1950s, these photographs did not aggrandize or glorify the American Dream and the success of a growing American economy.

Another documentary photographer, Chauncey Hare, made more explicit statements, both visual and verbal, of his personal opinions than did Owens. In his book, *Interior America*, published in 1978, Hare talked about his family and the impact of the American Dream on him and them. His book is also an indictment of the consequences of American industrial production on individuals and the society from the 1950s to the 1970s. Many of the photographs in the book are of bleak interiors of American domestic life. There "were middle-class people looking as if they have been stuffed by taxidermists, in stuffy, old-fashioned living rooms; lower-middle-class adults staring like zombies at television sets; working-class men and women stagnating in tiny apartments, drab rooming houses, and flop houses."[57] Hare's second book, *This Was Corporate America* (1984), went further in visually indicting the workplace as the cause of distress in "interior America."

While these photographers explored domestic interiors, several young women, including Miriam Schapiro and Judy Chicago, who were active in the woman's movement, also explored domestic imagery. In 1970 Schapiro and Chicago sponsored Womanhouse at the California Institute of the Arts in Los Angeles. Through women's experiences, they searched for a collective past and present that could preserve and honor women's contributions to society. Womanhouse, created with students, was the transformation of an abandoned building into a "female" environment based on women's dreams and fantasies. The house or home, which might have once represented a prison of domestic chores, came to represent a world of new possibilities and new dreams, particularly as the women's movement grew in force.

In her own work, Schapiro began to use imagery, as well as actual materials from "women's" history and art, such as scraps of material, yarns, and buttons. She created what she came to call Femmages, a type of feminist collage, a contraction of the words feminine and *image*. Her work not only employed fabric in a beautiful and significantly decorative way, but, in many instances, connected women around the country. Schapiro made these connections by collecting "souvenirs" from women all over the country—tea towels, aprons, handkerchiefs, and embroidered items, all of which she "recycled" in her paintings. She later wrote this about her continuing immersion in the concept of Femmage:

> Femmage is many things. It is work by women of history who saved, pieced, hooked, cut, appliquéd, quilted, tatted, wrote, painted and combined materials using traditional women's techniques to achieve their art activities "also engaged in by men but assigned in history to women." Femmage is also practiced by contemporary women, who like their ancestors, are clear about their womanly life and how it shapes their view of the world. Such artists, like Betye Saar, Mimi Smith, Harmony Hammond, Faith Ringgold, Marybeth Edelson, and I were to reshape artifacts from women's culture and give them new voice.[58]

A major Femmage of the seventies was Schapiro's 1976 *Cabinet for All Seasons*, a monumental piece composed of four 70-by-40-inch panels that were doorlike shapes with trompe l'oeil windows representing each season. The household piece of furniture was also transformed to represent the cyclical role of the seasons and life itself through her shapes and forms. The domestic tasks and artistry of women became globally connected through the overlaid grid work of embroidered handkerchiefs from all over the world.

In a later piece consisting of fabric and canvas, *Welcome to Our Home* [54], Schapiro incorporated images from the house and home—stenciled quilt designs, teapots, heart shapes, tulips, and actual pieces of handmade lace—into a large canvas whose central image is a woman's dress. In the center of the apron is a fetal image. The smaller stenciled images float around the dress and womb, connected to the womb by jagged linear paths, and serve as nourishment for the undeveloped child. Here, Schapiro celebrates elements of domestic life associated traditionally with women, the family, and the home as the tools for and content of mainstream art. The woman as wife, mother, and artist, not simply one or another role, was important. In Schapiro's view, domestic roles were now to have layers added to them by using a collage technique, whereby fragments of various realities could be layered, juxtaposed, and/or fused to create a new reality.

Faith Ringgold also turned to the use of fabric in her work in

54. Miriam Schapiro, *Welcome to Our Home*, 1983. Steinbaum Krauss Gallery, New York.

55. Faith Ringgold, *Mrs. Jones and Family*, 1973. Collection of the artist.

the 1970s as she focused on Afro-American life and her African roots. In 1972 she began painting on cloth, framing her pieces with stitched-together quiltlike pieces. She did a number of three-dimensional images of women and children that reflected her growing feminist consciousness. These life-size doll-like figures were made of brightly colored fabrics with faces inspired by African masks made of beads, shells, and stitched fabric. *Mrs. Jones and Family* [55] is in memory of a woman whom Ringgold loved and admired as a child growing up in Harlem. Three children are gathered around the mother figure, whose masklike head has a wide-eyed and wide-mouthed face made of tapestry, with strings of colored beads at her neck.

In 1976 Ringgold created a series of pieces entitled *The Wake and Resurrection of the Bicentennial Negro* (Steinbaum Krauss Gallery), which focused on events from the private lives of black citizens. One part, entitled *Nana and Moma*, shows two women, Nana and Moma, in mourning. The mixed-media pieces stand 67 inches and 62 inches high, respectively. Another part, *Bena and Buba*, is a soft sculpture of large figures of a black couple lying in state. The entire funeral tableau used five masked figures and four life-size soft sculptures to tell the story of death and resurrection. Originally a performance piece, with music accompanying the sculpture, it told the tale of Buba's death from a heroin overdose and his wife's subsequent death from grief. The performance concluded with a miraculous return to life, which Ringgold presented as a statement of maternal love, represented by Moma. Ringgold said this about the larger political, social, and economic implications of her piece: "I was trying to point to what happened to us in the 200 years of our country, and the resurrection was meant to say, let it not happen again; let us not have the same story to tell in another 200 years."[59]

Ringgold continued to emphasize the quilted elements in her pieces as she used fragments of cloth to create new realities. In tribute to her mother, Ringgold created *Who's Afraid of Aunt Jemima?* in 1983. This dyed, painted, and pieced patchwork-quilt piece combined written black dialect, traditional patterns, and embroidered portraits to tell the fanciful story of the family of Aunt Jemima, who was depicted as a successful and beautiful businesswoman, as well as a family-oriented person.

In 1988 Ringgold created *Tar Beach* (Solomon R. Guggenheim Museum, New York), which lovingly depicted a gathering of family and friends, in a combined painted-and-pieced, dyed-fabric work. The setting is a warm, summer evening on a rooftop in Harlem where the artist was born. Four adults are playing cards while two children lie on a blanket looking up at the stars. The written text at the top and bottom of the quilt tells the story from the perspective of the young girl, who sees the evening as filled with magic and the "stuff" of dreams while she imagines such things as the George Washington Bridge strung with lights as a "giant diamond necklace."

During the 1970s, a number of artists, inspired by the feminist movement, researched their own cultural and actual "foremothers." Betye Saar, for example, in *Veil of Tears*, 1976 (collection of Mr. and Mrs. Alvin P. Johnson), focused on her mother and grandmother in the mixed-media construction in a silverware box. Memories of family are evoked through photographs, kid gloves, handkerchiefs, and jewelry that have been sensitively placed in this assemblage, forming a portrait of the artist's relatives.

Audrey Flack, in her large-scale *Queen* [56], used her photore-

56. Audrey Flack, *Queen*, 1975–76. Louis K. Meisel Gallery, New York.

alist techniques to combine still-life imagery with autobiographical elements and a feminist historical sense. The painting, with its luxurious colors and reflective surfaces, combines locket photographs of the artist as a young girl and of her mother with traditional metaphoric images of flowers and fruit related to the female; cosmetic pots; perfume vials; personal mementos, such as a key chain with the letter "F" or a jar of model airplane paint; and the queen of hearts playing cards, along with the queen from a chess set—the game's most mobile player. A pocket watch marks the passage of time. Here is a portrait of specific individuals, as well as of connections with universal female symbols, connecting Flack's family, at least the female members of it, to a wider "herstory."

It is perhaps not surprising that a number of the images discussed here, particularly the painted and cloth pieces, were done by women as they sought to combine issues of the feminist movement with traditional domestic materials and images, such as quilted fragments and pieces. It is noteworthy that these surfaces are not smooth and coherent overall. Rather, they are fragmented, pieced, and sometimes layered, as woman's and family's lives were increasingly to become, especially as more and more women entered the workforce and the demands on and difficulties of two-career families and of one-parent families grew. In some of these works, there is a new sense of optimism, different from the disillusionment of the 1960s. Some of the interest in collage elements also reflected the rise of Postmodernism, in which narrative, historical quotation, appropriation, complexity, ornament, and metaphor came to have a role because the spare, sleek, flat forms of Modernism no longer had as much relevance in artistic expression.

Nicholas Africano explored the role of narrative and modes of communication between individuals in his work, in which his small figures appear as if they were on an empty stage set. In *The Cruel Discussion* [57], the space may be seen as a metaphor for a psychological and spiritual emptiness in a world where it is often difficult to communicate truly with others. The placement of the two figures, slightly off center, close but not too close for any real communication, sets off a wave of discomfort within the viewer who may confront his or her own loneliness, or sense of alienation.

Not a large number of artists were concerned with family and domestic imagery, to some extent because the feminist movement

57. Nicholas Africano, *The Cruel Discussion*, 1977. Holly Solomon Gallery, New York.

was urging women to explore opportunities outside the home. During the 1970s, the "number of unmarried couples who were living together tripled; among those age 25 and under with no children, it increased eightfold. Although living together usually represented a postponement rather than a rejection of marriage, it changed the pattern of dating and mating that had characterized earlier decades."[60]

There was also an increasing visibility of gay men and lesbians, who were calling for freedom of choice in sexual matters, thereby decreasing the "need" for heterosexual marriages. Marriage and family, in general, were no longer necessarily normative. Divorce was also becoming more prevalent. By the end of the 1970s, the image of the lovely, clear picture window in the house of the American Dream not only had cracks, but, in some instances, had actually shattered, leaving only shards and fragments of broken glass to be reassembled, replaced, or discarded completely.

8

The Eighties and Early Nineties

W hereas the journalist and novelist Tom Wolfe called the seventies "the Me decade," he called the eighties the decade of money fever. In the United States, in particular, there was an emphasis on making money, on commodities, on entrepreneurial projects. Donald Trump and Trump Tower were, for many, at the top of the ladder to be climbed. Works of art became an integral part of the emphasis on commodities and big business. By the end of the decade, the art world was a complex web of big money, the politics of exhibition, dealer-gallery relationships, and conflicts between the artist's studio and the marketplace. Art was becoming a type of status symbol in certain affluent circles.

While some thirsted for economic power and status, others thirsted for spiritual fulfillment. For some baby boomers who were entering midlife (in the United States there were over 60 million of them) the fixation on money, power, and materialism caused a spiritual void and the quest for something more. It was also a time of remembrance, a time to assimilate decades of war; antiwar protests; the women's, environmental, and civil rights movements; and the ferment caused by Mikhail S. Gorbachev and leaders in Europe, Japan, the Middle East, and Latin America. Joseph Campbell, a scholar and specialist in comparative mythology, became somewhat of a new cult figure as his reissued 1949 book

The Hero with a Thousand Faces, a comparative study of Eastern and Western myths, was on the *New York Times* best-seller list for sixteen weeks in 1988. A second book, *The Power of Myth*, based on Campbell's conversations with Bill Moyers, was on the list for over twenty-five weeks, and more than thirty-five thousand video-tapes of the Moyers-Campbell conversations were sold. The search for a new spiritual energy led to further religious emphasis, in the exploration of a variety of Christian, Jewish, Islamic, and Buddhist beliefs, as well as to individualized prayer outside any specific religious orientation.

The quest for renewed spiritual meanings may also be seen as a response to events in the world at large. The decade opened with the eruption of Mount St. Helens in Washington State in 1980. Also in 1980, there was a botched U.S.-Iran hostage rescue, Ronald Reagan was elected president, and the Iran-Iraq War began. In 1981 both President Reagan and Pope John Paul II were victims of assassination attempts, and Egyptian President Anwar Sadat was murdered. In the same year, France elected its first Socialist president, François Mitterrand, while martial law was declared in Poland. The year 1982 brought the Falklands War, the United States' backing of the Nicaraguan Contras versus the San-dinistas, and the death of Soviet President Leonid Brezhnev. In 1983 Lech Walesa, leader of the Solidarity movement in Poland, was awarded the Nobel Prize for Peace. In 1984 India's prime minister, Indira Gandhi, was assassinated and Ronald Reagan was reelected. Mikhail Gorbachev became leader of the Soviet Union in 1985 and introduced his policies of glasnost and perestroika, which created a new openness in the Soviet Union and increased contact and cultural exchanges with the West. In 1989 the opening of the Congress of People's Deputies marked the first national assembly in seven decades in the Soviet Union in which most members were chosen through competitive elections. In late 1989, the Berlin Wall was torn down, bringing promises of a more open Europe and hopes for a united Germany.

A push toward openness was also felt in China, where in early 1989, massive student demonstrations called for the ouster of Primer Minister Li Peng and democratic reforms. A group of art students constructed and erected a twenty-seven-foot sculpture of plaster and plastic foam, modeled after the Statue of Liberty, in Tiananmen Square, in the heart of Beijing. Called the *Goddess of Democracy and Freedom,* the statue symbolized the students' common hopes for democracy. But "Freedom Spring" was short-lived and ended in violence and suppression, when hundreds were injured and killed by Chinese government troops.

If there was increased tolerance in Soviet-Western relations, there was decreased tolerance of apartheid policies in South Africa. By the mid–1980s, there were frequent antiapartheid protests in both the United States and Europe. There were more terrorist attacks, too, by the mid–1980s—in particular, the 1985 Palestinian attacks on the Rome and Vienna airports. In 1988 a terrorist bomb smuggled onto a Pan Am plane exploded over Scotland, killing most of its innocent passengers.

A 1986 nuclear accident in Chernobyl in the USSR brought home the perils of nuclear power and further inspired antinuclear movements and demonstrations. That same year also brought the tragic explosion of the Challenger space shuttle seconds after its take-off. A nation watched television in horror as the crew of seven, including a New Hampshire schoolteacher, was killed before its very eyes. The U.S. Iran-Contra scandal was also exposed that year.

"Black Monday" came in 1987, when world stock markets plunged downward and many feared a severe depression similar to the one that followed the 1929 crash. But the market rallied and revived, leaving the fever for money still much a part of the decade. Another positive sign in 1987 was the Reagan-Gorbachev Washington Summit and the signing of the INF (Intermediate-range Nuclear Forces) treaty, aimed at reducing missile arsenals in Europe. In 1988 a Reagan-Gorbachev Moscow Summit was held, and the USSR's withdrawal from its war in Afghanistan began. In 1988 the Republican George Bush was elected president of the United States, after a campaign that illustrated the immense power of the media, particularly television.

In 1989, the world watched as the Berlin Wall came down; in 1990 Germany was united for the first time since 1945. The early nineties brought the end of Communist hegemony in eastern Europe as the Soviet Union was broken up. Civil war was unleashed in the former Yugoslavia, and the siege of Sarajevo began in 1992. In the same year Bill Clinton was elected U.S. president, and the United States sent troops to a starving Somalia to restore order and protect relief shipments. In 1990 Nelson Mandela won release from prison after twenty-seven years, and free elections for black and white voters were held in South Africa several years later as promises to end apartheid were made. In the United States the early 1990s brought the Clarence Thomas–Anita Hill hearings in the Senate as questions about sexual discrimination rose to the forefront. The tragedy of Waco, Texas, also burned heavily in the hearts of many, when children and families died in the explosive flames of the Branch Davidian complex. And, in April 1995, the chilling bombing of a federal building in Oklahoma City took away the innocence of many, when children and adults were killed in a senseless act of terrorism.

Outside the political arena, the world of science brought forth the first artificial heart transplant at the Utah Medical Center. Other than the 1986 Challenger disaster, the space program had launched the first woman, Sally K. Ride, into space in 1983; brought back photographs of Saturn's rings with Voyager II; and sent up Giotto, a mission to Halley's Comet in 1986. What the world of science could not conquer was the scourge of AIDS, which brought death to growing numbers of both the homosexual and heterosexual population in the 1980s and 1990s. The disease inspired a number of artists to help raise money for research for its cure.

In music, the experimental compositions of Philip Glass and Steve Reich became more widely accepted. John Cage served as Charles Eliot Norton Lecturer at Harvard University. His composition *101* was created from 487 quotations from political, literary, and philosophical sources, chopped up by a computer using a program based on the I Ching.

Literary achievements included William Golding's *Rites of Passage* (1980), Gabriel García Márquez's *Chronicle of a Death Foretold* (1982), Keri Hulmes's *The Bone People* (1986), and Garrison Keillor's *Lake Wobegon Days* (1986). In 1988 Toni Morrison received the Pulitzer Prize for her novel *Beloved*, in which a mother, Sethe, kills her children, rather than return them to slavery. Powerful and compelling, the book forced the reader to confront issues surrounding family and love in a chronicle of slavery and its aftermath, set in rural Ohio shortly after the Civil War.

By the 1980s, the influence of deconstructionism was widespread, and figures such as Jacques Derrida and Michel Foucault were popular in American graduate schools. In broad terms, to deconstruct a "text," such as the Declaration of Independence or a painting by Van Gogh, meant to pick it apart, in search of ways in which it failed to make the points it seemed to be trying to make. The world was not to be seen as a simple and certain reality. "Texts, works of art, merely transform other texts and other works of art in a reticulative and spiralling continuum across time. The informing fabric, common to all, is that of the medium and of available conventions. Individual poetic 'genius' or historical singularity are totemic notions, largely illusory. . . . In the poststructuralist and deconstructive model, it is the reader who produces the text, the viewer who generates the painting."[61]

Foucault emphasized the role of the principle of power in studying history and culture. Culture was to be studied through technologies and systems of power—not through class, "progress," or the human spirit. For Foucault, one was never outside some type of power relationship. "Relations of power are interwoven with other kinds of relations (production, kinship, family, sexuality),"[62] and are to be studied through their discourses. For some, the language of discourse was to become a prison.

The term *deconstruction* was used more specifically in relation to some art forms, as traditional forms and shapes were "deconstructed" by artists while questioning assumptions about the very nature of art and architecture. Frank Gehry, for example, designed a home in 1983 for a screen writer, the Norton House, Venice, California, which was an assemblage of cheap materials and odd forms that resembled a lifeguard station (the screen writer had, at one time, been a lifeguard). For his own home in Santa Monica, begun a few years earlier, Gehry had wrapped his small pink stucco house on an ordinary street with a layer of new rooms constructed from "junk" materials, such as corrugated metal and raw wood.

If part of our sense of self is somehow influenced by the spaces we inhabit, and/or if the design of architectural spaces is a reflection or extension of "self," then deconstructivist designs also spoke about a perception of self as layered and/or fragmented. Foucault, though, would state that one cannot recognize anything as given. "Nothing in man—not even his body—is sufficiently stable to serve as the basis for self-recognition or for understanding other men."[63]

The role of power was also seen in the power of the media, which was becoming increasingly significant. The artist Thomas Lawson spoke of the

insistent penetration of the mass media into every facet of our daily lives [that] has made the possibility of authentic experience difficult, if not impossible. Our daily encounters with one another, and with nature, our gestures, our speech are so thoroughly impregnated with a rhetoric absorbed through the airwaves, that we can have no certain claim to the originality of any of our actions. Every cigarette, every love affair echoes down a never-ending passage-way of references—to advertisements, to television shows, to movies, to the point where we no longer know if we mimic or are mimicked.[64]

The question, "What is real?" readily arose. Is the media representation more "real" than the event or person? Which comes first: the map or the territory? Jean Baudrillard spoke of the "precession of the simulacra," that "illusion is no longer possible, because the real is no longer possible."[65]

A number of artists and writers demonstrated that "'reality,' whether concrete or abstract, is a fiction, produced and sustained only by its cultural representation."[66] The self was viewed by some as a construct made by "cultural representation."

The challenges concerning absolute representation and notions of what constituted reality reflected, to some extent, continuing challenges to the notion of what a family was. During the 1980s, the consequences of the sexual revolution of the 1970s, the rising divorce rate, the growing number of working mothers, the demands for gay rights, and so on led to a rethinking and reshaping of the family. Issues related to day care, abused children, abducted children, and teenage pregnancies also became part of public discussion and controversy.

In the 1980 presidential campaign, Ronald Reagan used issues of the family for his conservative campaign. "Family, work, and neighborhood" were near the top of his rhetorical vocabulary. While in office, though, Reagan limited or cut spending in a number of programs that involved children and social services between 1981 and 1984. While cutting governmental spending to assist families, the Reagan administration encouraged Americans to live by "traditional" family values.

During the 1980s and early 1990s, the "family" became a buzzword for both political parties. Conservatives tended to voice opposition to governmental programs to aid individuals and families, while liberals defended governmental programs designed to help those suffering from poverty, abuse, and other problems. Debates on such issues as abortion, women's rights, the prerogatives of parents, the authority of husbands and/or fathers, the rights of children, adolescent sexuality, child care, and the like were frequently controversial or ended in deadlock.

As the eighties and now the nineties pass us by, conceptions of the family and domesticity have been pervaded by images of divorce, the working mother, the single parent, gay parents, *Roe vs. Wade*, *Murphy Brown*, Los Angeles riots, or *Iron John*. The darker, shadowy side of domesticity seems to be even more clearly and strongly expressed. Just as the turn of the nineteenth century was characterized by some as a period of malaise, so may the turn of the twentieth century be characterized as a time of dis-ease, of fragmentation; the breaking down of traditions and values are a part of everyday lives for individuals and entire countries. In his book, *The Saturated Self*, Kenneth Gergen pointed to the problems of social saturation by which we are bombarded with emerging technologies, with rapid change, and frequent fragmentation, thus making it difficult to have any sense of an "authentic" self. As he noted:

> This fragmentation of self-conceptions corresponds to a multiplicity of incoherent and disconnected relationships. These relationships pull in myriad directions. Each reality of self gives way to reflexive questioning, irony, and ultimately the playful probing of yet another reality, the center fails to hold.[67]

Lorie Novak's 1987 work, *Fragments* [58], may serve to illustrate, in part, this phenomenon. The photograph consists of a couple standing with a little girl in front of a child's portrait. Before them is a table filled with fragments of photographs and reflections of photographs. Where is the self?—in a painted portrait, in a photograph of the little girl's portrait, in the reflections, in the cut-up pieces? There is no longer a definitive answer to such a question.

A later installation piece by Novak, entitled *Traces*, which was placed in a darkened side gallery at Tufts University's 1993 exhibit, *Betrayal of Means; Means of Betrayal*, explored photography's role as a conveyor of cultural information and family identity. This piece involved projected photographic images from Novak's past ("standard" family-album shots) that were interspersed with scenes from concurrent public events, including civil rights marches, the Vietnam War, Woodstock, and the explosion of the atomic bomb. The feeling of a suburban backyard was simulated by the simultaneously projected images of water on a portable swimming pool. A sound track of live radio scanning accompanied the visual images.

58. Lorie Novak, *Fragments*, 1987. Collection of the artist.

This montage of public and private images suggested the influence of the intersection of public and private photography in the shaping of individual and family identities. The piece also implied, through its structure, the interchangeability of such public and private experiences in a world of instant media presentation. In a piece such as this, photography was seen as a possible manipulator of the truth, not necessarily as a "guardian" of the "truth" (which, in itself, may be debatable), as it was once traditionally viewed. The concept and image of the family album is thus deconstructed and reconstituted.

The concept of the family album and the myth of the American family were further explored by photographer Nan Goldin in her *The Ballad of Sexual Dependency*. The work appeared as a body of 35 mm color slides with a musical soundtrack that Goldin presented to audiences and as a book published by the Aperture Foundation in 1986. This is Goldin's extended family taken over a ten-year period. But these figures are primarily economically and socially unstable. The book opens with a shot of Goldin hugging "her man," juxtaposed with a photograph of her stiff, formal-looking, tight-lipped parents at a French restaurant. The parents are juxtaposed with a picture of wax effigies of the Duke and Duchess of Windsor at the Coney Island Wax Museum. We later see images of tension, estrangement, erotic desire, frustration, and regret. We see strange weddings, raunchy parties; we see Goldin after she was battered. The work is presented in a manner similar to a family snapshot album. But this album is filled not with the joy of remembered family events and rites of passage, but with the sadness of difficult and unsuccessful relationships with Goldin's immediate and "extended" family.

A somewhat different depiction of family scenes was found in the staged photographs of Sandy Skoglund. What might be images from a family album appear to be invaded. Skoglund created eerie room-size environments, such as *Radioactive Cats*, 1980 (collection of the artist) or her *Revenge of the Goldfish* [59]. In *Radioactive Cats*, which can be viewed as both humorous and horrifying, one sees an aging couple in an impoverished kitchen, invaded by sculpted fluorescent green-colored cats, searching for food. The entire room—furnishings and clothes, except for the skin tones of the couple—are a mottled gray color. The older

59. Sandy Skoglund, *The Revenge of the Goldfish*, 1981. Collection of the artist.

woman, whose back is to the viewer, peers into the empty refrigerator. *The Revenge of the Goldfish* depicts a young boy and his sleeping mother in a blue bedroom that has been invaded by a school of one hundred forty ceramic goldfish painted in high-key orange. The fish are on the floor, in the air, in drawers—everywhere. In both these photographs, what could have been somewhat harmonious domestic scenes are now invaded by outside, fantastic elements. Skoglund's images, at once witty and frightening, point to domestic scenes that can quickly change owing to constructions of our minds or to actual alien forces and to how we deal with such changes.

A number of photographers used primarily their own families as the main subjects of their work, in both positive and negative depictions. Some artists, such as Sally Mann and Tina Barney, worked exclusively with family subject matter. Some worked on family imagery over a period of years, visually portraying changes in individuals and family groups over time. Tom Bamberger, an adjunct curator of photography at the Milwaukee Art Museum,

noted some of the complexities and difficulties inherent in photographing one's own family in a modern and postmodern world:
"Modernism . . . with its heroic posture and quest for universal
truth . . . is inconsistent with the specificity and the vulnerability
inherent in family stories. Post Modernism's denial of *self* (the idea
we are a species of the mass media), and its theoretical posturing, is
at odds with what can be understood as the most self-indulgent
and intimate quest for *self* imaginable."[68]

In her photographic installation work, *Valuable Papers: Con-
structing My Father/Myself*, 1992, Karen Ellen Johnson attempted
to explore her complicated relations with her estranged father,
Ernie Johnson. She combined "valuable papers," such as military-
discharge papers, divorce papers, food stamp agreements, court
summons, and the like, from her father's life with visual images, in
an attempt both to deconstruct and to reconstruct her father's life
after his death and her life with him. For example, around a reproduction of her paternal grandparents' wedding portrait, in a piece
entitled *Dad Never Told Me*, 1992, Johnson hand wrote the following text:

> Wedding picture—Lillie Belle Murray Johnson and Albin Amil
> Johnson. Grandpa Johnson died with his feet propped on the oven
> door, age 51. Dad never told me. Grandpa thought it was indiges-
> tion. Dad never told me. Grandma Johnson tried to hold death
> back by pulling him close to her. Dad never told me. Grandma
> Johnson died in the Topeka State Mental Hospital, age 49. Dad
> never told me. She died covered with bruises. Dad never told me.
> Grandpa Johnson got Dad drunk with him. Dad never told me. . . .

In a series of photographs entitled *Enough?* Johnson took old
snapshots from a family album and blackened out her father's
image. In one photograph, she appears as a little girl floating in an
ominous black field (the arms of her father).

Beginning in 1983, the photographer Larry Sultan began to
spend much time with his parents, going through family albums
and movies, talking with his parents, and taking photographs. His
photographs, *Pictures from Home*, were shown in installation form,
and Sultan also completed a book, *Pictures from Home* (1992),

which included a text, photographs by Sultan, and photographs from the family albums. The project started as one with a sociological and deconstructive emphasis, but became a continuing constructive process in which Sultan and his parents came to know each other and themselves as individuals better. In the text, Sultan referred to his ongoing search for identity, which he came to realize had begun years before. He wrote:

> Mine was a collage of personalities and themes taken from various television shows. I was Tim Tyler of the Ivory Patrol, Spin from "The Mickey Mouse Club," Robbie from "My Three Sons." I made up stories about losing my teeth in a bad fight. I shaved my head to look tough. . . .
>
> It has taken me years to remember, or to admit to myself, that included in this repertoire of fictional selves was my father, or at least some younger version of him. I usually pictured him (me) standing off to the side of the school yard, leaning against the wall, wearing a clean white T-shirt stretched loose around the neck, looking real good without having to think about it or try too hard. . . . He may have been Frank Sinatra to my mother, but to me he was James Dean.[69]

In this quote, one cannot help but notice Sultan's mention of movie and television figures as points of reference in the formation and articulation of identity. We see the role of the mass media again in a photograph of Sultan's parents, entitled *My Mother Posing for Me*, 1984 (Janet Borden, Inc.). Sultan's mother stands tall and thin, with white pants and a silk shirt with a wide black belt, leaning against the backdrop of a pea-green wall. To her right, we see the back of Sultan's father as he intently watches a baseball game, seemingly oblivious to his wife posing for her son. The posed and unposed are thus juxtaposed in this somewhat eerie portrait.

In her large-format color photographs, Tina Barney also depicted her family, as well as friends—all white, upper-middle-class Americans. The settings of her large-scale pieces, which are filled with alluring colors and textures, are the richly decorated apartments, country homes, gardens, and beaches of the affluent.

Barney, a descendant of the Lehman family of New York, who are known to the art world for their endowment of a wing at the Metropolitan Museum of Art, had no formal art training and was introduced to photography when she was asked to join the Junior Council of the Museum of Modern Art in 1971. In 1973, when she moved to Sun Valley, Idaho, she began to take photography classes.

In her work, she invites the viewer into her almost life-size photographs that speak of intimacy, good taste, and informality (although her pieces are carefully arranged in advance). Barney said of her work, "I'm documenting something that's important historically, that has never been done before, in photography at least, from the inside—a way of life that I don't think might ever happen again in America, because our priorities, or the ways people choose to spend their time, have changed so much. The time that it takes to live with quality—in a style of life that has quality—is disappearing."[70] She also noted, "Everyone is afraid of her own life."[71] Some of this fear–of the unknown or of fear itself—is taken away as we are invited to share in the preparations for a Thanksgiving meal in the kitchen in *Thanksgiving* [60] or as we sit in the kitchen on a summer day as three little girls sit around a table with paper cups and various snacks, including a graham cracker box, in *The Graham Cracker Box*, 1983. A teenager, talking on the phone, lounges on a chair in the background, while a woman in white tennis clothes stands by the stove. Although Barney's photographs are of the upper class, they are not pretentious and appear accessible to a variety of viewers because of the informality and intimacy of the images. Some of the photographs, particularly those that emphasize the furnishings of the setting, such as *John's Den* (1985), are like large still-lifes in which the figures are an integral part of the total scene. As in *John's Den*, Barney's figures are frequently arranged in a triangular format, bringing a harmony and sense of repose to the pieces in a classical manner. Her large, color, atmospheric works are, in some ways, akin to those of the intimist painters Édouard Vuillard and Pierre Bonnard, who frequently painted domestic scenes. Barney's photographs also evidence a great deal of trust and intensity of relationships between the photographer and her subjects. Barney stated, "I want this pure con-

60. Tina Barney, *Thanksgiving*, 1992. Museum of Fine Arts, Boston.

centrated attention, one-on-one, that most family members do not give today. It's pure, rich, and intense. When we finish I know that. Afterwards, we sense a feeling of accomplishment, that we made art based on a one-to-one communication. . . . Most important to me is the question: how can you possibly express the extent of how much you love someone? There is no way. The feeling is so powerful."[72] Barney's photographs are testimonials and memorials to those she loves, in formal and informal settings.

Sally Mann also photographed those she loved—her children, in particular. Working in black and white, with a large-format camera and frequently staging her images, Mann presents a sensuality and precociousness in her children that has been difficult for some to deal with. Prior to her 1992 book *Immediate Family*, some of the images in her book *At Twelve* (1988) were attacked by some as pornographic as Mann explored the territory between childhood and adulthood in adolescent young girls. In *Immediate Family* (Aperture Foundation, 1992) some of the images are both disturb-

61. Sally Mann, *The New Mothers*, 1989. Houk Friedman Gallery, New York.

ing and alluring. For example, in *The New Mothers* [61], one sees two children playing with their dolls. The little girls stand in provocative poses, hands on their hips, one in sunglasses, one with a cigarette in her hand. The serious looks on their young innocent faces suggest that although this is "play," childhood is indeed short, or even nonexistent. In *Emmett's Bloody Nose* (1985), we see two young boys lying hand in hand, Emmett with blood gushing from his nose, dripping down to his shirt. Emmett's angelic, pure face is stained and marred, just as the innocence of childhood will be at some point.

In many of Mann's photographs, the children appear nude, sometimes innocent, sometimes provocative, suggesting a latent sexuality and the journey to adulthood and sexuality. Mann has spoken of the role of memory in her work, that her photographs "open doors into the past, but they also look into the future. . . . In this confluence of past and future, reality and symbol are Emmett, Jessie, and Virginia. Their strength and confidence, there to be seen in their eyes, are compelling—for nothing is so seductive as a gift casually possessed."[73]

To counter comments that she has exploited her children in some ways, Mann stated:

> There are times when I look at my life, and the lives of my children and I think, when is the bubble going to burst. We have ordinary problems but we have such a profoundly happy and cohesive life here. It's grounded in a piece of land; we actually have roots, real genuine southern roots. . . .
>
> So when I show these pictures it's with an enormous sense of certainty. I've expressed a lot of uncertainty about the ultimate implications of these photographs as they get out into the greater world. But as they are taken, and as they are displayed, or as I hold them in my hands, they really only express the beauty, individuality, and love that exists in this family.[74]

On a positive note, Nicholas Nixon celebrates the everyday gestures of his family, especially his two young children, Sam and Clementine, and his wife Bebe. We see close-ups of these little children, alone and with their mother. Nixon's pictures merge the spontaneity of snapshots and the intentionality of the large-format process. For example, in a close-up of a child nursing, with wide eyes, we see the details of eyelashes, eyebrows, and skin tones as the baby is absorbed in sucking at her mother's breast. Or we see Sam and Bebe embracing each other on Sam's bed with a teddy bear at its head. Nixon photographed his family intensively between 1985 and 1991. A book of some of these *Family Pictures* (Smithsonian Institution Press) appeared in 1991. In these photographs, we also feel Nixon's own presence in the heightened sense of intimacy that is depicted. The separation between Nixon and those he is photographing seems to disappear.

Beginning in 1975, Nixon also photographed his wife Bebe and her three sisters, Heather, Mimi, and Laurie, once a year every year for a number of years. His scenes of the Brown sisters mark a journey through time as the sisters age and change over time. The group portraits are simple and direct but speak eloquently about relationships through gestures and pose. Taken singularly, they may be little more than sensitive family portraits lifted from an album. But as a group, they stand as a provocative and universal reflection of the implications of growing older. It has been asked why images such as these do not remain in a family album, rather than appear in an exhibition like the Museum of Modern Art's 1978 *Mirrors and Windows* exhibition (a retrospective of American photography since 1960), curated by John Szarkowski, or later in *Artforum* (December 1981 and 1986). By being called art and placed in a museum setting, the photographs quickly raise the question, Who decides what is art, and what kind of meanings can be elicited from such specific portraits? But as Henry Sayre noted, "the ultimate source of the 'window' photograph's [as these of the Brown Sisters] power and interest is, I think, its very specificity, its complicity with the exigencies of historical time, its *documentary* status. The question is just what meanings such documents can begin to elicit."[75] Nixon's photograph challenged notions of "high" art and pointed to the power of a vernacular aesthetic. Also significant was the repetitive quality of the photographs of the Brown Sisters—a repetition that could generate a sense of the family as a simulacrum.[76]

Nixon photographed not only his own family, but family images of some people who were afflicted with AIDS. Although the photographs were considered controversial by some because of the difficult subject matter, they are compelling. At times, the images are difficult to view for an extended period because the ravages of the dreaded disease are captured on film. But the dignity of the subject is always maintained. The viewer may be both sympathetic to the subject and outraged at the devastation of the incurable disease. The depiction of family relations, such as *Tom Moran and His Mother, Catherine* [62], points to the power of human tenderness and love as we see Catherine Moran embrace the cheek of her haggard, disease-ridden son.

The photographer Sage Sohier chose to examine the lives and homes of gay couples. Between August 1985 and September 1988, she photographed approximately one hundred thirty couples in a number of different cities across the United States. She wrote of her work:

62. Nicholas Nixon, *Tom Moran and His Mother, Catherine*, 1987. Zabriskie
Gallery, New York.

I undertook the project because I was moved by the profound
impact of AIDS on the gay community. My goal was to make pictures of gay couples that would "ring true" to the straight viewer.
At the same time, any photograph that strikes us as both familiar
and unfamiliar causes us to question our own premises—our own
view of the world, our own sexuality—and thus brings about a
certain discomfort. My hope was to lead the viewer through a process of self-questioning and discomfort to a feeling of greater
openness and to an understanding of common ground. . . . My
intention was to show the abundance and diversity of gay and lesbian couples, as well as their range of tastes and styles.[77]

Instead of the "abnormal" some may associate with gay
lifestyles, one finds in Sohier's photographs many of the accou-
trements of the idealized home—including loving hugs, the family
dogs, and stuffed animals. Although these things may not necessarily imply that gay homes may be exactly like straight homes,
they do convey a tenderness without sentimentality. For example,

one sees Sohier's photograph of *Gordon and Jim, with Gordon's Mother Margot, San Diego, California,* 1987 (Museum of Modern Art, New York), in which the three are seated on a large, comfortable, floral-print couch. Gordon embraces his frail-looking mother with one hand while clasping the hand of Jim with the other hand.

This photograph appeared in a significant show mounted by the Museum of Modern Art in 1991—*Pleasures and Terrors of Domestic Comfort,* curated by Peter Galassi. The exhibit included approximately one hundred fifty images by diverse artists, such as Lee Friedlander, Sally Mann, Nicholas Nixon, Carrie Mae Weems, William Eggleston, Nan Goldin, Tom Bamberger, Lorie Novak, and Tina Barney. The show dealt with both positive and negative aspects and images of domestic life—both a bright side and, at times, intimations of a dark underside. The photographers, in general, did not take on the detached views of social critics, but had frequently chosen to photograph "at home" as an opportunity to explore and perhaps unravel threads of a complicated present and past that were tangled in the complexities of contemporary life. Some critics complained that the show was not political enough and lacked any serious reflection or concern for the "personal as political."[78]

Other artists have enlisted the computer as a tool to present photographic images, to enter the maze of memory, and to create narratives that give a visual reality to various views of our lives. The computer has enabled some photographers not only to construct images related to individual and collective memories, but to mirror in their work the very process of memory itself. Editing and selection of fragments or parts to contribute to a whole are a significant part of the process.

Martina Lopez used the computer to make a collage of landscapes and groups of family images from her own albums and from other photographs she found. *In the Way of Tradition 2* [63], for example, juxtaposes a young woman in nineteenth-century dress with two peasant women, a young girl dressed in a fairy princess costume, and a baby. In the distance is an old castle, a group on bicycles, and several tiny silhouetted "modern" couples. The figures are set in a large, open, dreamlike landscape. Juxtaposing and layering different generations and families, Lopez seems to suggest that

63. Martina Lopez, *In the Way of Tradition 2*, 1992. Collection of the artist.

our memories are like the fragments of the seen, the unseen, and the synthesized that have been combined into this presentation of a new reality. The notion of "a truth" remains open in her collages. When the viewer sees that the artist's process may be akin to the viewer's own way of establishing personal histories, Lopez's "family" may, in some instances, become the viewer's family. The large-scale format of the piece makes the images all the more alluring, and compelling.

The computer also has the capacity to invent totally new images, thereby eliminating a relationship between an artist and the figures portrayed, as well as any dialogue with past images, as in the works of Meyer and Lopez. The cover of a special issue of *Time* (Fall 1993), for example, featured an image of a young woman by imaging specialist Kin Wah Lam, totally done on the computer (over sixty-five hours of work), to dramatize the impact of interethnic marriage, which has increased dramatically in the United States in recent years. This creation of cybergenesis was chosen as a symbol of the future multiethnic face of America. "She" (or whoever may be created) did not exist in flesh and blood, but only on the computer. Questions of self and images of self thus become increasingly complex as computers come to have a role in the presentation and representation of individuals and families.

Questions about "a self" and the actual erosion of self, as well as the failure of a sense of any center in our beings, may be seen as part of the demise of the traditional nuclear family and the resulting lives of fragmentation, with little sense of integration, as was seen in the work of some of the photographers discussed here, such as Novak, Goldin, Johnson, and Skoglund. In the 1980s and early 1990s, tales of alcoholism, sexual abuse, violence, voyeurism, and other ills that were once part of stories one often read about only in newspapers and magazines began to dominate television more pervasively than in printed media and became more frequently the subject of artists' works. The title of a 1992 exhibit at the DeCordova Museum in Lincoln, Massachusetts, *Good-bye to Apple Pie: Contemporary Artists View the Family in Crisis,* suggested that the family was in crisis—a crisis that, in the eyes of some artists, should no longer be hidden by politeness and propriety. The artists in this exhibit explored domestic stress, violence, and abuse in a

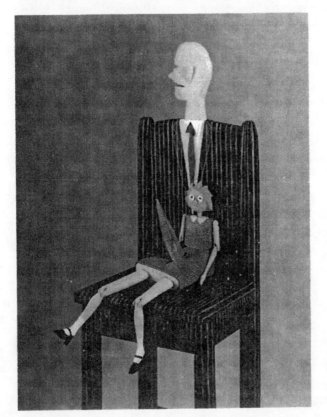

64. Marilyn Keating, *Father Knows Best*, 1986. Collection of the artist.

variety of media, using diverse techniques, such as humor, wit, irony, and Expressionism.

Marilyn Keating's beautifully colored and well-crafted wood sculptures drew on folk traditions. Colorful and playful forms are quickly jarred by the violence of the image with the intrusion of large phallic-like knives. Her titles, such as *Father Knows Best* [64] and *Beaver Cleaver Sickness* (1989), demanded a reevaluation of the role that the illusions of popular culture have played in various domestic situations. In *Father Knows Best*, one sees a little girl seated in the large lap (the seat of a chair) of a man in a pin-striped business suit; she is violated by the "phallic" knife thrust between her legs. Keating's interest in family abuse was stimulated by listening to stories of abused women when she worked for Tradeswomen of Philadelphia, teaching carpentry and electrical skills to low-income women. Her anger and frustration on hearing such stories led her to create this series of painted wood sculptures.

Mark Greenwold explored scenes of family violence through tiny gouache paintings with meticulous, realistic details that, from a distance, appear to be intimate genre paintings. But the middle-class interiors are stage sets for family violence. The disproportionate heads of the adults suggest a freakishness or abnormality that is analogous to the abnormal behavior that is being played out. In

65. Mark Greenwold, *The Broken Home*, 1983–84. Phyllis Kind Gallery, New York and Chicago.

The Broken Home [65], one sees a couple in conflict. The man is about to throw something at his wife. A young boy stands with his arm outstretched, a gun in his hand.

Yochwed Weinfeld juxtaposed appropriated classical Renaissance images of the Madonna and child (the classical parent-child image) next to the abusive horrors that Jews, women, and children may experience or have experienced. Under the central panels of her polyptychs, which are part of a series on motherhood, are familiar comforting phrases, such as "It's just a fairy tale" and "Mommy loves you, Sweetie." On one level, these words are "sweet nothings," that reflect a mother's desire to protect her child from the perils and possible terrors of the wider world. They point to the dilemma of many parents and children who must grow up in a world that is often beset with insensitivity, inhumanity, and/or violence. On either side of the harmonious mother-and-child images in Weinfeld's works, there are frequently images of fear—of prisoners in concentration camps, of rape victims, of a drug addict, or of a menacing wolf.

Power struggles between parents and between parents and children are the subject of Sharon Harper's expressionistic paintings that recall the anguish of some of Edvard Munch's work. With their sketchy figures, these paintings suggest the memories of events that live on to haunt the minds and behavior of family members. Memory becomes a cruel trick. For example, in *Wait Until We Get Home*, 1988 (Different Angle Gallery, Boston), an overpowering man sits beating a child on his lap, while a young girl stands rigidly next to him. A darkened house looms in the background of the shadowy painting, whose main colors are black, white, blood red, and its complementary green. The dripping expressionistic brush strokes emphasize the brutality of the painting. In *Too Hot to Handle*, 1990 (Asuah-Irving Gallery), a young boy stretches his arms toward a mother who stands in a threatening manner with hot kitchen utensils in her hands. Adults in these works are not protective, but menacing. A house is not a warm shelter, but a subterfuge or entrapment; the kitchen is a kind of torture chamber.

S. A. Bachman's collage work explores the mass media's invasion of the home and its representations of the family. The artist frequently juxtaposes found images, particularly those from Cold War-era magazines and advertisements, with texts that may reveal sexism, conformity, consumer issues, or the denial of domestic dysfunction as the bases of the media's images of the American family. Questions thus arise: What is fact, and what is fiction? Can families match the examples of an idealized media image, if that image is or becomes a desired goal? What kind of stress results from such media influence and/or manipulation, particularly when distinctions between fact and fiction become blurred? For instance, in an untitled image from her *Attraction/Repulsion* series, 1987–92, Bachman juxtaposed a photograph of a well-dressed family of the 1950s at the front door of their house with an image of a child's hands reaching up to a counter with a delicious pie on it. Laid over the pie is a photograph of a charging, ferocious dog, with its mouth wide open. An image from Bachman's *Double Entry* series, 1984–87, *Selective Fictions*, juxtaposes posed photographs of two harmonious families—an extended family and a "nuclear" family. The son in the family of four is pointing a gun at his mother. Although the gun seems like any harmless toy, the potential for violence lies beneath the surface of this tranquil, ordered image. Beneath the photographs are the words, "I suppose that in most ways my family is like any other American family. If you saw all of us standing together in a room we'd probably look as though we could be doing advertisements for Maxwell House Coffee."[79] Bachman's work is didactic in many ways, but it points strongly to the impact of the media in shaping and defining individual and family identities, which, in Bachman's eyes, could become entirely fictionalized.

Ida Applebroog examined issues of sexual power and isolation through domestic imagery combined with frightening fantastic figures, often set in scorched or barren landscapes. Her 1986 *Tomorrowland* (Denver Art Museum), for example, depicts a mother and child embracing in a pumpkin field that is dry and faded, as if it will never bear fruit again. To the left, in a separate panel, is a well-formed male figure, with a deformed head, menacing crossed eyes, and protruding horns. An early study done for the painting suggests that Picasso's *Guernica* was an influence for this frightening figure. Close to the dying landscape and imposing male figure are small linear sketches of innocent children and embracing adults. Innocence and the tender expression of feelings seem clearly threatened. A small sketch of somewhat provocative "chorus girl" figures further suggests a future loss of innocence. Applebroog's paintings, in general, frequently depicted a world permeated by irrational violence.

Eric Fischl explored subtle types of abuse or violence in looking at middle-class taboos in his rich painterly paintings. His suburban figures, often naked, frequently hint at an underlying alcoholism, voyeurism, or homosexuality. His subjects often seem vulnerable and psychologically naked. As Fischl noted, "Central to my work is the feeling of awkwardness and self-consciousness that one experiences in the face of profound emotional events in one's life. . . . I want people to feel they are present at a scene they shouldn't be at, and don't want to be at."[80]

Fischl's paintings are a kind of suburban vernacular that prompts narrative and calls for the viewer to participate in or finish that narrative. Through these paintings, it seems possible for the viewer to act out the fictions of hidden selves.

A 1981 painting, *Bad Boy* [66], showed a woman sleeping

66. Eric Fischl, *Bad Boy*, 1981. Saatchi Collection, London.

nude, her legs askew, while a young boy, possibly her son, watches her, his hands on her purse. The bowl of fruit in the painting, particularly the apples and bananas, carries further the themes of masculine and feminine sexuality and temptation. Beyond the sexual themes, it is the moment of self-consciousness for the subjects of the painting, as well as for the viewer, that is an important component of the piece. One may further ask why the boy is bad. Is it because he stands observing the woman or because he is going through her purse? Money and sexuality are thus subtly intertwined.

Fischl's 1982 painting *Barbecue* depicts a family scene in the backyard of an affluent home with a large in-ground polygon swimming pool. In this otherwise typical domestic summer scene, a young boy, eating fire, stands before a picnic table on which the only article is a large whole fish in a glass bowl, peering up at him. The viewer's position is close by, on the other side of the picnic table.

A painting of the same year, *The Old Man's Boat and the Old Man's Dog*, shows a family of five—all nude except for a life preserver around one figure's neck—on a boat. The family appears oblivious to the threatening sky, rising waves, and seemingly frantic barking of a sinister-looking dalmatian. Metaphorically, the family is "at sea" in a world of danger and peril, vulnerable and naked, psychologically, if not physically, in dealing with some of life's dilemmas.

Some of Fischl's paintings of the early eighties have been seen as analogous to Fischl's own childhood and his experiences growing up with an alcoholic mother. In response, he said: "It's really like fiction. All fiction comes from some kind of experience. Parents, people you've met, places you've lived, things that happened to you or that you feared might happen. And again, like fiction, I want the viewer to enter the picture—as a reader might get 'into' a book—and then work his way out."[81]

While Fischl explored aspects of suburban, primarily white middle-class, domestic life, some artists chose to examine and articulate aspects of immigrant family life. Henk Pander, an immigrant from The Netherlands who resides in Portland, Oregon, chose to reflect on generations past, on exile, on loss, on gain, and

67. Henk Pander, *The Deer and the Antelope*, 1992. Collection of the artist.

unsureness, in his paintings. His large-scale epic painting, *The Deer and the Antelope* [67], traces the journey of the immigrant. A ship, a dramatic sunset landscape, and symbolic iconography, using the conventions of Dutch still-life painting, Spanish Baroque painting, and Romantic landscape painting, pull the past and present together. A tall mirror on the left reflects Pander's childhood in Haarlem, while a mirror on the right shows his sons, as light shines on a new land. Pander wrote of his piece: "As an immigrant, I see myself as a transitional figure, filled with a longing for that which has gone. I see the painting as a metaphor for all of us, somewhat lost in a vastly changing, unstable world, a small CNN world in which everyone is an alien.[82]

Paul Sierra, born in Havana, Cuba, in 1944, has dealt with not only the passage of an immigrant to a new country, but with the concept of passage in various points of our lives. When he was sixteen, his family left Cuba and moved to Chicago, where in 1963, Sierra began studying painting at the Art Institute of Chicago. In *Family Portrait* [68], one sees the artist and his family leaving Cuba, finding their way in the manner of an epic myth, across difficult waters, led or pursued by a column of fire. In the distance appear blue skies, green-leaved trees, and a gentle terrain. Sierra portrayed himself as an adolescent painting in the lower right cor-

68. Paul Sierra, *Family Portrait*, 1991. Phyllis Kind Gallery, Chicago.

ner of the canvas. The act of painting was a way of piecing
together threads of Sierra's own life, from past and present.

In other paintings, such as *Charon* (1991), Sierra uses archetypal, mythical figures, such as Charon and Icarus, as he paints
moments of upheaval and passage. Sierra has grounded his own
story in the monumental terms of myth. In his use of myth, he
appears to search for, and at least partially recover, the self and the
past in which the self is rooted. Through myth, Sierra is able to
look into the past, which may be painful, and overcome some of
the pain.

Working in three dimensions, the artist John Ahearn, although
not an immigrant, turned away from the mainstream art world to
work in an alternative space in the South Bronx, New York, and on
an inner-city project. In 1979 he presented an exhibit, entitled *The
South Bronx Hall of Fame*, in the Bronx at Fashion Moda. In it
were about forty new portrait sculptures of people in that neighborhood. Ahearn and his collaborator, Rigoberto Torres, worked
with mold casting and acrylic paints, often turning the creation
process into a community event on the street for all to see.

Between 1981 and 1985 Ahearn and Torres collaborated on

four outdoor sculpture murals in the Bronx, funded by the Bronx Council of the Arts, the U.S. Department of Housing and Urban Development, and the National Endowment for the Arts. One, installed at 877 Intervale Avenue in the South Bronx in 1982, is entitled *We Are Family*. It depicts nine figures of various ages, couples embracing and individuals, looking out at their community from a barren cement wall overlooking an empty building lot.

A typical smaller piece by Ahearn is *Raymond and Freddy* [69]. This piece shows the Garcia brothers, who lived on Walton Avenue near the artist. Freddy, with a white shirt, who was HIV positive, appears tentative and unsure as he looks out. His brother Raymond, with a bright orange shirt, embraces his brother from above with a secure smile on his face. Ahearn usually made two

69. John Ahearn, *Raymond and Freddy*, 1992. Museum of Fine Arts, Boston.

sculptures of each sitter, one given to the subject and the other des-
ignated for the art market. In general, his goal was to celebrate a
sense of family and community, racial equality, and ordinary
heroes. But some projects, such as a 1991 installation project in
front of the Forty-fourth Precinct Police Building in the South
Bronx, were criticized for presenting a white man's perspective on
people of color. Questions thus arise as to who should depict, and
how, marginalized groups in a society, particularly in American
society.

The Canadian-born Micah Lexier chose to investigate individual and family identities in a number of three-dimensional pieces.
Locket, a wall piece from 1989, contains photographs of a daughter,
mother, and grandmother in a multichannel hologram, set in the
steel cutout of an open locket. As the viewer changes his or her
angle, one face changes into another, and one generation is thereby
replacing another. The piece refers not only to intergenerational

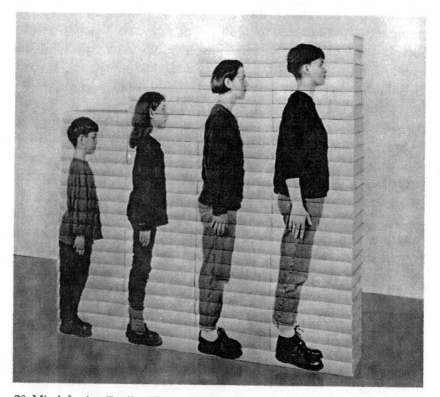

70. Micah Lexier, *Family of Four*, 1993. Jack Shainman Gallery, New York.

family relationships, but to memory, stages of life, and aging, as well as to concepts of motherhood.

In a 1991 floor sculpture, *My Father and Myself*, words cut out of steel—"He was the same age as I as I write this"—were placed on and around a white fluorescent light. The phrase, taken from J. R. Ackerley's novel, *My Father and Myself*, was repeated three times, mirroring a circumstance common to three generations of men in the fictional family story.

In later work Lexier explored family relationships in a series of sculptures made from life-size photographs of real people reproduced on stacks of large books. He lined up his subjects like children being measured on a door and used only enough books to fit a figure's height. His groups are not necessarily stereotypical middle-class families. They have included a lesbian couple and two children; seven siblings photographed in their parents' home; a grandmother, mother, and daughter; and the *Family of Four* [70]. In these pieces, family members measure themselves against each other. For Lexier, the "empirical" measurements also stand for things that cannot be measured, such as temperament. The "books" also serve to emphasize how identity can be shaped by the media, family, histories, and social conditioning in general.

Charles Ray, in looking at the nature of family identity in his provocative piece, *Family Romance* [71], stripped the family bare. In this realistic tableau of four mannequins a mother, father, young son, and toddler daughter stand nude in a row. However, the parents have been scaled down and the children have been scaled up, so they are all approximately the same size. This piece could be interpreted in a variety of ways—as a search for inner identities without the confines of outside apparel and generational and gender definitions, as an exploration of a child's fantasy about his or her parents, or as a consideration of repressed sexuality within a family group. The figures, all fair skinned and healthy, stand hand in hand, facing the viewer as a group, not as separate individuals.

Mike Kelley dealt with concepts of the family in primarily nonfigurative two- and three-dimensional ways. In 1987 he began a project, *Halt a Man*, which was to address issues of gender-specific imagery and the family. The project included felt banners,

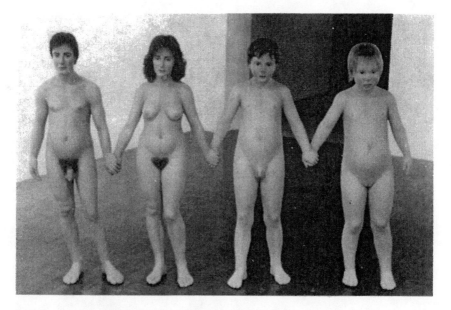

71. Charles Ray, *Family Romance*, 1993. Donald Young Gallery, Seattle.

black-and-white "symmetrical" drawings, "garbage" drawings, refinished furniture, and stuffed animal objects. In his stuffed animal pieces, Kelley used old, dirty toys—the "stuff" of family memories, childhood, and innocence. He tied the toys together and placed them on baby blankets or hung them from a wall or ceiling. Sometimes he used hand-sewn or crocheted dolls and blankets. The myth of childhood innocence is quickly exploded in these pieces, which frequently have a sexual presence. *Fruit of Thy Loins* [72], for instance, is a stuffed rabbit whose offspring emerge from its torso. In *Four Sock Dolls*, 1990, the dolls hang upside down, so their skirts fall over their heads, exposing the stuffed socks that represent "private parts." Ironically, the upended dolls look like phallic symbols. By using materials that are sewn and that have traditionally been associated with women's work, Kelley also presents crafts and "low" art as a way to confront the limitations of "high art" and Modernism, contradicting a heroic modernist image of the male artist using industrial materials to produce monumental sculptures.

Like photographers, painters, and sculptors, filmmakers in the 1980s and early 1990s dealt with the family in diverse ways and

72. Mike Kelley, *Fruit of Thy Loins*,
1990. Linda and Barry Macklowe
Collection, New York.

reflected the growing number of different family constellations, including single-parent homes, stepparent homes, and gay couples' homes. In a variety of ways, the film industry continued to represent, comment on, influence, and participate in social history, in general, and in family issues, in particular.

In 1982, an extraterrestrial creature, the beloved E.T., a lost alien, befriended a ten-year-old boy named Elliott (Henry Thomas) in Steven Spielberg's film *E.T.—The Extra-Terrestrial*. Elliott's home is fatherless, and E.T. seems to fill a gap in the child's life as the whole family learns that friendship does not have to have earthly limitations. The film portrays childhood innocence, frustration, and love. And, at times, E.T. appears to be a Christlike figure whom very few have faith in.

In 1983 John Sayles directed *Lianna*, starring Linda Griffiths, Jane Hallaren, Jon DeVries, and Jo Henderson. The film depicts a young woman, Lianna (Griffiths), trapped in an unhappy marriage with two children. Her husband (DeVries) teaches cinema and literature and is caught sexually "playing around" at a party. Lianna finds herself attracted to another woman, Ruth, who, in the end, does not want Lianna. But the film's real focus is the sensitive portrayal of a woman trying to come to grips with being a lesbian, and the consequences thereof, in a primarily heterosexual society.

The year 1984 brought several films related to the family farm, as thousands of real families were fighting to save real family farms. There was *Places in the Heart*, written and directed by Robert Benton, in which Sally Field plays a widow in Waxahachie, Texas, in 1935, who is determined to survive as a cotton farmer. She is helped by John Malkovich, who plays a blind man, and by a black man (Danny Glover). Field won an Oscar for her performance, as did Benton for his original screenplay. Mark Rydell's *The River* (1984), starring Sissy Spacek and Mel Gibson, also dealt with a family's struggles to make its farm work in an area that was constantly threatened by the nearby river. Also in that year, Jessica Lange and Sam Shepard starred in *Country* [73], directed by Richard Pearce. The film is about a modern family, the Ivys, who are torn apart when the government threatens to foreclose on a

73. *Country*, 1984. Touchstone Films. Photofest.

loan and take their land away. Here, the woman is portrayed with the strength to hold the family together.

A number of films dealt with "yuppie" issues—of a lifestyle that frequently valued success and materialism over idealism and social consciousness—and the possible redefinition of the concept of a family in relation to such a lifestyle. When numerous couples realized that the biological clock was ticking quickly and loudly, birthrates rose. In 1987, 3.8 million babies were born in the United States, the largest number since 1964. And beginning in 1987, a number of films dealt with babies, some humorous, some more serious. In 1987 alone, there were *Raising Arizona*, *Baby Boom*, *Made in Heaven*, *Three Men and a Baby*, and *She's Having a Baby*.

In *Baby Boom*, directed by Charles Shyer, J. C. Wiatt (Diane Keaton) is a Madison Avenue business executive, known as the "Tiger Lady" at work, with an MBA from Harvard and a six-fig-ure salary. She lives with a Wall Street broker. Her life changes dramatically when she suddenly "inherits" a baby, Elizabeth. The career woman has to learn to be a mother and becomes involved in conflict with her male bosses as she tries to do so. She ultimately has to retreat to the country and rebuild an old farmhouse to con-tinue being a mother and to maintain her career. In a good-natured and humorous manner, this film parodies the yuppie lifestyle that seems obsessed with success.

A more serious "baby" film was *Immediate Family* (1989), directed by Jonathan Kaplan. This film is about the frustrations of infertility and the difficulties surrounding adoption. The Spectors, Julie (Glenn Close) and Michael (James Woods), an affluent pro-fessional couple, turn to a lawyer after unsuccessful attempts to have a child. The lawyer puts them in touch with a pregnant teenager, Lucy, and her boyfriend, Sam. The film examines the emotions of all four persons in the baby's immediate family.

The Good Mother [74], directed by Leonard Nimoy and based on the novel by Sue Miller, explored the subject of divorce and family breakup, carrying the themes of *Kramer vs. Kramer* further. In *Kramer vs. Kramer,* a young son of a soon-to-be-divorced father meets his father's girlfriend, naked in the hall, but this incident is never mentioned in the custody trial. In *The Good Mother*, Anna

74. *The Good Mother*, 1989. Touchstone Films. Photofest.

Dunlop (Diane Keaton) is a single mother living with her daughter Molly. She is portrayed as a responsible mother, who subsequently becomes involved with another man, Leo (Liam Neeson). Anna's former husband takes her to court again and wins custody of Molly because Anna is open about her sexuality. The film explores the double standard set for women and the patriarchal world in which a woman cannot be a mother and herself and in which divorce simply becomes a new kind of imprisonment.

By the early nineties, a number of films did not include a mother at all. The 1994 season had *Angels in the Outfield*, in which the hero's mother was dead and his father abandons him to a foster system; *Lassie*, in which a loving dog helps a boy overcome his grief for this mother; and *Corrina, Corrina*, which opened with a grieving seven-year-old hiding at her mother's funeral. Earlier films, including *Sleepless in Seattle* (1993) and *My Girl* (1991), also revolved around dead mothers. And on television, comedies, such as *Full House* and *The Nanny*, feature widowed fathers. Why? Was the proliferation of such scenarios due to increased attention to fathers' roles in parenting and to fathers' "rights"? Or were these films, as some fairy tales, ways for children to confront unconscious fears? But for very young children, who have difficulty distinguishing between fantasy and reality, such films were considered by some to be inappropriate.[83]

A quite different film from those just discussed was Oliver Stone's powerful *Born on the Fourth of July* [75], starring Tom Cruise. The film was based on the real-life saga of Vietnam veteran Ron Kovic, who joined the marines as an enthusiastic recruit in the 1960s and came home paralyzed from the chest down. It depicts a small-town family who believe in war, in patriotism, and in America's power before Kovic leaves for Vietnam, but afterward are unable to cope well with and help their son. Nor can society at large. Kovic is disillusioned and bitter before he emerges as an antiwar activist. Stone won an Oscar for Best Director for this film. This film and a number of other Stone films of the latter part of the decade—*Salvador, Platoon, Wall Street,* and *Talk Radio*—marked Stone as a forceful cultural critic.

Several other films in this period were about families who were trying to deal with the disability or disease of their members. Jim Sheridan's *My Left Foot,* starring Daniel Day-Lewis, tells the story of a Dublin Catholic boy, Christy Brown, who is born with cerebral palsy and condemned to live as a vegetable. His father (Ray McAnally) is confused and angry about the situation, but his

75. *Born on the Fourth of July,* 1989. Universal Pictures. Photofest.

mother (Brenda Fricker) seems to understand Christy, and his siblings try to help him. He escapes from his handicap by learning to paint with his foot. Both Day-Lewis and Fricker won Oscars for their performances.

Lorenzo's Oil, a 1992 film directed by George Miller (a former doctor), was based on the true story of Augusto (Nick Nolte) and Michaela (Susan Sarandon) Odone and their five-year-old son Lorenzo, who has a rare form of muscular sclerosis. Against all professional advice from doctors, support groups, and scientists, the couple sets forth to save their child. Their struggles test their marriage and the boundaries of traditional medicine. These determined parents offer hope to those whose children have been proclaimed critically ill with the disease. At the time the film was made, the boy was still alive, and the lives of numerous children had been extended because of Lorenzo's oil and the Odones' heroic efforts.

In 1993, *Philadelphia*, directed by Jonathan Demme, depicted a family rallying lovingly around their AIDS-stricken son, played by Tom Hanks (who won an Oscar for the role). Although the film is primarily about the dilemmas of AIDS in the workplace, in this case, a prestigious law firm, the role of Hanks's family is significant. Not only do they support him and accept his gay lifestyle, but, together with his partner, they see him through his sickness and grieve together at his death.

Thus, a number of films in the eighties and early nineties dealt with some substantive issues related to family life in a variety of ways, both humorous and serious. As one writer noted, "Film is a social practice for its makers and its audience; in its narratives and meanings we can locate evidence of ways in which our culture makes sense of itself."[84]

In general, artists of the eighties and early nineties appeared to interpret their experiences and concepts of self and family in chaotic and dark, brooding images, as well as in more quiet, tranquil, and intimate images. Some were hopeful; some were not. It seems important to note, though, that as there have been increased alternatives to traditional family life, increased forces that have had an impact on family life, and an increased skepticism about lasting family bonds, the idea of family has more and more become the subject of art.

Epilogue:
Identities, Images, and Stories

Identity would seem to be the garment with which one covers the nakedness of the self; in which case, it is best that the garment be loose, a little
like the robes of the desert, through which robes one's nakedness can
always be felt and sometimes discerned. This trust in one's nakedness is
all that gives one the power to change one's robes. [1]

JAMES BALDWIN

Common to both [authority and legitimacy] is the idea of coherence,
that the meanings, mundane and transcendental, of one's life experience
should cohere in some intelligible pattern. What modernity has done—in
its drive to enhance experience, in its repudiation of tradition and the
past, in its sanction for the new and the idea that the individual could
remake his self in accordance solely with desire—is to disrupt that coherence in the name of an unbounded self. The radicalism of post-mod-
ernism now drives the individual into the beyond. [2]

DANIEL BELL

Concepts of identity and self, as individuals, and as families,
as has been shown, are complex and changing. As I indicated in the preface, this book may have raised more questions than it provided answers. Various notions of self and identity
have been raised—a self defined by one's birth, one's wealth, one's
faith; a fragmented self; a "saturated" self; a "minimal" self; a "protean" self; and so forth. Where are we in this maze that seems to be
part of modern and postmodern life? As O. B. Hardison noted,
"The central fact of cultural history is that the mind and the world

are mirrors. Sometimes the images appear to be accurate; sometimes they seem as wildly distorted as images in mirrors in the maze of an amusement park."[3]

As indicated in the pages of this book, it is the artist's and the media's vision and voice that have articulated some of these images of the mind and of the heart, images that can be seen either as mirrors or as lamps for ourselves and our families, depending on the time and circumstances. As mirrors, the images may reflect, in clear as well as distorted ways, a sense of self, family, and culture. As lamps, they may light a new path and help shape and articulate a new sense of identity, individually and collectively. In general, the artists discussed here have truly portrayed, or drawn forth, as the root word *protrahere* suggests, some aspect of self and family, at times reflecting social conventions and at times piercing beneath the surface, beneath our garments to our nakedness, both physical and psychological.

We have seen images of the self and family that have served as propaganda, as preservers of the status quo, as documents of a particular time and place, as voices of protest, as minority and majority voices, as voices in pain, and as voices in celebration. We have seen the sometimes complicated relationships among the artist, the popular media, those portrayed, and the viewer. In this twentieth-century world, which has frequently viewed reality as being found in material things and "truth" only as that which can be verified empirically, it is the artist who can help shed light on how people construct meaning for themselves and their families and on how the tensions between the material and nonmaterial, the visible and the invisible, may be eased or surmounted. It is the work of art, in its "real presence," that is able to help us truly enter our own psyches, which certain types of verbal language can perhaps never do or only vaguely suggest. As George Steiner wrote, "Serious painting, music, literature or sculpture make palpable to us, as do no other means of communication, the unassuaged, unhoused instability and estrangement of our condition."[4]

The artists and works discussed in this book may be viewed as a kind of collage of voices over time, from the past to the present. Their "stories," like other his/her stories, are part of a larger cultural tapestry to which we may all belong in one way or another at different times in our lives—in the center or on the fringe, in a dangling thread, tangled, straight, strong, or weak. One may ask such questions as: Are these artists to be seen as social critics, documentarians, prophets of doom, or prophets of hope? Do the dark images serve as a way of illuminating a shadowed world and of pointing the way to change? Thomas Mann's question *"Was ist das?"* is still there, too. There is no one quick and easy answer to any question surrounding identity, self, and family. But raising the questions of what, who, why, how, and where related to ourselves and to our families is sometimes as important as finding an answer.

As I suggested at the beginning of this book, we all need stories in various ways. Taken together or singly, these visual stories may help us to gain a better understanding of ourselves, our families, and the role of the family in the larger society. If it is true that the self has been eroded or even erased in this postmodern world, then perhaps images such as those in this book may indeed help us discover more about who we are and where we are going as we enter the twenty-first century.

Notes

Preface

1. Wallace Stegner, *Angle of Repose* (New York: Penguin Books, 1971), p. 18.
2. Donald Katz, *Homefires: An Intimate Portrait of One Middle Class Family in Postwar America* (New York: Harper Perennial, 1991), p. xiii.
3. Ibid.

Introduction

1. David Popenoe, "Scholars Should Worry About the Distintegration of the American Family," *Chronicle of Higher Education* (April 14, 1993), p. A48.
2. E. H. Gombrich, *Art and Illusion: Study in the Psychology of Pictorial Representation* (New York: Bollingen Foundation, 1959), pp. 87–90.
3. Édouard Vuillard, quoted in Heather McPherson, *Fin de Siècle Faces: Portraiture in the Age of Proust* (Birmingham: University of Alabama, 1988), p. 19.
4. Marcia Pointon, *Hanging the Head: Portraiture and Social Formation in 18th Century England* (New Haven, Conn.: Yale University Press, 1993), p. 1.
5. John Pope-Hennessy, *The Portrait in the Renaissance* (New York: Bollingen Foundation, 1966), p. 3.
6. Oscar Wilde, *The Picture of Dorian Gray* (London: Penguin Classics, 1985), p. 27.
7. Ibid., p. 72.
8. For an additional in-depth discussion of the issues of likeness, see Richard Brilliant, "Portraits: The Limitations of Likeness," *Art Journal* (Fall 1987), p. 171. See also Richard Brilliant's theoretical study devoted entirely to portraiture, *Portraiture* (London: Reaktion Books, 1991), for a further analysis of connections between the subject matter of portraits and the viewer's response.
9. Lorne Campbell, *Renaissance Portraits* (New Haven, Conn.: Yale University Press, 1990), p. 1.
10. R. G. Collingwood, *The Principles of Art* (New York: Oxford University Press, 1958), pp. 52–53.

11. Robert Jay Lifton, *The Protean Self* (New York: Basic Books, 1993), pp. 1–2.
12. Diane Arbus, quoted in Susan Sontag, *On Photography* (New York: Farrar, Straus and Giroux, 1977), p. 23.
13. Yousuf Karsh, quoted in Estelle Jussim, "The Psychological Portrait," in James Borcoman, Estelle Jussim, and Philip Pocock, *Karsh: The Art of the Portrait* (Ottawa: National Gallery of Canada, 1989), p. 93.
14. George Steiner, *Martin Heidegger* (London: Penguin Books, 1978), p. 134.

Part I

1. E. Panofsky, *Tomb Sculpture* (New York: Harry N. Abrams, Inc., 1964), p. 16.
2. Sheldon Nodelman, "How to Read a Roman Portrait," *Art in America* (January–February, 1975), p. 27.
3. Juvenal 6, 448–51.
4. John Pope-Hennessy, *The Portrait in the Renaissance* (New York: Bollingen Foundation, 1966), p. 3.
5. Lorne Campbell, *Renaissance Portraits: European Portrait Painting in the 14th, 15th and 16th Centuries* (New Haven, Conn.: Yale University Press, 1990), pp. 209–10.
6. For a further discussion of how concepts of "home" have changed over time, see Witold Rybczynski, *Home: A Short History of an Idea* (New York: Penguin Books, 1986).
7. Marcia Pointon, *Hanging the Head: Portraiture and Social Formation in 18th Century England* (New Haven, Conn.: Yale University Press, 1993), pp. 178–80.
8. W. Craven, *Colonial American Portraiture: The Economic, Religious, Social, Cultural, Philosophical, Scientific, and Aesthetic Foundations* (New York: Cambridge University Press, 1986), p. 268.
9. Karin Covert, "Children in American Family Portraiture, 1670–1810," *William and Mary Quarterly* 39 (January, 1982), p. 109.
10. Eugène Delacroix, *The Journal of Eugène Delacroix*, trans. W. Pach (New York: Covici-Friede, 1937), p. 93.
11. Erika Langmuir, "Portraiture," *Encyclopedia of Visual Art*, vol. 10 (Danbury, Conn.: Grolier Education Corporation, 1983), p. 69.
12. From J. F. C. Harrison, "The Victorian Gospel of Success," quoted in *St. Anselm College Humanities Reader* (Manchester, N.H.: St. Anselm College Humanities Program, 1993), p. 434.
13. Henry Fox Talbot, quoted in Asa Briggs with Archie Mills, *A Victorian Portrait* (New York: Harper & Row, 1989), p. 12.
14. Reprinted by Beaumont Newhall in *On Photography: A Source Book of Photo History* (New York: Century House, 1956), p. 59.
15. Anon., "One Day in My Life," *Harper's Weekly*, January 2, 1858.
16. George Fuller to Harriet Fuller, January 12, 1857, in Sarah Burns, "Images of Slavery: George Fuller's Depictions of the Antebellum South," *American Art Journal* 15 (Summer 1983), p. 37.
17. Henry T. Tuckerman, *Book of the Artists* (New York: 1867), in Ellwood Parry, *The Image of the Indian and the Black Man in American Art, 1590–1900* (New York: Gordon Press, 1974), p. 102.

18. Paul Valéry, quoted in Baroness Frances Pellenc, *Mother and Child*, ed. Mary Lawrence (New York: Crowell, 1975), p. 174.

19. Vincent Van Gogh, *The Complete Letters of Vincent Van Gogh* (Greenwich, Conn.: Bulfinch Press, 1958), Letter 192.

20. Vincent Van Gogh, quoted in John Walker, *Portraits: Five Thousand Years* (New York: Harry N. Abrams, Inc., 1983), p. 227.

21. Quoted in L. Stone, *The Family, Sex and Marriage in England, 1506–1800* (New York: Harper & Row, 1977), p. 277.

22. Fantin-Latour, quoted in Douglas Druick and Michael Hoog, *Fantin-Latour* (Ottawa: National Gallery of Art, 1983), p. 87.

23. Heather McPherson, *Fin-de-Siècle Faces: Portraiture in the Age of Proust* (Birmingham: University of Alabama, 1988), p. 29.

Part II

1. John Thomson and Adolphe Smith, quoted in Ben Maddow, *Faces: A Narrative History of the Portrait in Photography* (Greenwich, Conn.: New York Graphic Society, 1977), p. 236.

2. Roland Penrose, *Picasso: His Life and Work* (New York: Schocken, 1976), p. 108.

3. Guillaume Apollinaire, "Phantom of the Clouds," in *Selected Writings of Guillaume Apollinaire*, ed. and trans. Roger Shattuck (New York: New Directions, 1949), p. 165.

4. E. L. Kirchner, Künstlergruppe Brücke Manifesto, 1906, cited in P. Selz, *German Expressionist Painting* (Berkeley: University of California Press, 1957), p. 95.

5. Max Beckmann, quoted in Bernard S. Myers, *The German Expressionists* (New York: Praeger, 1956), p. 307.

6. Paula Modersohn-Becker, quoted in Whitney Chadwick, *Women, Art, and Society* (London: Thames and Hudson, 1990), p. 270.

7. Rainer Maria Rilke, *Selected Works*, vol. 2, trans. by J. B. Leishman (London: Hogarth Press, 1976), p. 654.

8. Käthe Kollwitz, Letter to Romain Rolland, October 23, 1922, quoted in Elizabeth Prelinger, *Käthe Kollwitz* (New Haven, Conn.: Yale University Press, 1992), pp. 57, 59.

9. Edvard Munch, quoted in R. Stenersen, *Edvard Munch* (Stockholm: 1950), p. 119.

10. Pablo Picasso, "Picasso Speaks," *The Arts* (New York: May 1923).

11. Karl Jaspers, *On the Intellectual State of the Time* (London: G. Routledge & Sons, Ltd., 1933), pp. 180–81.

12. Paul Hermann, *Deutsche Rassenhygiene*, pp. 17–21. Translation in *Nazi Culture: Intellectual, Cultural, and Social Life in the Third Reich*, ed. George Mosse (New York: Schocken Books, Inc., 1966).

13. Adolf Hitler, cited in *Völkischer Beobachter*, September 15, 1935.

14. Charlotte Perkins Gilman, *The Home: Its Work and Influence* (New York: McClure, Phillips & Co., 1903), pp. 34–35.

15. Steven Mintz and Susan Kellogg, *Domestic Revolutions: A Social History of American Family Life* (New York: Free Press, 1988), pp. 108–9.

16. Advertisements reproduced in Donald M. Scott and Bernard Wishy, *America's*

Families: A Documentary History (New York: Harper & Row, 1982), pp. 620–21.

17. Herbert Seligmann, "Georgia O'Keeffe, American," *Manuscript*, no. 5 (March 1923), p. 16.
18. Louis Kalonyme, "Georgia O'Keeffe: A Woman Painting," *Creative Art* (January 1928), p. 37.
19. Robert Henri, *The Art Spirit* (Philadelphia: J. P. Lippincott, 1923), p. 67.
20. Elizabeth McCausland, "Rural Life in America as the Camera Shows It," quoted in James Guimond, *American Photography and the American Dream* (Chapel Hill: University of North Carolina Press, 1991), p. 109.
21. James Agee and Walker Evans, *Let Us Now Praise Famous Men* (Boston: Houghton Mifflin, 1941), p. 445.
22. Dorothea Lange, quoted in Beaumont Newhall, *The History of Photography* (New York: Museum of Modern Art, 1964), p. 143.
23. See Richard Bolton, ed., *The Contest of Meaning: Critical Histories of Photography* (Cambridge, Mass.: MIT Press, 1989), Martha Rosler, "In, around, and afterthoughts (on documentary photography)," p. 315. See also *New York Times Magazine*, May 25, 1980, pp. 31–45, for the story related to Allie Mae Burroughs.
24. Roy Stryker, February 19, 1942, quoted in Guimond, *American Photography and the American Dream*, p. 138.
25. Milton Brown, Sam Hunter, and John Jabocus, *American Art* (New York: Prentice-Hall, 1979), p. 451.
26. James Van Der Zee, quoted in Mary Schmidt Campbell, *Harlem Heyday: The Photography of James Van Der Zee* (New York: Studio Museum of Harlem, 1982), n.p.
27. Martha Wolfenstein and Nathan Leites, *Movies: A Psychological Study* (New York: Atheneum, 1977), pp. 101–2.
28. Elaine Tyler May, *Homeward Bound: American Families in the Cold War Era* (New York: Basic Books, 1988), p. 45.
29. Quoted in John Morton Blum, *V is for Victory: Politics and American Culture During World War II* (New York: Harcourt Brace Jovanovich, 1976), p. 28.
30. Christopher Lasch, *The True and Only Heaven: Progress and Its Critics* (New York: W. W. Norton, 1991), pp. 83, 118.
31. Joseph Adelson, "Is Women's Lib a Passing Fad?" *New York Times Magazine*, March 19, 1972, p. 94.
32. Barnett Newman, "The Sublime Is Now," *The Tiger's Eye*, no. 6 (December 1948), p. 51.
33. David Burnett, *Colville* (Ontario: Art Gallery of Ontario, 1983), p. 92.
34. Jean Paul Lemieux, quoted in "Notes sur le dessin," *Lejour*, October 1, 1938.
35. Henry Moore, quoted in *The Listener* 18 (August 18, 1937), p. 339.
36. James Schuyler, quoted in John Spike, *Fairfield Porter: An American Classic* (New York: Harry N. Abrams, 1992), p. 190.
37. Stuart Preston, *New York Times* review of a 1965 Porter exhibit, quoted in ibid.
38. William T. Levitt, quoted in Kenneth Jackson, *Crabgrass Frontier: The Suburbanization of the United States* (New York: Oxford University Press, 1985), p. 231.
39. Richard Nixon, text of speech quoted in *Newsweek*, August 3, 1959, pp. 15–19.

40. Gerry Badger, "From Humanism to Formalism: Thoughts on Post-War American Photography," in *American Images: Photography 1945–1980*, ed. Peter Turner (New York: Viking Press and Barbican Gallery, 1985), p. 13.

41. Roland Barthes, quoted in Guimond, *American Photography and the American Dream*, p. 198.

42. Gilles Peress, interview with Miriam Horn, p. 89, quoted in ibid., p. 197.

43. John F. Kennedy, January 20, 1961, quoted in *This Fabulous Century, 1960–1970* (New York: Time Life Books, 1988), p. 10.

44. Martin Luther King, Jr., quoted in *This Fabulous Century*, p. 30.

45. Mort Drucker and Stan Hart, "The Nilson Family," *Mad*, January 1966, p. 13.

46. Michael Paul Rogin, *Ronald Reagan, the Movie, and Other Episodes in Political Demonology* (Berkeley: University of California Press, 1987), p. 252.

47. Ibid., p. 253.

48. Diane Arbus, in *Diane Arbus* (Millerton, N.Y.: Aperture Foundation, 1972), p. 3, copyright © 1972, the Estate of Diane Arbus.

49. Frank H. Goodyear, Jr., *Contemporary American Realism since 1960* (Boston: New York Graphic Society, 1981), p. 67.

50. See Christopher Lasch, *The Minimal Self* (New York: W. W. Norton, 1984).

51. Ibid., p. 151.

52. Cindy Nemser, quoted in "Alice Neel–Teller of Truth," in *Alice Neel: The Woman and Her Work* (Athens: Georgia Museum of Art, 1975), n.p.

53. Critics' citations concerning Freud are from Marina Warner, "Lucian Freud— The Blinking Eye," *New York Times Magazine*, December 4, 1988, p. 68.

54. Ibid.

55. Todd Gitlin, *The Sixties: Years of Hope, Days of Rage* (New York: Bantam Books, 1987), p. 433.

56. Vivian Sobchack, "Child/Alien/Father: Patriarchal Crisis and Generic Exchange," in *Close Encounters: Film, Feminism and Science Fiction*, eds. Constance Penley, Elisabeth Lyon, Lynn Spiegel, and Janet Bergstrom (Minneapolis: University of Minnesota Press, 1991), p. 6.

57. Chauncey Hare, *Interior America*, p. 19, in Guimond, *American Photography and the American Dream*, p. 269.

58. Miriam Schapiro, "Femmage," in *Collage: Critical Views*, ed. Katherine Hoffman (Ann Arbor, Mich.: UMI Research Press, 1989), p. 296.

59. Faith Ringgold, in Grace Glueck, "An Artist Who Turns Cloth into Social Commentary," *New York Times*, July 29, 1984.

60. May, *Homeward Bound*, p. 222.

61. George Steiner, *Real Presences* (Chicago: University of Chicago Press, 1989), pp. 118–26.

62. Michel Foucault, *Power/Knowledge: Selected Interviews and Other Writings, 1972–77*, ed. Colin Gordon (New York: Pantheon Books, 1980), p. 141.

63. Michel Foucault, "Nietzsche, Genealogy, History," in *Language, Counter-Memory, Practice*, ed. Donald Bouchard (Ithaca, N.Y.: Cornell University Press, 1977), p. 153.

64. Thomas Lawson, *A Fatal Attraction: Art and the Media* (Chicago: Renaissance Society, University of Chicago, 1982).

65. Jean Baudrillard, "The Precession of Simulacra," in *Art After Modernism: Rethinking Representation*, ed. Brian Wallis (New York and Boston: The New Museum of Contemporary Art, in association with David Godine Publishers, 1984), p. 253.

66. Craig Owens, "Representation, Appropriation, and Power," *Art in America* (May 1982), p. 21.

67. Kenneth Gergen, *The Saturated Self* (New York: Basic Books, 1991), p. 7.

68. Tom Bamberger, *Blood Relatives* (Milwaukee: Milwaukee Art Museum, 1991), p. 6.

69. Larry Sultan, *Pictures from Home* (New York: Harry N. Abrams, 1992), p. 26.

70. Tina Barney, quoted in *Friends and Relations* (Washington, D.C.: Smithsonian Institute Press, 1991), p. 6.

71. Tina Barney, quoted in Bamberger, *Blood Relatives*, p. 5.

72. Ibid., p. 9.

73. Sally Mann, *Immediate Family* (New York: Aperture Foundation, 1992), n.p.

74. Sally Mann, quoted in Bamberger, *Blood Relatives*, p. 11.

75. Henry M. Sayre, *The Object of Performance: The American Avant-Garde Since 1970* (Chicago: University of Chicago Press, 1989), p. 39.

76. See ibid., p. 65.

77. Sage Sohier, "At Home with Themselves: Photographs and Interviews with Gay and Lesbian Couples," artist's statement (Andover, Mass: Addison Gallery of Art, 1990).

78. For example, see the feminist critic, Deborah Bright, "Family Practices," *Views* (Summer 1992), p. 8.

79. The text above the photographs reads, "Recently, sociologists at the University of California at Los Angeles have completed studies which indicate that individuals born during the 1950's or the so-called 'First Television Generation' have great difficulty making distinctions between fact and fiction. The studies' findings confirm the previous belief that there is a tendency for this generation to be confused about reality. In fact, these individuals come to define their existence through the media by creating a personal fiction that is a synthesis of their real life experience and the cultural images they have absorbed. This cultural phenomenon has been termed, 'Selective Fictionalization.'"

80. Quoted in Sayre, *The Object of Performance*, p. 25.

81. Eric Fischl, quoted in Paul Gardner, "Fear and Desire," *Artnews* (September 1994), p. 162.

82. Henk Pander, quoted in *Documents Northwest: The Poncho Series*, "1492/1992," Seattle Art Museum, October 22, 1992–January 3, 1993, artist's statement.

83. See Melinda Beck, "Movies Without Mothers," *Newsweek*, August 29, 1994, p. 56.

84. Graeme Turner, quoted in William Palmer, *The Films of the Eighties: A Social History* (Carbondale: Southern Illinois University Press, 1992), p. 309.

Epilogue

1. James Baldwin, installation banner, Museum of Fine Arts, Boston, Fall 1993.

2. Daniel Bell, "Beyond Modernism, Beyond Self," in *Art, Politics, and Will*, eds. Quentin Anderson, Stephen Donadio, and Steve Marcus (New York: Basic Books, 1977), pp. 251–52.

3. O. B. Hardison, Jr., *Entering the Maze: Identity and Change in Modern Culture* (New York: Oxford University Press, 1981), pp. x–xi.

4. George Steiner, *Real Presences* (Chicago: University of Chicago Press, 1989), p. 139.

Selected Bibliography

Adam, Peter. *Art of the Third Reich*. New York: Harry N. Abrams, 1992.

Agee, James, and Walker Evans. *Let Us Now Praise Famous Men*. Boston: Houghton Mifflin Co., 1941.

Alice Neel. Athens: Georgia Museum of Art, 1975.

Alvarez, Ronald A. F., and Susan Calhoun Kline. *A Family Album: The American Family in Literature and History*. New York: Walker and Co., 1988.

Anderson, Quentin, Stephen Donadio, and Steve Marcus, eds. *Art, Politics, and Will*. New York: Basic Books, 1977.

Anderson, Ross. *Abbott Handerson Thayer*. Syracuse, N.Y.: Everson Museum, 1982.

Anthony, Carolyn. *Family Portraits: Remembrances by Twenty Distinguished Writers*. New York: Doubleday, 1989.

Arbus, Doon, and Marvin Israel, eds. *Diane Arbus: Magazine Work*. New York: Aperture Foundation, 1984.

Ariès, Philippe. *Centuries of Childhood: A Social History of Family Life*. New York: Vintage Books, 1962.

Art in America. Issue on Portraiture, January–February, 1975.

Atkinson, Tracy. *Inner Circle*. Milwaukee: Milwaukee Art Center, September 15–October 23, 1966.

Ballerini, Julia, curator. *The Surrogate Figure: Intercepted Identities in Contemporary Photography*. Woodstock, N.Y.: Center for Photography at Woodstock, 1991.

Bamberger, Tom. *Blood Relatives: The Family in Contemporary Photography*. Milwaukee: Milwaukee Art Museum, 1991.

Banner, L. W. *American Beauty*. Chicago: University of Chicago Press, 1984.

Barney, Tina. *Friends and Relations*. Washington, D.C.: Smithsonian Institution Press, 1991.

Bauer, Fred. *The Faith of America*. New York: Artabras Books, 1980.

Baumeister, Roy. *Identity—Cultural Change and the Struggle for Self*. New York: Oxford University Press, 1986.

Beattie, Ann. *Alex Katz*. New York: Harry N. Abrams, 1976.

————, and Andy Grundberg. *Flesh and Blood—Photographers' Images of Their Own Families*. New York: Picture Project, 1992.

Blum, John Morton. *V Is for Victory: Politics and American Culture During World War II*. New York: Harcourt Brace Jovanovich, 1976.

Bolton, Richard, ed. *The Contest of Meaning: Critical Histories of Photography*. Cambridge, Mass.: MIT Press, 1990.

Borcoman, James, Estelle Jussim, and Philip Pocock. *Karsh: The Art of the Portrait*. Ottawa: National Gallery of Canada, 1989.

Brekenridge, James. *Likeness: A Conceptual History of Ancient Portraiture*. Evanston, Ill.: Northwestern University Press, 1968.

Briggs, Asa. *A Victorian Portrait*. New York: Harper & Row, 1989.

Brilliant, Richard, ed. "Portraits: The Limitations of Likeness." *The Art Journal* (College Art Association), Fall 1987.

————. *Portraiture*. London: Reaktion Books, 1991.

Brophy, John. *The Face of Western Art*. London: George G. Harrap, 1963.

Brunette, Peter, and David Wills, eds. *Deconstruction and the Visual Arts*. Cambridge, England: Cambridge University Press, 1994.

Burnett, David. *Colville*. Toronto: Art Gallery of Toronto, 1987.

Campbell, Lorne. *Renaissance Portraits*. New Haven, Conn.: Yale University Press, 1990.

Campbell, Mary Schmidt. *Harlem Heyday: The Photography of James Van Der Zee*. New York: Study Museum of Harlem, 1982.

Carcopino, Jerome. *Daily Life in Rome*. New Haven, Conn.: Yale University Press, 1940.

Carr. Carolyn Kinder. *Then and Now: American Portraits of the Past Century from the National Portrait Gallery*. Washington, D.C.: National Portrait Gallery, Smithsonian Institution, 1987.

Carrani, Marie. *Jean Paul Lemieux*. Quebec: Musée du Québec, 1992.

Center Gallery. *Faces Since the 50's: A Generation of American Portraiture*. Lewisburg, Penn.: Bucknell University, March 11–April 17, 1983.

Chadwick, Whitney. *Women, Art and Society*. London: Thames and Hudson, 1990.

Clark, Clifford Edward, Jr. *The American Family Home: 1800–1960*. Chapel Hill: University of North Carolina Press, 1986.

Clarke, Graham. *The Portrait in Photography*. London: Reaktion Books, 1992.

Close, Chuck, and Kirk Varnedoe. *Artist's Choice—Chuck Close—Head-On/The Modern Portrait*. New York: Museum of Modern Art, January 10–March 19, 1991.

Collingwood, R. G. *The Principles of Art*. New York: Oxford University Press, 1967.

Colomina, Beatriz, ed. *Sexuality and Space*. Princeton Papers on Architecture. Princeton, N.J.: Princeton Architectural Press, 1992.

Coontz, Stephanie. *The Social Origins of Private Life: A History of American Families, 1600–1900*. London: Verso, 1988.

————. *The Way We Never Were: American Families and the Nostalgia Trap*. New York: HarperCollins, 1992.

Cottle, Thomas. *A Family Album—Portraits of Intimacy and Kinship*. New York: Harper & Row, 1985.

Covert, Karin. "Children in American Family Portraiture, 1670–1810." *William and Mary Quarterly* 39 (January 1982), pp. 87–113.

Craven, W. *Colonial American Portraiture: The Economic, Religious, Social, Cultural, Philosophical, Scientific, and Aesthetic Foundations.* New York: Cambridge University Press, 1986.

Dault, Gary, and Jane Corkin. *Children in Photography: 150 years.* Willowdale, Ontario, Canada: Firefly Books, 1990.

De Cock, Liliane, and Reginald McGhee, eds. *James Van Der Zee.* New York: Morgan and Morgan, 1973.

Degler, Carl. *At Odds—Women and the Family in America from the Revolution to the Present.* Oxford, England: Oxford University Press, 1980.

De Lauretis, Teresa. *Alice Doesn't—Feminism, Semiotics, Cinema.* Bloomington: Indiana University Press, 1984.

Demos, John. *Past, Present, and Personal: The Family and the Life Course in American History.* Oxford, England: Oxford University Press, 1989.

Desmarais, Charles. *The Portrait Extended.* Chicago: Museum of Contemporary Art, 1981.

Duncan, Carol. *The Aesthetics of Power.* Cambridge, England: Cambridge University Press, 1993.

Edwards, Lee. *Family Life in American Painting, 1840–1910.* New York: Hudson River Museum, 1985.

Fairbrother, Trevor, and Kathryn Potts. *In and Out of Place: Contemporary Art and the American Social Landscape.* Boston: Museum of Fine Arts, 1993.

Feldman, Melissa, and Benjamin H. D. Buchloh. *The Portrait in Recent Art—Face-Off.* Philadelphia: Institute of Contemporary Art, 1994.

Flacelière, Robert. *Daily Life in Greece at the Time of Pericles.* New York: Macmillan, 1966.

Flexner, James Thomas. *America's Old Masters.* New York: McGraw-Hill, 1980.

Franits, Wayne. *Paragons of Virtue: Women and Domesticity in Seventeenth Century Dutch Art.* Cambridge, England: Cambridge University Press, 1993.

Fuenmayor, Jésus, Kate Haug, and Frazer Ward. *Dirt and Domesticity: Construction of the Feminine.* New York: Whitney Museum of American Art at the Equitable Center, June 12–August 14, 1992.

Furst, Herbert. *Portrait Painting, Its Nature and Function.* London: John Lane, Bodley Head, 1927.

Fussell, Paul. *The Great War and Modern Memory.* Oxford, England: Oxford University Press, 1975.

Gadamer, Hans-Georg. *Truth and Method* (2d rev. ed.). New York: Crossroad, 1989.

Galassi, Peter. *Pleasures and Terrors of Domestic Comfort.* New York: Museum of Modern Art, 1991.

Galloway, David. *A Family Album.* London: John Calder, 1978.

Garrett, Elisabeth D. *At Home: The American Family: 1750–1870.* New York: Harry N. Abrams, 1990.

Gergen, Kenneth. *The Saturated Self: Dilemmas of Identity in Contemporary Life.* New York: Basic Books, 1991.

Gibson, Robin. *The Portrait Now.* London: National Portrait Gallery, 1993.

Giddens, Anthony. *Modernity and Self-Identity.* Stanford, CA: Stanford University Press, 1991.

Gledhill, Christine. *Home Is Where the Heart Is—Studies in Melodrama and the Woman's Film.* London: British Film Institute, 1987.

Glover, Jonathan. *The Philosophy and Psychology of Personal Identity*. New York: Penguin Press, 1988.

Godfrey, F. M. *Child Portraiture from Bellini to Cézanne*. London: Studio Publications, 1979.

Goldin, Nan. *The Ballad of Sexual Dependency*. New York: Aperture Foundation, 1986.

Goldscheider, Frances K. *New Families, No Families? The Transformation of the American Home*. Berkeley: University of California Press, 1991.

Gombrich, E. H. *Art and Illusion: Study in the Psychology of Pictorial Representation*. Princeton, N.J.: Princeton University Press, 1989.

Goodyear, Frank H., Jr. *Contemporary American Realism Since 1960*. Boston: New York Graphic Society, 1981.

Green, Martin, and John Swan. *The Triumph of Pierrot: The Commedia dell'Arte and the Modern Imagination*. New York: Macmillan, 1986.

Guarino, Guido, trans. and ed. *The Albertis of Florence: Leon Battista Alberti's Della Famiglia*. Lewisburg, Penn.: Bucknell University Press, 1971.

Guimond, James. *American Photography and the American Dream*. Chapel Hill: University of North Carolina Press, 1991.

Halle, David. *Inside Culture, Art and Class in the American Home*. Chicago: University of Chicago Press, 1992.

Hardison, O. B., Jr. *Entering the Maze: Identity and Change in Modern Culture*. New York: Oxford University Press, 1981.

Hareven, Tamara. *Good-bye to Apple Pie: Contemporary Artists View the Family in Crisis*. Lincoln, Mass.: DeCordova Museum, September 19–November 29, 1992.

Hawes, Joseph, and Elizabeth Nybakken, eds. *American Families: A Research Guide and Historical Handbook*. Westport, Conn.: Greenwood Press, 1991.

Higonnet, Anne. *Berthe Morisot*. New York: Harper & Row, 1990.

Hills, Patricia. *Alice Neel*. New York: Harry N. Abrams, 1983.

——. *John Singer Sargent*. New York: Harry N. Abrams, 1986.

Hirsch, Julia. *Family Photographs: Content, Meaning and Effect*. New York: Oxford University Press, 1981.

Hoffman, Katherine. *Explorations: The Visual Arts Since 1945*. New York: HarperCollins, 1991.

Hooton, Bruce, and Nina Kaiden, eds. *Mother and Child in Modern Art*. New York: Duell, Sloan, and Pearce, 1963.

House, John, Anne Distel, and Lawrence Gowing. *Renoir*. Boston: Museum of Fine Arts, 1985.

Hunt, Lynn, ed. *The New Cultural History*. Berkeley: University of California Press, 1989.

Hunter, Jean, and Paul Mason, eds. *The American Family: Historical Perspectives*. Pittsburgh: Duquesne University Press, 1991.

Jackson, Kenneth. *Crabgrass Frontier: The Suburbanization of the United States*. New York: Oxford University Press, 1985.

Kaplan, E. Ann. *Motherhood and Representation: The Mother in Popular Culture and Melodrama*. New York: Routledge, 1992.

Katz, Donald. *Homefires: An Intimate Portrait of One Middle Class Family in Post War America*. New York: Harper Perennial, 1992.

Kearney, Richard. *The Wake of Imagination*. Minneapolis: University of Minnesota Press, 1988.

Küchler, Susanne, and Walter Melion, eds. *Images of Memory.* Washington, D.C.: Smithsonian Institution Press, 1991.

Lampert, Catherine. *Lucian Freud: Recent Work.* New York: Rizzoli Publications, 1993.

Langer, Cassandra. *Mother and Child in Art.* New York: Crescent Books, 1992.

Lasch, Christopher. *The Minimal Self.* New York: W. W. Norton, 1984.

———. *The True and Only Heaven: Progress and Its Critics.* New York: W. W. Norton, 1991.

Lavin, Maud. *Cut with a Kitchen Knife: The Weimar Photomontages of Hannah Höch.* New Haven, Conn.: Yale University Press, 1993.

Lexier, Micah. *Name and Family Name.* Calgary, Alberta, Canada: Stride Gallery, September 9–October 3, 1992.

Lifson, Ben. *Faces Photographed: Contemporary Camera Images.* New York: Grey Art Gallery, 1982.

Lifton, Robert Jay. *The Protean Self.* New York: Basic Books, 1993.

Lipsitz, George. *Time Passages: Collective Memory and American Popular Culture.* Minneapolis: University of Minnesota Press, 1990.

Lovell, Margaretta. "Reading Eighteenth-Century American Family Portraits." *Winterthur Portfolio* (Henry Francis duPont Winterthur Museum), 1987, pp. 243–65.

McGrath, Jerry. "A Sense of Measure: Notes on Recent Works by Micah Lexier." *Parachute 61,* January–March 1991, pp. 43–46.

McPherson, Heather. *Fin de Siècle Faces: Portraiture in the Age of Proust.* Birmingham: University of Alabama, 1988.

McQuillan, Melissa. *Impressionist Portraits.* Boston: New York Graphic Society, 1986.

Maddow, Ben. *Faces, A Narrative History of the Portrait in Photography.* Boston: New York Graphic Society, 1977.

Mann, Sally. *Immediate Family.* New York: Aperture Foundation, 1992.

Mann, Thomas. *Buddenbrooks.* New York: Vintage Books, 1992.

Masnick, George, and Mary Jo Bane. *The Nation's Families: 1960–1990.* Cambridge, Mass.: Joint Center for Urban Studies of MIT and Harvard University, 1991.

May, Elaine Tyler. *Homeward Bound: American Families of the Cold War Era.* New York: Basic Books, 1988.

Mead, Margaret, and Ken Heyman. *Family.* New York: Macmillan, 1965.

Mersand, Joseph, ed. *Three Comedies of American Family Life.* New York: Pocket Books, 1961.

Mike Kelley—Three Projects: Half a Man, From My Institution to Yours, Pay for Your Pleasure. Chicago: Renaissance Society, University of Chicago, May 4–June 30, 1988.

Miller, Toby. *The Well-Tempered Self: Citizenship, Culture, and the Postmodern Subject.* Baltimore: Johns Hopkins University Press, 1993.

Mintz, Steven, and Susan Kellogg. *Domestic Revolutions: A Social History of American Family Life.* New York: Free Press, 1988.

Mook, Bertha. *The Dutch Family in the 17th and 18th Centuries: An Explorative-Descriptive Study.* Ottawa: University of Ottawa Press, 1977.

Morgan, David. "Paul Sierra: Images of Passage." *Sierra-Paintings.* Chicago: Gwenda Jay Gallery, April 24–May 30, 1992.

Morrison, Toni. *Beloved.* New York: Knopf, 1987.

Muncaster, Alice, Ellen Sawyer, and Ken Kapson. *The Baby Made Me Buy It! A Treasury of Babies Who Sold Yesterday's Products.* New York: Crown, 1991.

Murray, Stuart. *Norman Rockwell's Four Freedoms.* Stockbridge, Mass.: Berkshire House, 1993.

National Portrait Gallery: Illustrated Checklist. Washington, D.C.: Smithsonian Institution Press, 1987.

Nestor, Helen. *Family Portraits in Changing Times.* Troutdale, Ore.: New Sage Press, 1992.

Nixon, Nicholas. *Family Pictures.* Washington, D.C.: Smithsonian Institution Press, 1991.

————. *Pictures of People.* New York: Museum of Modern Art, 1988.

Nochlin, Linda. *Women, Art and Power and Other Essays.* New York: Harper & Row, 1988.

Norman, Barry. *The 100 Best Films of the Century.* New York: Citadel Press, 1993.

Olsen, Tillie, and Estelle Jussim. *Mothers and Daughters: That Special Quality.* New York: Aperture Foundation, 1987.

Olson, Stanley. *John Singer Sargent.* New York: St. Martin's Press, 1986.

Orvell, Miles. *The Real Thing—Imitation and Authenticity in American Culture, 1880–1940.* Chapel Hill: University of North Carolina Press, 1989.

Pacey, Philip. *Family Art.* London: Polity Press, 1989.

Palmer, William. *The Films of the Eighties, A Social History.* Carbondale: Southern Illinois University Press, 1993.

Panofsky, E. *Tomb Sculpture.* New York: Harry N. Abrams, Inc., 1964.

Parfit, Derek. *Reasons and Persons.* Oxford, England: Clarendon Press, 1984.

Penley, Constance, Elisabeth Lyon, Lynn Spiegel, and Janet Bergstrom, eds. *Close Encounters, Film, Feminism and Science Fiction.* Minneapolis: University of Minnesota Press, 1991.

Penrose, Roland. *Picasso: His Life and Work.* New York: Schocken Books, 1976.

Pettigrew, Jane. *An Edwardian Childhood.* Boston: Bulfinch Press, 1992.

Piper, David. *The English Face.* London: Thames and Hudson, 1957.

Pointon, Marcia. *Hanging the Head: Portraiture and Social Formation in Eighteenth Century England.* New Haven, Conn.: Yale University Press, 1993.

Pope-Hennessy, John. *The Portrait in the Renaissance.* New York: Bollingen Foundation, 1966.

Praz, Mario. *Conversation Pieces: A Survey of the Informal Group Portrait in Europe and America.* London: Methuen, 1971.

Prelinger, Elizabeth. *Käthe Kollwitz.* New Haven, Conn.: Yale University Press, 1992.

Ramsden, E. H. *"Come, Take This Lute," A Quest for Identities in Renaissance Portraiture.* Great Britain: Element Books, 1983.

Reff, Theodore. *Degas: The Artist's Mind.* New York: Harper & Row, 1976.

Rogin, Michael Paul. *Ronald Reagan, the Movie, and Other Episodes in Political Demonology.* Berkeley: University of California Press, 1987.

Rosen, Randy, curator. *Making Their Mark: Women Artists Move into the Mainstream, 1970–85.* New York: Abbeville Press, 1989.

Rosenberg, Harold. *Richard Avedon Portraits.* New York: Farrar, Straus and Giroux, 1976.

Rosenblum, Robert. *The Romantic Child: From Runge to Sendak.* New York: Thames and Hudson, 1988.

Roskill, Mark, and David Carrier. *Truth and Falsehood in Visual Images.* Amherst: University of Massachusetts Press, 1983.

Rutherford, Paul. *The New Icons? The Art of Television Advertising.* Toronto: University of Toronto Press, 1994.

Rybczynski, Witold. *Home: A Short History of an Idea.* New York: Penguin Books, 1986.

Saisselin, Rémy G. *Style, Truth and the Portrait.* New York: Harry N. Abrams, 1963.

Sander, Gunther, ed. *August Sander: Citizens of the Twentieth Century.* Cambridge, Mass.: MIT Press, 1986.

Sayre, Henry M. *The Object of Performance: The American Avant-Garde Since 1970.* Chicago: University of Chicago Press, 1992.

Schickel, Richard, and Sid Avery. *Hollywood at Home: A Family Album, 1950–1965.* New York: Crown, 1990.

Schiff, Nancy Rica. *A Celebration of the 80's—Portraits.* New York: Harry N. Abrams, 1983.

Schmoll, Anne W. *Charles Hopkinson, N.A.: Moods and Moments.* Boston: Vose Galleries, 1991.

Scott, Donald, and Bernard Wishy, eds. *America's Families: A Documentary History.* New York: Harper & Row, 1982.

Seidel, Linda. *Jan Van Eyck's Arnolfini Portrait: Stories of an Icon.* Cambridge, England: Cambridge University Press, 1993.

Self and Shadow. New York: Aperture Foundation, Spring 1989.

Shawe-Taylor, Desmond. *The Georgians: Eighteenth Century Portraiture and Society.* London: Barrie and Jenkins, 1980.

Sheldon, James, curator. *Within Memory.* Andover, Mass.: Addison Gallery of Art, 1993.

Shipman, David. *Cinema: The First Hundred Years.* New York: St. Martin's Press, 1993.

Simon, Robin. *The Portrait in Britain and America.* Boston: G. K. Hall, 1984.

Skolnick, Arlene. *Embattled Paradise.* New York: Basic Books, 1991.

Smith, David. "Irony and Civility: Notes on the Convergence of Genre and Portraiture in Seventeenth-Century Dutch Painting." *Art Bulletin,* September 1987, pp. 407–30.

Smith, Edward Lucie. *Impressionist Women.* New York: Harmony Books, 1985.

Southall, Thomas W. *Likeness: Portrait Photographs from the Collection.* Lawrence, Kans.: Helen Foresman Spencer Museum of Art, 1990.

Spike, John. *Fairfield Porter: An American Classic.* New York: Harry N. Abrams, 1992.

Stacey, Judith. *Brave New Families.* New York: Basic Books, 1990.

Stegner, Wallace. *Angle of Repose.* New York: Penguin Books, 1971.

Steichen, Edward, curator. *The Family of Man.* New York: Museum of Modern Art, 1955.

Steiner, George. *Martin Heidegger.* New York: Penguin Books, 1980.

———. *Real Presences.* Chicago: University of Chicago Press, 1989.

Stenersen, R. *Edvard Munch.* Stockholm: Frankfurt A.M. Zurich, 1950.

Stone, L. *The Family, Sex and Marriage in England, 1506–1800.* New York: Harper & Row, 1977.

Stuckey, Charles, and William Scott. *Berthe Morisot: Impressionist.* New York: Hudson Hills, 1987.

Suleiman, Susan, ed. *The Female Body in Western Culture.* Cambridge, Mass.: Harvard University Press, 1986.

Suleiman, Susan Rubin. *Risking Who One Is: Encounters with Contemporary Art and Literature.* Cambridge, Mass.: Harvard University Press, 1994.

Sultan, Larry. *Pictures From Home.* New York: Harry N. Abrams, 1993.

Sutton, Peter C. *The Age of Rubens.* Boston: Museum of Fine Arts, 1993.

Taylor, Charles. *Sources of the Self: The Making of the Modern Identity.* Cambridge, Mass.: Harvard University Press, 1989.

Timm, Werner. *The Graphic Art of Edvard Munch.* Boston: New York Graphic Society, 1972.

Tobey, Susan Bracaglia. *Art of Motherhood.* New York: Abbeville Press, 1991.

Traube, Elizabeth. *Dreaming Identities: Class, Gender, and Generation in 1980's Hollywood Movies.* Boulder, CO: Westview Press, 1992.

Tremblay, Hélène. *Families of the World—Family Life at the Close of the 20th Century—The Americas and the Caribbean.* New York: Farrar, Straus and Giroux, 1988.

Trilling, Lionel. *Sincerity and Authenticity.* Cambridge, Mass.: Harvard University Press, 1972.

Turner, Peter, ed. *American Images: Photography 1945–1980.* New York: Viking Press and Barbican Gallery, 1985.

Waetzoldt, Wilhelm. *Die Kunst Des Porträts.* Leipzig: Ferdinand Hirt and Sohn, 1908.

Wagner, Viqi, ed. *The Family in America—Opposing Viewpoints.* San Diego, Calif.: Greenhaven Press, 1992.

Walker, John. *Portraits: 5000 Years.* New York: Harry N. Abrams, 1983.

Walters, Suzanna. *Lives Together/Worlds Apart—Mothers and Daughters in Popular Culture.* Berkeley: University of California Press, 1992.

Wendorf, Richard. *The Elements of Life, Biography and Portrait: Painting in Stuart and Georgian England.* Oxford, England: Clarendon Press, 1990.

————, ed. *Word and Image* (Taylor and Francis) 6 (October–December 1990).

Wengraf, Paul, ed. "Portrait Painting," *Apropos* (London), no. 3, 1946.

Wheeler, Monroe. *20th Century Portraits.* New York: Museum of Modern Art, 1942.

Whitford, Frank. *Expressionistic Portraits.* London: Thames and Hudson, 1987.

Wigley, Mark. *The Architecture of Deconstruction: Derrida's Haunt.* Cambridge, Mass.: MIT Press, 1990.

Wilde, Oscar. *The Picture of Dorian Gray.* New York: Penguin Books, 1985.

Wind, Edgar. *Hume and the Heroic Portrait: Studies in Eighteenth Century Imagery.* Oxford, England: Clarendon Press, 1986.

Wise, Kelly. *Portrait: Theory.* New York: Lustrum Press, 1982.

Wolfenstein, Martha, and Nathan Leites. *Movies: A Psychological Study.* New York: Atheneum, 1977.

Wood, Christopher. *Victorian Panorama—Paintings of Victorian Life.* London: Faber and Faber, 1976.

Zemel, Carol. "Sorrowing Women, Rescuing Men: Van Gogh's Images of Women and Family." *Art History* (September 1987), pp. 351–68.

Zimmerman, Patricia. "Filming Adventures in Beauty—Pictorialism, Amateur Cinematography and the Filmic Pleasures of the Nuclear Family from 1897–1923." *Afterimage* (December 1986), pp. 8–11.

Index

Page numbers in *italics* refer to illustrations.

253

LaVergne, TN USA
03 November 2009
162835LV00002B/22/A